Recruiting, Retaining and Releasing People

To Jan, with love ...

...Mac

Recruiting, Retaining and Releasing People

Managing redeployment, return, retirement and redundancy

Adrian Mackay

AMSTERDAM • BOSTON • HEIDELBERG • LONDON • NEW YORK • OXFORD
PARIS • SAN DIEGO • SAN FRANCISCO • SINGAPORE • SYDNEY • TOKYO
Butterworth-Heinemann is an imprint of Elsevier

ELSEVIER

Butterworth-Heinemann is an imprint of Elsevier
Linacre House, Jordan Hill, Oxford OX2 8DP
30 Corporate Drive, Suite 400, Burlington, MA 01803, USA

First edition 2007

British Library Cataloguing in Publication Data
A catalogue record for this book is available from the British Library

Library of Congress Cataloguing in Publication Data
A catalogue record for this book is available from the Library of Congress

ISBN–13: 978-0-7506-8306-7
ISBN–10: 0-7506-8036-6

For information on all Butterworth-Heinemann publications
visit our web site at http://books.elsevier.com

Printed and bound in Great Britain

07 08 09 10 11   10 9 8 7 6 5 4 3 2 1

Working together to grow
libraries in developing countries

www.elsevier.com | www.bookaid.org | www.sabre.org

ELSEVIER   BOOK AID
International   Sabre Foundation

Contents

List of Figures

List of Tables

Preface

As part of the working party developing the new National Management Standards, and as a subject specialist with the Chartered Management Institute, I realised that there were many new initiatives, changing legislation, and shifts in society affecting the 'hiring and firing' of people. To reflect these changes this text and its companion website, (found at http://books.elsevier.com/management?isbn=0750683066), aims to provide employers with a practical guide to the key management processes in recruiting, retaining and releasing people. It has been written to meet the requirements of the Chartered Management Institute and CIPD programmes of study, and each chapter introduction highlights which particular parts of each syllabus are being addressed.

While the book's title defines the main text, there is much more useful detail than the front cover might allow, particularly in the area of retaining and releasing people.

Part 1 looks at the world of recruiting people. With the influence of the Internet we start by looking at graduate recruitment, the recruitment of general managers and recruiting more senior people – the need to address diversity issues throughout is underlined with practical advice. How to write job descriptions and person specifications are covered before exploring the main selection methods. There is a whole raft of developments in the area of what questions one may or may not ask at interview – before you run your next one, read this section carefully! Once the decision on who to take on is made we look at induction programmes best practice to ensure the full integration of our new recruit.

Part 2 explores many facets of the retention of people, whether that is through the particular case of women returning to work after a career break – where I have to thank my dear wife, Jan, who provides a hands-on perspective way beyond that possible of even the most doting husband – or through redeployment. While there may be people that you clearly want to get rid of, redeployment of good people is often overlooked, and a practical guide is included here! The section on job evaluation schemes comes from a review of the literature on what might constitute best practice and my observations are included here; you'll get a clear overview of what to think about before establishing a system for your organisation or ideas on how to improve one that is already in place. Many managers fear delivering appraisals almost as much as their staff fears receiving them – so the chapter on my 'goals-orientated approach' may come as a relief to both parties concerned! I also developed a BARC® management workshop to guide managers on the key elements of managing people – *B*riefing work, *A*ssessing work, *R*einforcing good behaviours and *C*oaching to address any shortfalls – and have included the key elements of the supporting materials as a practical guide for the busy manager. Finally in this section, the new approaches to discipline and grievance procedures have been covered, along with an outline of the new practices required from the new legislation – so be warned!

Part 3 deals with the difficult and sensitive subject when people leave work, whether through retirement, redundancy or employers 'having to let people go'. Having experienced redundancy three times from my last three appointments in industry, this section is written with some empathy for the difficulties faced by employees and should guide managers on how to approach the subject with due consideration. This section gives advice for both the employer in an HR advisory function, the line manager and the employee dealing with 'removal'. The final chapter takes a view into the future of work, providing the opportunity to consider how technology can enable differing working practices, including flexible working, working part-time, interim working and balancing the demands of work/life – and how to achieve that balance. (Having the good fortune to share five 'children' – the youngest is 15 – my wife and I wish we could put into practice some of the ideas written here!)

It must be emphasised that at no stage is this text intended to replace sound advice from an experienced legal advisor, but it is hoped that it represents a collection of pragmatic approaches to recruiting, retaining and releasing people built up through both experience and study.

Acknowledgements are due to my wife, Jan, not only for her contribution already mentioned, but also her patience with me as the book evolved from *Motivation, Ability and Confidence Building in People,* written at the same time.

I would also like to thank Maggie Smith at Butterworth-Heinemann for her considerable patience and ingenuity in developing the text – and also to all others at the publisher's for not shouting at me once.

Adrian 'Mac' Mackay
Moreton Pinkney

About the author

Adrian 'Mac' Mackay is Managing Partner with Duncan Alexander and Wilmshurst, Training and Development Advisors, and is a Director of DAW Limited, that specialises in providing innovative marketing solutions. Mac's interests are advising professional people on marketing, as well as management skills, leadership and improved performance, and client care. He has recent international experience in Europe and the USA and has worked with many varied organisations, both large and small.

He co-authored *Below-the-Line Promotion* (1992), *Fundamentals of Advertising, second edition* (1999) and *The Fundamentals* and *Practice of Marketing, fourth edition* (2002) with John Wilmshurst; is editor of *The Practice of Advertising, fifth edition* (2004); he co-authored *The Veterinary Receptionist* with John Corsan and is also sole author of *Motivation, Ability and Confidence Building in People* (2007) – a companion text to this book.

Mac is an Honours graduate in Physiology and Nutrition from Leeds University (1977), he holds a Diploma from the Chartered Institute of Marketing (1983), a Masters Degree in Strategic Marketing (1994), was elected to the Faculty of the Chartered Institute of Marketing and is a full Member of the Chartered Management Institute (2002); he is a former subject specialist on their accredited programmes. He achieved a Postgraduate Certificate in Management from University College Northampton (2006).

Mac coaches a local junior rugby team and is an East Midlands RFU Society Referee. He is married to Jan – who wrote Chapter 4 – and they share five fabulous children and live in Northamptonshire.

Part 1

Recruiting People

1

Recruitment – A Modern Perspective

Technologies can be bought; what we need is the talent to implement them.
Lord Brown of Madingley, CEO of BP

Learning Outcomes

This chapter has been written with three objectives:

1. To serve as a practical guide for today's manager aiming to recruit the right person for an identified position.
2. To meet the needs of the Chartered Management Institute's Diploma in Management optional module *Unit O41 – Recruitment and Selection.*
3. To meet the needs of the CIPD Professional Development Scheme – particularly regarding recruitment as part of the *People Management and Development* core module.

This chapter aims to help you learn how to identify personnel requirements and to select the required people.

By the end of this chapter you will:

- Have a clear understanding of the main influences on today's recruitment market
- Explore an employer's responsibility concerning diversity and equal opportunities
- Know how to write a job description and person specification

- Understand the various recruitment methods and the purpose and validity of each
- Review best practice when making a decision and offering the job
- Have both the employer and employee views on induction programmes – and learn how to ensure they are effective.

Recruitment Today

The UK recruitment market is the most developed and competitive in the world. While the US market may be worth three times as much as Britain's (see Table 1.1), the US has a labour force almost five times as large.

Figures from the Government Turnover Inquiry (GTI), the Recruitment and Employment Confederation (REC) and the marketing intelligence firm Key Note valued the UK recruitment industry between £20 and £24.5 billion in 2004.

The results published in January 2006 showed a decline in the demand for temporary/contract labour and a marked switch to permanent business. While the recruitment market grew some 571 per cent over 10 years – explaining the highly fragmented market – recent figures show there has been a 4.2 per cent decline in total industry turnover, which now stands at just under £23.5 billion. This reduction in overall turnover, for only the second time in the history of the survey, is mirrored by government VAT data.

The recruitment market is split into essentially two areas:

- Retained firms work on senior roles and require part-payment upfront (typically one-third of the final fee), and further payments are made on representation of a shortlist and the new employee starting.
- Contingency agencies are paid on success only.

Table 1.1 Top five recruitment markets worldwide

	Value 2003 ($bn)	Value 2004 ($bn)	Change (%)
US	94.5	95.0	0.05
UK	33.6	33.0	−1.80
Japan	15.0	15.1	0.70
France	14.7	14.3	−2.70
Netherlands	8.4	9.2	9.50

Source: Key Note.

A tightening job market brings good and bad news for recruitment firms. Figures from the National Office of Statistics (http://www.statistics.gov.uk) sourced in May 2006 confirm that in the three months to February 2006 the trend in the employment rate is falling, while the trend in the unemployment rate is increasing. The number of people claiming Jobseeker's Allowance benefit has increased, while the number of job vacancies has fallen. Growth in average earnings excluding bonuses is unchanged, while growth in average earnings including bonuses has increased.

Box 1.1 shows the recent figures published by the National Office of Statistics for Great Britain.

Box 1.1: Employment trends for the three months to February 2006 published by the National Office of Statistics for Great Britain (http://www.statistics.gov.uk/)

- The employment rate for people of working age was 74.5 per cent for the three months ending in February 2006. This is unchanged over the quarter but down 0.4 per cent over the year.
- The number of people in employment for the three months ending in February 2006 was 28.84 million. This is the highest figure since comparable records began in 1971. Employment increased by 76 000 over the quarter and by 147 000 over the year. The quarterly increase in employment was mainly due to more women employees.
- Total hours worked per week were 926.1 million, the highest figure since comparable records began in 1971. This is up 4.3 million over the quarter and up 3.6 million over the year.
- The unemployment rate was 5.1 per cent, up 0.1 per cent over the quarter and up 0.4 per cent over the year. The number of unemployed people increased by 30 000 over the quarter and by 120 000 over the year, to reach 1.56 million. The quarterly increase in unemployment was due to more unemployed women.
- The claimant count was 937 600 in March 2006, up 12 600 on the previous month and up 106 200 on the year.

(*Continued*)

Box 1.1: Continued

- The inactivity rate for people of working age was 21.3 per cent for the three months ending in February 2006, down 0.1 per cent over the quarter but up 0.1 per cent over the year. The number of economically inactive people of working age fell by 13 000 over the quarter, to reach 7.93 million.
- The annual rate of growth in average earnings (the AEI), excluding bonuses, was 3.8 per cent in February 2006, unchanged from the previous month. Including bonuses it was 4.2 per cent, up from 3.6 per cent the previous month.
- The average number of job vacancies for the three months to March 2006 was 593 200. This was down 3300 on the previous quarter and down 43 300 over the year.
- The redundancy rate for the three months to February 2006 was 5.7 per 1000 employees, up 0.1 from the previous quarter.

While this is good news for agency fees, the figures show unemployment to be *generally* at its lowest for nearly 30 years, the competition for a declining pool of people will be fiercer than ever.

This demand for executives moving in the opposite direction to supply is particularly acute in the USA, where demographic predictions suggest that the number of 35- to 44-year-olds will fall by 15 per cent by 2015 while that of 45- to 55-year-olds will rise. Moreover, the demands companies place on executives is increasing, which in turn affects the escalating talent shortfall. Complex global markets require more sophisticated management skills, including international sensitivity, cultural fluency, technological literacy, entrepreneurial flair and, most critically, leadership. Add to this the third factor – the rise of the high-potential small and medium-sized companies – and larger companies now have to compete with and provide career opportunities and earnings on a par with the more modest organisation. A host of high-tech start-ups, especially Internet-based businesses, are going to attract a growing proportion of top people who might otherwise have joined 'blue-chips'. Many people do not want to work for what they see as 'faceless corporations' when they can have more fun working for an exciting start-up business. These factors mean that the competition for talented people is intensifying.

The Influence of the Internet

Finding the right people at the right time has never been more important and the Internet provides a sound solution. Recruitment via the Internet widens the sphere of people who can be accessed.

It is estimated that 1.2 million people every month in the UK use the Internet to search for a job and that there are 4700 recruitment agencies on the Internet. Recent research by the Institute of Personnel Development found that nearly half of all employers are now using the Internet to recruit staff; numbers are rising from 36 to 47 per cent in a year. The IPD research identifies three main approaches:

- Sending application forms by e-mail (66 per cent of companies)
- Advertising jobs on corporate intranets (62 per cent)
- Using corporate websites to advertise vacancies (43 per cent).

Research by Reed shows that it is the most skilled 'AB' social group who are most likely to use the Internet for job-seeking, usage among the 25–34 age group being particularly high. However, it is not just high-fliers who are looking for their next move online. Companies like New Look and Harrods, for example, have successfully used the Internet to help them recruit front-line staff to cover seasonal peaks, while FedEx Express has used it to hire couriers and clerical staff. Tesco also targets 'silver surfers' through its careers website, as part of its drive to recruit more over-fifties into its workforce.

Part of the online recruitment approach will be to get people thinking about their careers constantly. A number of recruitment agencies are using WAP services, where their websites can be accessed by mobile phone. Users can create their personal job profile and a daily search then matches a user's profile with any vacancies and e-mails. People can be sitting at their place of work while fielding a host of potential new jobs on their mobile phones.

Graduate recruitment

While today's graduates use the Internet, frequently in place of direct conversation, employers have to do more to attract them. Recently, marketing stunts and offering free entertainment are among the successful tactics businesses have used to attract graduates.

- In November 2004, Barclays Bank treated Warwick University students to popcorn, fizzy drinks and a private viewing of a popular new release. The bank used the opportunity to show a short video explaining what its business was about and why it was a natural career choice for graduates.
- Students at Oxford, Cambridge and other leading universities have ridden in rickshaws (accountants KPMG), watched street artists (professional service firm Deloitte), and other 'stunts' provided by corporations such as Shell, Asda and PriceWaterhouseCoopers (PwC).
- LloydsTSB aimed to recruit high-calibre students who typically look for a career in management consultancy or a big accounting firm – they used a campaign that featured the unexpected appearance at universities of life-sized models of its iconic black horse. They noticed an appreciable improvement in the quality of students applying to its scheme. In 2002/3, one in five candidates seen by its assessment centres was appointable; in 2003/4 it was one in four.

Knowing how to target students is crucial to success. Organisations need to understand which elements of recruiting work globally and which should be localised. As more undergraduates combine studying with part-time jobs, which take them away from their universities, employers are finding it increasingly difficult to attract graduates through established recruiting channels. Organisations are increasingly bolstering their annual recruitment drives with continuous campaigns aimed at making students aware of their employer brand from the moment they first set foot on campus. Such initiatives include running business games, sponsoring sports clubs and societies and even, in the case of Shell, providing specialist projects for course work.

Offering holiday work, scholarships and placements are well-established methods of gaining prior access to the most promising candidates. However, as more recruiters adopt such strategies, the most opportunistic are going to extreme lengths to secure an early lead on young talent.

In October 2004, Deloitte launched a pre-university scholarship programme for 26 outstanding school leavers. The programme combines periods of paid work experience with finance for gap year travel and an annual bursary paid throughout the scholar's undergraduate life. Deloitte are confident that, when they leave university, most of the scholars will apply to the graduate programme and be taken on full-time.

A 2006 survey by the Higher Education Careers Services Unit (Hecsu) of more than 200 000 former students found that 8 per cent of male graduates remain jobless six months after leaving university – a whole 3 per cent higher than the UK overall unemployment rate and nearly double the number of women who remain unemployed in the same time frame. Moreover, many graduate careers advisory services find that three of every five people on their books are women.

In *The Independent* (4 May 2006) Mike Hill, CEO of Hecsu, puts their findings down to two perceived masculine traits – poor organisation and arrogance – and believes that parallels can be drawn throughout the education system. 'Over the past 10 years, women have been outperforming men in terms of diligence and organisation that is apparent at GCSE, A-level and increasingly at higher levels.' It is also true that some graduates taking longer to find jobs than others might mean that they weren't on the right courses in the first place – itself suggesting a gender gap in forward planning.

General management recruitment

While the common-sense consensus is that online recruitment can work effectively at a junior or technical level, for the foreseeable future at least, it is going to struggle to compete at a general management level. If someone is going to be running a company, it is good to meet them in the flesh before offering them a salary and comprehensive rewards package. The IPD research suggests that only 1 per cent of recruiters for professional positions viewed online recruiting as a useful method, and only 2 per cent of those recruiting for managerial or skilled positions viewed it as more effective than other ways of recruiting.

As there will be 11.8 million people over 50 in the UK by 2011, representing a sizeable part of the working population, some recruitment agencies are partnering with sites that target over-45-year-olds.

Senior executives are often uncomfortable with the Internet as a medium and demand confidentiality. Online recruitment in its various forms lacks the personal touch. This applies to both sides. Actually seeing people, talking to them face to face and interacting with them remain central issues to recruit anyone, anywhere.

While the Internet can help screen applicants during the recruitment process, there is no place for online assessment for general managers. Screening is one thing; clear assessment of abilities and inadequacies is another. For all the technology available to recruiters, talent appraisal seems to be a personal thing.

Director recruitment

Learning from the experiences of nine former board members of Equitable Life, facing a court case in which the insurance company seeks more than £3 billion from them, the attraction of being a company director has faded somewhat.

The liabilities and risks on individual non-executive directors have increased substantially, and the amount of time one has to put in has increased dramatically. Non-executive directors have been in the spotlight since the Enron affair first erupted in 2001. Sir Derek Higgs was appointed by the British government to look at how the role of non-executive directors should be tightened. His 2003 report not only increased the number of non-executive directors a company must have, but also spelt out their increased responsibilities.

The result, head-hunters have discovered, is that high-calibre non-execs are becoming harder to recruit. The problem is particularly acute with chairmen of FTSE 100 companies and chairs of audit committees. Whereas inside the FTSE 250, candidates for non-executive roles are becoming more choosy and exercising more due diligence, those in smaller companies are demanding higher rewards for the increased workload.

While the advantages of being invited include opportunities for networking, a sense of flattery and the challenge of the appointment, the downsides – like a damaged reputation – are putting many possible candidates off the idea altogether, to say nothing of the financial liability. The financial liability against Equitable's former board may be considered exceptional in the UK; in the USA, such suits have become common.

Directors and Officers (D&O) insurance has plenty of exemptions – not least if you are no longer serving – so sound advice for potential directors would be to study the policy carefully and take legal advice before signing on the dotted line.

The burden of increased time and commitment is a different issue. While a few years ago the commitment may have been a few days a year, today the number of meetings, their duration and the amount of preparation required has grown. The immediate consequence is a demand for bigger rewards to compensate. Until recently, £25 000–30 000 was the usual remuneration for a non-executive director with a mid-cap company. Already the fees are now about £35 000–40 000 and a few bigger firms are paying £75 000–80 000 a year. Recent research by Income Data Services found that the average remuneration for FTSE 100 non-execs rose 36 per cent to £40 000 in 2004.

Companies in difficulties are finding it particularly hard to recruit new board members when they need the help the most. Why would anyone risk being associated with an organisation where there was the hint of mismanagement or financial wrongdoing?

So much for the part-timers – but what of the other executives? There is a growing reluctance to take on even these roles due to the constant scrutiny and relentless pressure, when there are plenty of easier ways to earn top salaries.

Among smaller public companies, the cost of bearing a larger number of non-executive directors, in conformance with the Higgs recommendations, is prohibitive. With five or six executives on the board, under the new rules one needs seven or eight non-executives too. As a result, many companies are taking most of their executives off the board and having an executive committee that runs the business. In the UK, therefore, the situation is tending towards the German-style two-tier board system, where all of the corporate governance is designed for a unitary board.

Face to face

Companies that are using online recruitment extensively may marginalise quite distinct sectors of the population who may not have access to the Internet, but who probably have a great deal to offer. Women on maternity leave and single parents have less access to the Internet and online recruitment. Companies also need to ensure that they do not miss the human touch, as sophisticated technology is no substitute for meeting and talking to others face to face.

Dr Alan Slater, a psychologist at Exeter University, presenting his findings to the British Association for the Advancement of Science in September 2004, stated that we are genetically programmed to prefer a pretty face. Babies were shown photographs of faces from glamorous magazines interspersed with pictures of office workers judged to be 'plain' or 'ugly'. The babies invariably spent longer studying the good-looking faces. He suggested that the explanation for babies' interest in attractive faces is that the size and shape of the features tend to be closer to the average face. If one were to take a wide selection of female faces and 'morph' or average them into one face, that face is not an average-looking face, but a very attractive face.

Dr Slater said:

Research has shown that if you have attractive individuals, people judge them to be more honest and trustworthy – any positive attributes are more likely to be associated with them. There is no doubt that attractive people tend to do a lot better in interviews than less attractive people – nobody ever said evolution was supposed to be fair.

For this reason, we need to have some objective standards in interviewing applicants face to face and not rely on subjective opinion (see Chapter 2).

A guide for online recruitment

- *Job application site.* Set up a specific area on your website and include information about jobs, the company and your recruitment process. Test to make sure jobseekers can find the information they want.
- *Internal advertising.* Make sure every one internally has the opportunity to find out about internal opportunities first. Use an intranet if you have one, company newsletter or team briefings, etc.
- *Tailor your recruitment process.* Don't just put your current process online, use the opportunity to improve the process.
- *Advertise your online process with other job advertising.* Make sure you mention the process in all adverts, including internal communications, and encourage interested applicants to apply online.
- *Use the online information.* The management information so obtained should be used to improve the process and help choose the best job boards.
- *Build a talent bank.* Even unsuccessful applicants can be your first resource for any new jobs you may have in the future.
- *Invest in dedicated software.* Worth the investment, especially if you want to publish jobs to all your job boards at the same time.
- *Match your applicants' chosen technologies.* If they use text messages as well as e-mail, this could improve your recruitment process.

- *Keep a human touch.* While online recruitment will reduce administration, you will still need able recruitment people to speak to applicants if the need arises.
- *Stay fresh.* As 'advertisements' for your organisation, don't let the information get out of date.
- *Make sure your data protection is in place.* You have a responsibility for all the personal information you are likely to collect.

(Adapted from information provided by Capital Consulting, www.capitalconsulting.co.uk.)

Diversity and Equal Opportunities

Politicians and social campaigners, at least as much as business women and men, feel obliged to make the business case for gender diversity, family-friendly policies or corporate social responsibility. In 2003 the Equal Opportunities Commission argued against gender stereotyping in the labour market on the grounds that it was impeding productivity growth. This is well-documented mainstream thinking, but few case studies make a robust case. So, to alter the mainstream course, it is argued that you need some people working outside it as well as within (Reeves, 2003).

Are family-friendly policies more often supported on social justice grounds than on business ones? Even with corporate social responsibility (CSR), the real attractions do not lie within a narrow business case but more in cultural ones (*Marketing Week*). The business case for gender equality, like that for CSR, is thin. If there is a business case, it is that in the long run, successful organisations have to be seen to reflect and enact our wishes for the world. Despite decades of trying, has anyone yet shown incontrovertibly that there is always and everywhere a clear commercial rationale for treating men and women equally? This may explain why gender equality remains more rhetoric than reality in most businesses.

However, discrimination need not be overt; it can be insidious. In efforts to assist in the development of diversity and improve working relationships, particularly between men and women, Procter & Gamble in the USA devised a scheme where senior male executives as mentors would help selected women learn to think and behave in ways that might get them promoted. However, when it was realised that the problem lay less with the women than with the men, the whole scheme was called into question. To effect change it was felt necessary to change the attitudes of the executives first. So, the women became mentors to the executives, with remarkably positive results all round. Not only did the women become more visible and learn about higher-level decision-making, but also the executives became sensitised to a whole range of diversity issues – many had a direct impact on how the company functioned and understood its customers. Thus, diversity in a mentoring relationship stimulates the examination of issues from different perspectives.

Diversity is here to stay and it is worth reviewing the situation from a number of perspectives.

Equal pay for women

There are a number of factors driving increasing pay parity for women managers, not least the equal pay provisions of the 2002 Employment Act. Equal pay law in Britain is set out in the Equal Pay Act (EPA) 1970 and subsequent amendments. European Union law also covers equal pay. Article 141 of the treaty of Amsterdam requires that women and men should receive equal pay for equal work.

Under the EPA, employees may claim equal pay with colleagues of the opposite sex where they are in the same employment and are doing work that is:

- The same or broadly similar
- Rated as equivalent under an analytical job evaluation scheme
- Different but which is of equal value in terms of the demands of the job.

The law covers full-time, part-time, casual or temporary contracts, regardless of the length of service.

As a result of the 2002 Employment Act, companies must examine their pay practices and eliminate discriminatory pay differences.

The National Management Salary Survey 2004 (published by the Chartered Management Institute and Remuneration Economics – see www.celre.co.uk) has been tracking earnings for about the same time that equal pay rights have been in existence. When the survey was launched in 1974, only 2 per cent of managers were women; this compared to one in three by 2004. It has been suggested that for women managers, qualifications and skills linked to the tight labour market have been as influential as the Equal Pay Act in giving them the necessary leverage to command earnings equal to pay levels of men. Petra Cook (2004), The Chartered Management Institute's head of policy, stated that, '. . . women managers are much more aware of their rights and are more confident about their roles in the workplace'. This premise is supported in the 2004 Marketing Rewards Survey (www.croner-reward.co.uk), conducted by Croner Reward on behalf of the Chartered Institute of Marketing. It found that pay increases for marketing professionals averaged 3 per cent in the previous 12 months, with senior marketing managers paid between 6 and 9 per cent more than those working in other functions. The pay gap between men and women working in marketing seems to have stabilised at around 3 per cent. While the average pay gap in the 2004 survey was wider than the year previously, it had closed on the 2002 figure. For middle and senior managers the pay for women is equal to that of men, but for other grades women were paid 3 per cent less than men. Some 16 per cent of marketing directors who responded to the survey were female (see Table 1.2).

However, in a report published in November 2004 by the Department of Trade and Industry (reported in the *Financial Times*, 25 November 2004), many organisations discriminated strongly against married women and women working part-time in particular. One in three companies were said to be guilty of discriminating against employing married women in finance jobs. The pay gap between men and women is assessed at an average of 22 per cent, although at finance director level the gap narrows to 12 per cent. Moreover, British women working part-time earned an average 22 per cent less per hour than those working full-time in the last year, the

Table 1.2 Women managers' pay compared to men in marketing jobs 2004

Croner Reward rank	Job level	Median basic pay (£)		Difference (%)	
		Women	Men	2004	2003
0	Director	67 000	69 000	−2.9	−0.8
1	Senior Manager	49 000	50 000	−2.0	−4.2
2	Senior/Middle Manager	37 000	38 000	−2.6	−
3	Middle Manager	30 000	30 000	−	−
4	Middle/Junior Manager	23 690	24 550	−3.5	2.5
5	Junior Manager	19 000	18 000	−	−2.7

biggest gap in the European Union. Companies are also accused of adopting unfriendly family policies – by underpaying women and being unsympathetic to the government's drive to encourage flexible working and give more generous maternity terms.

The Equal Opportunities Commission report issued in 2004 showed a stark picture: women make up 18 per cent of MPs, 12 per cent of council leaders, 13 per cent of Local Authority Chief Executive Officers, 7 per cent of senior police officers, 9 per cent of 'big-firm' directors, 9 per cent of national newspaper editors and 6 per cent of high court judges. The EOC chair, Julie Mellor, thinks that the imbalance is important because these organisations and others like them are fishing for talent in only half the pool and also that '. . . the legitimacy of decisions made by such a homogeneous group has to be questioned' (reported in *Management Today*, January 2004, p. 23).

It has been suggested that the 'glass ceiling' has been constructed in part by British women themselves, who consistently value the acquisition of power and status at a lower level than men. (Most of the women who have made senior positions in industry and commerce are from the USA – an industrial society in which women's aspirations more closely match those of their male peers.) However, this partial explanation is no justification. It is good to have a diverse society, in which some people are more ambitious for power than others, but it is profoundly inappropriate, regressive and unjust for those differences to be based on gender.

Two papers presented at the 2003 Royal Economic Society annual conference identified some interesting suggestions. Alan Manning, Professor at the London School of Economics, showed that although women and men now start their careers at absolute pay parity, within a few years men are pulling ahead – and they stay ahead throughout the lifecycle. Was this, as Manning speculated, because men were more 'bolshie' than women about their salaries? Anecdotal evidence from industry supports this claim. The second paper, presented by Maureen Paul of Warwick University, showed that women are significantly more likely than men to feel that they are paid 'fairly'.

Her work suggested that the source of women's job satisfaction is not primarily financial. Women rank social interaction, meaningful work and friendship more highly than men, who cite financial factors. While men have more money, are they happier? Beyond a certain threshold, there is scant evidence that money does little or nothing to make people feel better. Once an individual is financially comfortable, friendship, family life and meaningful work become much more important to happiness. We already know from Maslow's hierarchy of needs (see Mackay, 2007) that as a society we should have shifted beyond the stages of material acquisition and be moving up to 'self-actualisation'.

The pay gap can now be seen as a sign of women's success in rejecting a flawed financial philosophy. Perhaps the way to close the gap is not to encourage women to be as short-sighted as men; it is to encourage men to abandon their obsessive faith in the size of their wallets or the power of money.

Sadly, this does not seem to be happening – newspapers in March 2006 were reporting widely on the growing pay gap between the genders.

The Women and Work Commission, led by Baroness Prosser, published its final report in May 2006, concluding that inequality between men and women costs the British economy £23 billion a year in lost productivity and wasted talent. The report calls for employers to offer greater flexibility in senior management posts, through part-time working or job shares – and to make sure that managers at all levels are 'regularly and continually trained on diversity and flexibility issues'.

Women returning to work after a having a baby

In April 2004 new laws improved the situation for parents: those with children under six can request flexible working (the employer is obliged to listen, although not agree); parents can take up to 13 weeks unpaid leave during their child's first five years, and parents with dependants can take time off for emergencies. However, it seems that attitudes are harder to regulate.

A survey by the Chartered Institute of Personnel and Development found that employees in nearly 50 per cent of organisations say those who are not entitled to request flexible working resent those who can. Moreover, support from colleagues is crucial in determining whether mothers return to work – many women are worried whether they are performing at the level they were pre-baby. A useful resource for 'women returners' can be found at http://www.women-returners.co.uk – it is equally important for employers to be aware of the issues too (see Chapter 4).

Men

Work/life balance was a legitimate concern for women to worry about and to request a degree of flexibility when it came to workplace hours – but men? One study that made use of a dummy request for unpaid childcare leave discovered that employers were more likely to reject the attempt if it was thought to come from a man.

While 'family friendly' may have replaced the phrase 'work/life balance', the issues are the same: how can busy parents balance the demands of work and home? (Although today it seems that it is not just parents with young children that need the care at home, more and more 'children' have to care for their elderly parents. With changing demographics in the UK – and doubtful pension provision – this is going to become a more prevalent factor in the future.)

While it is tempting to widen the debate to include the childless, the truth is that parents are in the time-vice. Some 'work/life balance' campaigners take children out of the picture, but this probably undermines the cause of workplace flexibility. (After all, it is more important to collect a child than to catch a pottery class.) There may be a backlash from the childless, but perhaps this is a price worth paying!

However, the real problem with the debate about work and family today is the absence of men. Few seminars on the issue, despite the best efforts of organisers, attract many men. While women now define themselves in a variety of roles – mum, carer, career woman, working woman, friend, community activist, 'ladette', feminist, entrepreneur – most men remain stuck in the role of 'breadwinner'. More than half the population think that women with pre-school children should stay at home (and most do not); equally, about half the population think a father's primary responsibility is to bring home the bacon (and men still earn two-thirds of family income).

Men are doing more childcare and housework than their fathers ever did, often because their partners demand it. Thirty years ago, the family model of earning father and caring mother was ascendant. Today, there are twice as many dual-earning families as traditional ones. More than a third of mothers aged between 25 and 34 return to work within a year of having their first child, compared to one in 10 of their mothers. All this puts the same pressure on fathers as mothers, because mum is doing her part of the breadwinning, but their bosses often lack sympathy. Men are expected to be 'New Man' at home but 'Real Man' at work – small wonder that they are so stressed. While workplaces are often organised along gender lines they are powerfully constructed along generational lines too. Work is designed not just for men but for older men with 'stay-at-home' wives – a disproportionately powerful minority.

Management Today (2003) ran a telephone survey of 500 men's opinions on a variety of family-friendly issues and found a complex, varied and sometimes alarming state of affairs. There are clear signs, which cannot be ignored, that working life seriously impinges on the family commitments of some of the men in the survey and creates a serious sense of unhappiness that applies across the age range, decreasing slightly only when respondents had reached the age of 55 (see Figure 1.1).

	Yes	No	Don't know
Does your company offer family-friendly practices?	58%	41%	1%
Do you make use of your company's family-friendly practices?	69%	31%	
Do you think your firm does too much to accommodate staff who have families?	7%	77%	16%

What family-friendly practices does your company offer?	
Crèche	7%
Flexitime	76%
Job share	5%
Paternity leave	12%
Part-time working	5%
Home working	18%
Career break / sabbatical	4%

Do you think government policy on family-friendly practices goes far enough?		
	Under 45	Over 45
Goes far enough	37%	38%
Doesn't go far enough	46%	29%
Goes too far	9%	27%
	With children	Without children
Goes far enough	35%	39%
Doesn't go far enough	46%	31%
Goes too far	12%	21%

Figure 1.1 Companies' 'family-friendly' approaches (*Management Today* survey, 2003)

From April 2004, employees with children under the age of six were entitled to apply for flexible working and have their employer seriously consider the request. This was planned to lead to staff seeking part-time and flexitime work patterns, job sharing, term-time-only working and 'annual hours' contracts. However, it remains to be seen how effective the new right will be. Employers must now go through a rigorous procedure in assessing whether a proposed working arrangement is practicable, backed up by the right to complain to an employment tribunal. There will be limited scope to challenge a management decision backed by a 'business case' that refuses the request. The maximum compensation for an employee will be eight weeks' pay (with a £260 weekly maximum). It is likely that the right will be used mostly by women as a first stage in claiming the more powerful remedies available for sex discrimination.

It seems that small firms are particularly worried by plans that the UK government is proposing to give fathers six months' unpaid paternity leave from April 2007. This is part of the government's 'Work and Families Bill', aimed at reforming childcare, that also included measures to extend maternity leave for women to nine months. Clearly, small firms employing just a few staff would struggle to find short-term and qualified people to replace people on leave for long periods. While it is estimated that 400 000 men a year in the UK would qualify, few would take the unpaid leave with bills to pay – and more mouths to feed! As one SME business manager commented (*The Sunday Times*, 2005), 'If a man in my employment wanted to take six months off for paternity leave, I would probably question his motivation and his desire for work.'

So, while more companies will be offering more options to assist working parents, driven by government intervention, only in a few of them do men feel confident about taking it. Truly father-friendly workplaces will only come about when the younger dads join their female colleagues to change the old models of work based on antiquated models of the family.

Age

As one's customer base grows more varied in age, outlook and spending power, businesses need to take a hard look at how they present themselves to the outside world. To diverse customers, one needs a diverse workforce. As part of the anti-age discrimination campaign and to try to ensure that the world of work is fully involved, the UK government has set up a website (www.agepositive.gov.uk) that provides information on the continuing debate on age discrimination and the age-diverse workforce.

According to the National Audit Office (an executive summary of the report can be downloaded from www.noa.org.uk), it is estimated that relatively low levels of employment among older workers costs the economy £19–31 billion a year, in part due to lost output but also because of reduced taxes and increased welfare payments. Moreover, in a poll carried out by Age Concern and ICM Research (see more from Age Concern on www.ageconcern.org.uk), it was discovered that 66 per cent of workers are opposed to being forced to retire at a fixed age and say that more flexible working arrangements would be the biggest incentive to carry on working. Both issues were central proposals in the UK government's pensions Green Paper that was published in early 2003. By April 2005, the government introduced rules allowing workers to defer their state pension while working beyond state pension age.

From October 2006, employees will be able to bring tribunal age-bias claims with the prospect of unlimited compensation. Thus, employers need to start treating the older generation with greater respect. Having older people in the workplace is immensely beneficial; they tend to be more contented than their younger colleagues, they have years of experience and are more likely to see the bigger picture than focus entirely on their own position within the company.

The regulations only apply to employment and vocational training, and aim to stop unjustified direct and indirect discrimination of people of any age, and all harassment and victimisation on grounds of age. Advice from the Chartered Management Institute (*Professional Manager*, May 2006, p. 11) outlines the regulations from 1 October 2006 that will:

- Ban age discrimination in terms of recruitment, promotion and training
- Ban unjustified retirement ages below 65
- Remove the current age limit for unfair dismissal and redundancy rights.

They will also introduce:

- A right for employees to request working beyond retirement age and a duty on employers to consider that request
- A new requirement for employers to give a least six months' notice to employees about their intended retirement date so that individuals can

plan better for retirement, and be confident that 'retirement' is not being used as cover for unfair dismissal.

When the new legislation comes into effect it will be unlawful to set age limits for jobs and unsuccessful older applicants may challenge terms such as 'energetic' or 'dynamic' used in recruitment advertising. On the other hand, a requirement for a 'senior' manager or someone 'with gravitas' could be found to discriminate against younger people. ACAS advises employers to remove age or date of birth requests from application forms and create an 'equality policy'. Neither is a legal requirement, but would remove an easy trigger for a discrimination claim and provide a defence in a tribunal hearing.

Recruitment advertising in niche magazines could be indirectly discriminatory, ACAS warns, as a segment of the population may not read it. The choice of words and pictures becomes a minefield, with ACAS suggesting that employers avoid pictures with 'hidden' meanings – like a group of only young people or a group that do not reflect the ethnicity of the workforce – as Ford Motors found in the late 1980s when it was found that their 'diverse' ethnic workforce advertising did not, in fact, represent their Dagenham factory workforce profile.

Also, employers need to be wary of that teasing 'over the hill' birthday card. Terminating older workers' employment will be the hardest hurdle of all (see Chapter 9). Individuals forced out in their fifties could win huge awards, given the poor prospect of finding similar work. ACAS also warn that the rules would even cover a situation where a father and son worked in the same office and the son took offence at ageist jokes aimed at his father; it adds that it would be 'good practice' to make sure customers and suppliers did not make ageist jokes as well.

The regulations also have an impact on benefits relating to length of service (see Chapter 2). Thus far, ministers are still undecided on employers' scope to enforce mandatory retirement ages, although more will be said about this in the section on retirement (see Chapter 9).

Employers wanting further guidance on this issue are directed to ACAS (http://www.acas.org.uk), the government appointed agency to give advice on age issues, or Age Positive (http://www.agepositive.gov.uk).

Disability

There are estimated to be about 8.7 million people with disabilities in the UK, representing 15 per cent of the population. Contrary to popular belief, people who use wheelchairs actually account for the smallest proportion (only about 5 per cent) with disability. People with mental health problems are in fact the biggest category, followed by those with learning difficulties. People with sensory impairments are the third largest group. Often overlooked, these people are all potential customers who can choose where to spend their combined spending power, estimated to be between £50 and £80 billion a year (facts and figures about disability obtained from the Disability Rights Commission).

From 1 October 2004, their rights under the 1995 Disability Discrimination Act (DDA) were enhanced in various ways, placing new obligations on organisations in their capacity as both employers and suppliers of goods or services. While duty to make 'reasonable adjustments' were familiar to many businesses, as it has applied to disabled workers for nearly ten years, most changes affect business premises so that they are more accessible to people with various disabilities. However, the employment provisions of the DDA were also reviewed from 1 October to bring them into line with EU equality laws. This was aimed to enhance protection for staff with physical or mental disabilities – although most of the changes are technical and have most interest to employment law specialists.

However, the changes are further incentive for organisations to undertake a thorough review of policy and practice towards disabled people, particularly in their recruitment policies.

Ethnic groups

While the community appreciates the contribution of doctors, lawyers, bankers, engineers and scientists working in the UK, the largest proportion of migrant workers are unskilled, working in both cities and rural areas. We are increasingly becoming reliant on overseas nationals to fill vacancies in the agriculture, catering, hospitality and ancillary sectors – the health service and local government both employ large numbers of unskilled migrant workers. And for the community at large, there are considerable benefits: *The Economist* magazine (2004) quoted a Home Office study from 1999 that calculated that migrant workers contributed £2.5 billion more in taxes than they received in benefits and services such as health and education.

So, in a multicultural society, with the changing demographics of today's workforce, managing diversity is increasingly on the agenda for all UK organisations. Not only has the workforce changed but the consequences of not getting it right have changed too. Apart from the six-figure awards at employment tribunals, there is also the damage to company reputations to consider.

The Government Minority Ethnic Group has developed four diversity competencies, which are used on a regular basis with senior and top managers:

- Flexible thinking – being able to consider individual requests on merit; being able to consider unusual solutions; accepting different styles of working.
- Developing people – taking a development approach to all people; looking at mistakes as a learning opportunity; providing timely and helpful feedback.
- Championing diversity – being seen as a role model for diversity; living up to the values of an organisation; being prepared to accept feedback and acting upon it; challenging those who do not live up to the diversity values.
- Strategic diversity focus – how diversity fits into business; includes diversity within the business plan; can explain the benefits of having a diverse workforce.

A review of the diversity programme for one major UK organisation found that, after the programme, absenteeism in the divisions of the participating managers fell by 45 per cent – a saving equivalent to the £13 000 per month for each area director who had participated in the programme. In addition, staff turnover was reduced, the numbers of women promoted to senior management increased and there was greater use of flexible working.

Mental ill-health and recruitment

Employment is an area where people with mental health problems experience extensive discrimination and disadvantage. Employment is a central aspect of social inclusion and plays a critical part in recovery. At the same time, the workplace can be a source of damaging stress that causes mental ill-health. Mind (www.mind.org.uk) works for people's rights to employment free from discrimination, and for good mental health at work. However, we see human value and social inclusion as being much broader than employment and challenge measures that marginalise people who cannot work.

> **Box 1.2:** Better mental health at work (courtesy of Mind)
>
> If someone with a mental health problem applies for a job with you:
>
> - Don't make assumptions about their ability
> - Don't be afraid to talk about the issue in a constructive way
> - Don't discriminate.
>
> From 'Managing for Mental Health: The Mind Employers' Resource Pack'. E-mail: publications@mind.org.uk.

Mind is working for improvements to the Disability Discrimination Act and to improve the support available to people trying to get or keep jobs. Mind made a substantial response to the Social Exclusion Unit's consultation on mental health, in which employment featured prominently, and is supporting its implementation.

Employers have an obligation under the Disability Discrimination Act to make sure they treat people with mental health problems fairly. New Health and Safety Executive (HSE) standards also require them to assess the risk of work-related stress and take measures to control it within their organisation. Thus, existing employment and equal opportunities policies need to be reviewed and adapted to make sure they encompass people with mental health problems.

Mind provides the advice shown in Box 1.2 to guide employers on managing mental health problems at the recruitment stage; Chapter 2 deals with mental health problems experienced by existing employees.

Job Descriptions

Drawing up job descriptions for each person in the department helps to ensure that work is organised into jobs that occupy a person according to their time at work, and to check that each position is justified. Job descriptions provide the basis for the preparation of key results and objectives for the organisation (in output terms), each function and each person in it, making sure that these fit into a coherent whole.

Appropriately written, a job description can give a candidate a job overview and provide the recruiter with an objective checklist of requirements against which to match candidates. Once in post, an employee will have a list of main effectiveness areas and important contacts through direct working relationships. As we will see later in Chapter 5, the organisation will find job descriptions essential in job evaluation and assessments; they are also helpful when settling disputes about duties (Chapter 8), while permitting some flexibility.

So what are job descriptions? They are a structured and factual statement of a job's function and objectives, the acceptable standards of performance and the boundaries of the jobholder's authority. The job title, department, location, and to and for whom the jobholder is responsible are also included (*Management Checklists* 110 of the Chartered Management Institute).

While job descriptions are useful in the recruitment process, are an aid in defining objectives and agreeing training requirements, form the foundation of job evaluation schemes, and are essential for clarifying boundaries of responsibility and decision-making, they can create a 'that's not in my job description!' environment if too restrictive and need regular updating.

Job design and the work of organisations

Job design and work organisation are the specification of the contents, method and relationships of jobs to satisfy technological and organisational requirements, as well as the personal needs of the jobholder. While not a thorough thesis of a complex subject, consideration of these issues is fundamental to defining effective job descriptions.

Two basic assumptions dominated early thinking about the scientific management approach to the design of jobs and work organisation: management and workers.

The first assumption was that management can be most effective if it devises rules and procedures to govern the way in which the task is to be undertaken. Management is assumed to be more effective than labour at devising methods for executing the work and then planning and organising. By breaking the work down into simple elements:

- Worker training is simplified
- Worker substitution is easier
- Supervision is easier, as it is more apparent when workers are doing something that is not part of their specific task.

The second assumption was that human beings are rational economic beings. The prime goal is assumed to be monetary, and consequently reward systems that relate pay levels to output are seen as likely to result in maximum output. As such, humans will examine a situation and identify a course of action likely to maximise their self-interest and act accordingly.

All that is required to maximise output, from the organisation's perspective, is to hire the right people, train them properly and construct an appropriate reward system. If the work can be paced, say by a machine, a worker can develop a natural rhythm and momentum.

However, all too often in our post-industrial societies, despite much research on what constitutes a productive, rewarding work environment, examples of counter-productive organisational environments can all too easily be found. Job designers would appear to have ignored the psychological and social aspects of work to the detriment of the organisation, the workforce and society as a whole. Opportunities for (and the benefits flowing from) the development of problem-solving and other skills in employees, at all levels, are being squandered.

For instance, high levels of task rationalisation are associated with high levels of boredom, which in turn are associated with job dissatisfaction and counter-productive work behaviour – although such jobs have some appeal to some workers! Research suggests that there are no clear rules to job design, but it can be said that people bring a diverse range of skills and abilities to the workplace, together with a diverse range of experiences, aspirations and expectations.

Therefore, the task facing today's responsible organisations would be to strike a balance between the needs of the organisation to achieve its goals and the creation of a working environment that results in the job satisfaction of the employees (see Mackay, 2007).

In job descriptions inputs are deadly sins

The first step in developing more effective job descriptions is to think about the job in output terms as the effectiveness areas of the job in question. Jobs tend to have five or 10 of them and they must all be outputs. However, the problem is that too many jobs are described in terms of inputs, not outputs: in terms of input areas and not in terms of *effectiveness* areas.

The source of some of the problems which surround effectiveness is found in the way job descriptions are written. Lengthy job descriptions, or even crash programmes to write or update them, usually have little actual usefulness.

Many, if not most, managerial jobs are defined in terms of their input and behaviour requirements by such phrases as:

'administers'…'maintains'…'organises'…'plans'…'schedules'

Naturally enough, managers never refer to job descriptions like these; once made, they are not very useful as an operating guide. They are often proposed initially by those who want to use a seemingly scientific technique to justify a widespread change in salary differentials or a change in the organisation structure. They are often a negative influence, as they focus on input and behaviour, the less important aspects of the manager's job.

So, in order to improve the effectiveness of any job, one needs to give a statement of how the jobholder can be effective instead of focusing on the activities or input areas of their job. If the position is needed at all, most inputs can be converted to outputs. Some examples are:

- Insurance   to   Asset protection
- Maintain machines   to   Machine availability
- Customer satisfaction   to   Repeat sales
- Coach subordinates   to   Subordinate effectiveness
- Train staff   to   Change behaviour
- Speed reading   to   Speed learning.

One should beware of such areas as communication, relationships, liaison, coordination and staffing: these areas usually suggest inputs to the activity, rather than outputs that the activity produces.

The outputs must be based on the authority the jobholder is going to have. If they do not have the authority to achieve an output then they cannot take responsibility for it. Virtually no one in any situation has control of all the variance in an output. The key question to ask is, 'Will they have control of *most* of the variance in their part of the organisation?'

Sometimes when brand managers get promoted to marketing managers the person that replaces them finds the recently promoted manager has taken some authority upwards. So the new brand manager, so called, really becomes a brand planner because the position does not give the opportunity to make changes in the product or to change prices. The main output could be simply producing plans, while the title suggests that it is producing profits.

Producing plans, in this case, may be the output because the manager does not have the authority to go further – particularly in implementation.

While many initial attempts to set effectiveness areas turn out instead to be a list of activities, many attempts can go in the other direction. Sometimes everyone appears to think they are heading a profit centre. Of any proposed effectiveness area the question should be asked, 'Why is this being done?' or 'Why is this important?'

For example, training managers might go through the kind of process illustrated in Figure 1.2.

The correct area as an output written into their job description for these training managers would probably be 'To increase managerial skill in problem-solving'. It cannot be 'To improve the quality of managerial decisions' or 'To improve profit performance' as these are both influenced by many factors over which the training managers have no control and no authority. On the other hand, the areas cannot be simply 'programme design' or 'putting on courses', which are clearly inputs.

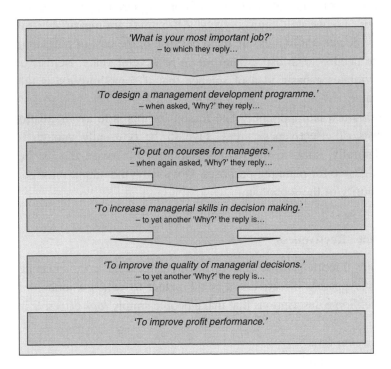

Figure 1.2 A process to define the outputs that a training manager might reasonably be expected to achieve

So, in short, the way you find the outputs of someone's job is to keep asking 'Why?' until you fall off the limit of their authority where they cannot take responsibility for variance in the output that you have arrived at. If we all keep asking 'Why?' beyond this point we all end up with 'improving the gross national product'. Things have to stop somewhere and they stop at the limit of the jobholder's authority.

So what are the tests for effectiveness areas? In essence, all effectiveness areas should meet four tests:

- Output
- Measurability
- Importance
- Authority.

Obviously, effectiveness areas must represent output not input. No less important, they must lead to associated objectives which are measurable. If you think your job has some element of non-measurability then simply forget it, because no one will know anyway. All outputs are measurable, although you may decide not to measure them because of the cost of measurement or the time needed to measure them might be several years. Neither of these points violates a basic idea of science that if something exists then it is measurable.

Another test is importance. The reason for this is to avoid creating very long lists of effectiveness areas. Five to 10 is usually enough for any job. Naturally, stick to the important things, otherwise the list becomes unmanageable for planning purposes. Obviously, the output must be within the authority of the jobholder.

Apparent effectiveness

It is quite important to be able to distinguish actual from apparent effectiveness. Apparent effectiveness is the extent to which a jobholder looks effective. Some descriptions that make people simply *look* effective include:

- Usually on time
- Answers promptly
- Makes quick decisions
- Liked by subordinates

- Good communicator
- Good at public relations
- Writes clearly.

While these qualities may be useful in some jobs at some times, they give absolutely no indication of level of effectiveness of the person in the job. They only point to a level of what seems to be effectiveness to the naive observer. Behaviour must be evaluated in terms of whether or not it is appropriate to the output requirements of the job. In short, apparent effectiveness may or may not lead to managerial effectiveness. There may be little wrong with the items listed above, but they do not necessarily point to managerial effectiveness.

Conventional job descriptions often lead to an emphasis on what could be called job efficiency, the ratio of output to input. The problem is that if both input and output are low, efficiency can still be 100 per cent. In fact, a keyboard operator, manager or department can easily be 100 per cent efficient yet 0 per cent effective.

Efficient managers are easily identified. They prefer to:

- Do things right   *rather than*   Do the right things
- Solve problems   *rather than*   Produce creative alternatives
- Safeguard resources   *rather than*   Optimise resource utilisation
- Discharge duties   *rather than*   Obtain results.

Conventional job descriptions lead to the apparent effectiveness of the behaviour as listed in the left column; a job *effectiveness* description which emphasised managerial effectiveness would lead to performance as listed in the column on the right.

The distinction between job effectiveness and apparent effectiveness can be further illustrated by what really happens when a 'steamroller' manager brings what appears to be chaos to an organisation but the situation clearly begins to improve. Unless outputs are the focus of attention, the result can be a serious distortion of what is really going on.

Revising, preparing and using job descriptions

Best practice (paraphrased from *Management Checklists* of the Chartered Management Institute) would include the following.

Inform staff of the reasons for reviewing and amending job descriptions

When existing job descriptions are reviewed, to guard against employees feeling threatened, it is important to inform employees what is happening and why. A statement should be made to the effect that the exercise will be carried out, with the full involvement of the jobholders, with the objectives being, for example:

- To ensure that people have the appropriate workload for their hours
- To ensure that department functions have the correct staff levels for their workload
- To help guide jobholders to improve their personal effectiveness and guide training programmes
- To give everyone a clear understanding of how the organisation is organised.

Assign responsibility to the jobholder and their manager

It is generally undesirable to have job descriptions prepared by personnel departments and then agreed with the jobholder and manager. Guidance about form and content should, however, be available from the personnel department. This department should be assigned to check job descriptions for consistency and overlap. In doing this, the following points should be considered:

- Does each jobholder have a clear line of authority, report to the right person and have their 360-degree relationship agreed?
- Is the job description written with the outputs of the job clearly defined, appropriate to their level of authority?
- Do too many employees report directly to one manager, who may be unable to cope with their supervision properly?
- Are some jobs so similar as to be essentially the same?
- Are similar functions grouped together or are there some specialised jobs in other departments which clearly belong elsewhere?
- Is there a clear relationship with job descriptions related to the job under review so that business processes across departmental functions are properly related?
- Are there any 'gaps', i.e. tasks related to the organisation's objectives for which no one has been assigned responsibility?

Work on objective criteria and gather information

The person responsible for compiling the job description should consider:

- What the outputs of the job are – they are often someone else's inputs
- What the jobholder *thinks* he or she is doing and what he or she is *actually* doing
- What others, over 360 degrees, whose work interacts with the jobholder, *think* he or she is doing and *ought* to be doing.

This information should be gained from informal interviews. If resources are limited, it is possible to use questionnaires, but the results tend to be ambiguous and the time required to analyse the completed questionnaires can exceed the interviewing time. While employees can be asked to complete a diary over a short period of time, generally employees dislike this and it should be avoided.

Write the job description to the following headings:

Basic information

- *Job title and department.* The job title should be readily understood inside and outside the organisation. Remember that other employees will consider the status of those with the same kind of job title to be equal. Do not use over-elaborate job titles.
- *Location.* If some flexibility is expected then it is wise not to define the location too tightly, but to state that the normal location may change from time to time.
- *Responsibility to.* The names of the people who are responsible for supervision, discipline, etc.
- *Responsibility for.* Include the total number of staff for whom they are responsible, with the job title of those reporting directly to the jobholder. For example, 'responsible for 30 staff through three supervisors'.
- *Major functional relationships.* An organisation chart will show how a job fits into the organisation and its relationship with other jobs. For example, a junior veterinary receptionist at a branch surgery may report directly to the duty veterinary surgeon at the branch, but a dotted line should also show the receptionist reporting to the practice manager at the main surgery.

Principal purpose or objective of the job   This should be a short statement describing why the job exists. For example, for support staff in a professional services firm, it could be simply 'to save the fee earner's time and to support the needs of clients'. Why else should their job exist?

Main duties/key tasks/key result areas – defined as outputs   Review the earlier section on job outputs before writing the main duties. Are you defining inputs or outputs? Will it be absolutely clear how the jobholder can be effective in the role? Key tasks, or responsibilities, are those which make a substantial contribution towards the job outputs that collectively, with other jobs, builds into the key goals of the organisation. These form the main part of the job description and there should be no more than eight to 10 outputs listed, rather than a list of all the jobholder's tasks. To ensure against too restrictive a job description, an open-ended statement should be included. One suggested standard statement is: 'Such duties as are considered essential for effective operations and services.' This should form the final key task. Distinguish between those tasks which are the direct responsibility of the jobholder and those which he or she delegates to others to carry out.

The job description should allow for an individual to use his or her initiative, and where results are measurable in some way, these should be stated. Results expected should be concrete, specific, attainable and worthwhile. Where levels of achievement are specified in measurements, it is particularly important that these are regularly updated.

Once the key tasks have been identified in output terms, they should be put into some sort of order, which might be chronological, by relative importance, by frequency of performance, by similar sorts of tasks, or by all tasks related to a particular aspect of the job. Each task should be described in a sentence or two that explains what is done, how and why. Sentences should begin with action verbs, with imprecise phrases like 'responsible for' avoided.

Update and review
The job description must be kept up to date and should be examined at least:

- Once a year when the jobholder is appraised
- When a job falls vacant, to ensure that the description still meets the department's requirements
- After the new jobholder has been in post a few months to take account of any significant changes in the jobholder's duties.

Box 1.3: Dos and don'ts for preparing a job description

Do

- Get the current jobholder involved
- Make sure that there are no clashes with other interrelated job descriptions
- Regularly update job descriptions.

Don't

- Write the job description in input terms – that will stifle effectiveness
- Amend or update job descriptions without letting staff know why they are being changed
- Let the job description restrict employees' initiative.

Person Specifications

A person specification describes the requirements a jobholder needs to be able to perform the job satisfactorily. These are likely to include:

- Education and qualifications
- Training and experience
- Personal attributes/qualities.

While a job description describes the job, a person specification describes the person needed to do the job. A person specification can therefore form the basis for the selection of the most suitable person to fill the job.

The most common approach now used by recruiters to create a person specification is to use what are known as 'competencies' to design the person specification. These are then classified as 'essential' or 'desired' to determine which are most important.

Competencies might include some or all of the following:

- Physical attributes (e.g. state of health, age, speech)
- Education (e.g. highest level of education completed)
- Attainments (e.g. relevant market experience, ability to supervise/manage)

PERSON SPECIFICATION: Head of Development and Promotions

1	Knowledge/ Understanding	Essential	Desirable	How assessed
		• Degree level preferably in business studies, marketing, law or human rights	• Full membership of Chartered Institute of Marketing qualification or equivalent	A
		• Appreciation of the role of the Not for Profit sector in the UK	• Appreciation of migration, immigration and asylum issues	AI
			• Appreciation of parliamentary/ legislative process in UK and or Europe	
2	Skills/Abilities	• To plan and manage a wide range of projects and activities	• Ability to assimilate new information quickly and effectively	AI
		• To foster effective marketing and promotion at all levels in the organisation		AI
		• To respond quickly, flexibly and imaginatively to events and to work calmly under pressure		AI
		• To provide creative solutions		AI
		• To develop project plans and budgets		AI
		• Excellent written and communication skills.		AT
		• Excellent negotiation and presentation skills		AI
		• Website management		AI
3	Experience	• Minimum of 5 years' experience of marketing, market analysis, fundraising and/or development function	• Experience of promotional work or lobbying at national, local or European levels	AI
		• Experience of using spreadsheets and databases for marketing and promotion		AT
		• Experience of identifying business opportunities from the results of market analysis and market audits		AI
4	Other Requirements	• Sensitivity to other cultures and related issues		AI
		• Commitment to the aims and principles of IAS		AI
		• Commitment to equal opportunities		AI
		• To work unsocial hours – weekends and evenings		AI
		• To travel within UK and abroad with stays of up to a week		AI

Abbreviations:
A = Application Form
T = Test
I = Interview

Figure 1.3 Person specification from the UK Immigration Advisory Service (2005)

- Aptitudes (e.g. verbal reasoning, numerical aptitude)
- Disposition (e.g. able to influence, persuade, team player, drive and initiative)
- Interests (e.g. social activities, sporting activities)
- Personal circumstances (e.g. freedom to travel, ability to work shifts, full- or part-time).

Person specifications have to be prepared and used with great care. In particular, it is important to ensure that the list of essential or desired competencies does not lead to unlawful discrimination against potential employees.

As we will see in Chapter 2, recruiting people that will align more readily with the existing organisational values and principles (psychological contract – see Chapter 2) is often considered; it is easier to train-in the skills required to do a job than to change someone's core values. However, it is very difficult to do this objectively in an interview, leaving the organisation open to complaint from interviewees who perceive they have been treated unfairly.

Selection Methods

Purpose and validity of selection methods

It is essential that two things happen in any selection method:

- The candidate's capacity and motivation to perform a particular job effectively within an organisation, to the satisfaction of the organisation, is evaluated fairly – and be seen to be so.
- The candidate must be able to formulate their assessment of the job and of the organisation.

While personal interviews may be the only selection method used, they may form one stage in a sequence of eliminating hurdles, including school reports, references, medical checks, intelligence tests, personality tests, aptitude tests and group assessment techniques.

Of key importance is the validity of any method or methods chosen. Much has been written about the validity of interviews as a selector tool – '. . . it's too subjective', '. . . biased interviewers', '. . . prejudice' and '. . . arrogance on the part of "experienced" people', all adding to the 'cons'. However, properly conducted job interviews should have a fairly significant place in the selection process – the key word, though, is 'properly'.

But properly conducted means something more than the 'I can spot one when I see one. . . ' approach. Equally, properly conducted does not mean that the interviewer pretends to be free from bias and prejudice and susceptibility to the halo effect. It is one where the interviewer has examined their own attitudes sufficiently thoroughly to be aware when these forces may be having an effect and to make appropriate allowances for them.

There are, of course, plenty of different tools used by organisations in their recruitment process. Any given résumé, curriculum vitae or application form may not have full candour and may often have been 'sexed up' for the particular vacancy. Many feel that personal references, which are usually only available if one has made a job offer 'subject to references', are too bland. One cannot give a bad reference and who would offer a referee that might speak ill of you? There is ability testing and psychometric testing (see below) as well as assessment centres, even calligraphy (handwriting tests).

In a recent article, Ivan Robertson and Mike Smith of the Manchester School of Management (2001) reviewed more than 120 articles and pieces of research, and devised a scale that scored various methods of recruitment on a scale of 0 to 1, where 1 would be a perfect fit between the candidate and the job. It was clear from the research that the poorest determinants of good future job performance are handwriting, leisure activities and even years of experience. Personal references and biographical data, susceptible as they are to distortion and exaggeration, score higher and personality tests (psychographics) higher still. Results of over 0.5 are achieved by cognitive ability tests, work sample tests and structured interviews, and the best results of all by a combination of these – usually in assessment centres.

Candidate evaluation and selection process

What is required during the applicant evaluation and selection process is a disciplined approach – discipline to work out what the organisation is looking for and why it is looking for it. The process must be able to:

- Recognise it when it is there
- Judge whether it in there in sufficient quantity
- Assess each candidate strictly in terms of the qualities and attributes sought, rather than by some subjective measure.

Square pegs in round holes do neither the peg nor the hole any good; it is positively detrimental to both. Equally, it is a lot easier to get square pegs in than out, as Chapter 8 points out. Correct selection is therefore of crucial importance. And this means that the organisation and the candidate are satisfied, in all circumstances, that the right decision has been made. The candidate who has been subjected to a battery of tests, particularly online, however thoroughly validated, will not necessarily feel satisfied if he or she has never had the chance to speak to someone in the organisation. Similarly, the interviewer who has never met the candidate cannot be sure that the approved ingredients detected by the test do really go to make up an acceptable whole whose approach to and impact on others match his or her test scores and whose tenacity and motivations augur well for success in the job.

Box 1.4: An outline job selection process

1. Decide if you have a vacancy or if the tasks can be reasonably incorporated into someone else's job. Is your vacancy full- or part-time, permanent or contract?
2. Consult with other staff – particularly those who will interact with the new post.
3. Define all the tasks and responsibilities that will be required of somebody holding that job and produce a detailed job description of effectiveness areas and outputs required.
4. Draw up a profile of the skills you believe somebody would need to be able to do the job successfully, and decide what competencies you will most require in the successful candidate – identify essential and desirable qualities.
5. Identify the selection tool(s) you will use.
6. Advertise the duties and responsibilities of the post in the appropriate media (remember internal candidates), giving clear instructions on how to apply and the closing date. Indicate salary range or type of salary, and other remuneration options.
7. Receive all the applications and decide how you will formulate your interview shortlist. Inform those people on the shortlist of arrangements for interviews and thank those who applied but have not been short-listed.
8. Go into the preparation stage of the interview process for each interview conducted.
9. Offer feedback to those candidates who would like it, to help them learn from the process.
10. After all the interviews have been completed, decide which candidate has been most successful and those who were not selected. Inform them all of your decisions.

It will be important to decide who in the organisation makes the candidate evaluation and selection decision. In larger organisations both operating managers and personnel specialists are involved in the process, and it is a general rule that if more than one person is involved, more effective candidate evaluation and selection decisions are made. Box 1.4 gives an outline to the job selection process and Table 1.3 illustrates the respective roles of operating managers and personnel managers in the scheme.

Person specifications as outlined above (pages 35–7) will be necessary for any effective evaluation/selection programme and these must be stated explicitly in the job specification.

Profile analysis

Unfortunately, there are no scientific formulae for defining position requirements and evaluating job applicants. The position/person match process seems more art than science and, while it is performed daily by managers, few feel comfortable with the required complexities. (Those that do are often insensitive to the suggestion that they could possibly be at fault when they have

Table 1.3 Operational and human resources management roles in the employee selection process

Selection functions	Operational management role	HR management role
Selection criteria	✓	Recommends and implements for criteria based on job specification/job analysis
Criteria validation		✓
Screening		✓
Process applications		✓
Interviewing	✓	Preliminary vetting interview and/or panel interviews
Testing		✓
Reference checks		✓
Physical checks		✓
Selection decision	Final decision	Recommends

'been in this game as long as I have'). One reason is that there is no analytical framework in place to address the process of balancing people with jobs.

Once we have the person specification (see Figure 1.3, page 36), a list of knowledge or skill constructs can be prepared and we can then determine the level of knowledge or skill required to work effectively in each area of their job. To do this we can place each factor on a continuum ranging from zero to a theoretical maximum of, say, 10 (see Figure 1.4).

For each construct identified in the person specification, determine the level required for someone to be effective in the job role. This process must acknowledge that while a range of knowledge/skill factors is required, the level required is not the same for each, nor is the highest (10) always the best. Not all factors can be quantified to the same extent and some might be quite subjective by nature. However, if it is important to the position and the outputs of the task are quantifiable, such factors should be listed and an attempt made to determine a level.

Let us take the person specified in Figure 1.3; among their 'essential' skill set was 'experience of using spreadsheets and databases for marketing and promotion'. If they were only required to input data accurately, the position required on the continuum might be 2 or 3. If they were expected to redesign a relational database to back up an e-commerce facility, one might be looking for 8 or 9. However, to use spreadsheets and databases for marketing and promotion purposes, within the context of the organisation concerned, one might look for skills somewhere on the midpoint of the scale. In this way, a candidate's profile can be evaluated to determine if they have the appropriate skill set that is a reasonable 'fit' to the job requirements.

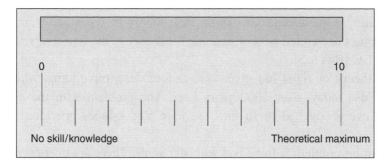

Figure 1.4 The knowledge/skill continuum

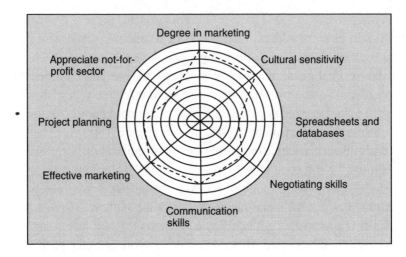

Figure 1.5 The ideal position profile

Across, say, eight primary knowledge/skill constructs, when the continua are combined, one for each knowledge/skill factor, the ideal candidate might have a profile similar to Figure 1.5.

Once the position requirements are established, attention can turn to evaluate each candidate in turn. The recruitment interview and the selection process basing one's decision-making on the ideal person profile are reviewed below.

Psychometric tests

The first attempt to solve the descriptive and causal problems of personality was made by the ancient Greeks, in their theory of types and 'humours'. Hippocrates is credited with originating the theory of the four temperaments in 400 BC (Box 1.5).

The theory of types has given rise to four descriptive terms which are still in use today, over 2000 years later. The problem with the concept is that everybody had to fit into the four pigeon-holes provided by the theory.

A similar problem is to be had with star signs. There are over 60 million people in the UK and it is difficult to believe that some 5 million similar Gemini people are going to have pretty much the same sort of day!

Box 1.5: The four 'humours'

Blood: (Latin: *sanguis*)	Sanguine: optimistic, hopeful
Black bile (Greek: *melan coln*)	Melancholic: sad, depressed
Bile (Greek: *coln*)	Choleric: irascible
Phlegm (Greek: *flegma*)	Phlegmatic: apathetic

Modern psychologists have developed a bewildering array of psychometric tests that more and more companies are using in recruitment and career development. Some of the tests available today include:

- Herrmann Brain Dominance Instrument
- Keirsey Temperament Sorter
- Thomas–Kilmann Conflict Mode Instrument
- Hogan Personality Inventory
- Myers–Briggs Type Indicator
- Occupational Personality Questionnaire
- Sixteen PF
- Fundamental Interpersonal Orientations Behaviour Instrument.

The practice in organisational recruitment dates back at least as far as World War II, when the British army experimented with the technique to measure officers' ability and leadership skills. Companies have been using it mostly since the 1970s and it was brought to the public's attention recently when James Murdoch (son of Rupert) was required to take one as part of the recruitment process for the chief executive job at BSkyB – the satellite broadcaster that is part of his father's media empire.

The annual survey of the Chartered Institute of Personnel and Development showed in 2003 that personality questionnaires, general ability tests, and literacy and numeracy tests were used by 45 per cent of 560 companies that responded – up by some 10 per cent on the previous year.

Fifty-nine of the 73 FTSE 100 companies that responded to a recent (2006) FT survey are using some form of psychometric testing. While online recruitment has meant that companies receive large volumes of applications, particularly from graduates, 80 per cent of respondents use psychometric testing for managers and some 13 per cent use it for board-level appointments.

Companies that develop and market the tests are producing increasingly persuasive evidence that using psychometric assessment can make the whole recruiting process cheaper, as well as reducing the risk of recruiting the wrong person. Certainly, psychometric assessment can save money when an organisation is dealing with a large number of applicants, and the extra cost involved in the detailed investigation of small numbers of senior candidates is usually relatively small. Some companies are providing 15-minute tests online in place of the usual sifting of CVs, followed by telephone interviews.

For executive recruitment, the cost would probably be between £500 and £1500 per head – just a fraction of the head-hunter's fee – yet this can be a concern for the more modest employer. Box 1.6 describes Virgin Mobile's experience.

The major reason why psychological tests are used in personnel selection is that they can tell us things which would otherwise be difficult to discover or difficult to get to know with any degree of confidence within the constraints of the selection situation. If tests are not used, our information about a job applicant is limited to what can be learnt about them from a CV or application form, from an *ad hoc* interview and perhaps also from references.

Each of these sources can be severely limited in terms of what can be learnt about the applicant with confidence. For instance, an *ad hoc* interview is known to be a highly unreliable means of judging a person's personality and character. This is because it is often an 'unstandardised' assessment device – there is no firm set of rules for assessing a person that can be

---

Box 1.6: Using psychometric testing to improve retention at Virgin Mobile

Virgin Mobile – a virtual mobile phone operator and FTSE 250 company – has seen the retention rate of new recruits show an encouraging rise after it started to use psychometric testing more consistently since 2004. Their Human Resources department claim that this is because the company has been better able to identify which individuals would enjoy and complement their 'self-directed' culture. Previously, newcomers might take up to a year to discover that they did not 'fit' with the way of working before becoming disenchanted and leaving the firm.

applied in precisely the same way on each occasion and for each applicant. Different interviewers will ask different questions of the applicant and different applicants will provoke different questions from the interviewer. Furthermore, there is a danger that whatever any one applicant might say may be interpreted in quite different ways by different interviewers. As a consequence, different interviewers may reach quite different impressions about the same candidate in relation to his/her job suitability. In such circumstances, it might conceivably be that one interviewer has judged the applicant 'correctly'. The problem is: how do we know which interviewer was right? We cannot simply allow ourselves to be guided by the interviewer 'with the most experience', since there is no guarantee that an interviewer with years of experience will necessarily be a good judge of people.

We have the same difficulty when trying to assess a person on the basis of an application form or CV. The possession of qualifications or attendance at courses may give us some idea about a person's level of knowledge and his/her general level of ability. However, the relationship between ability and qualifications is not particularly strong and, furthermore, we generally need information about abilities which are far more specific than those tested by written examinations at school and college. Similarly, there are difficulties in judging a person's experience on the basis of an application form or CV. To have worked for several years in a particular occupation is no guarantee that the individual has actually picked up any of the knowledge and skills relevant to that occupation.

References, of course, do not improve matters very much. If the name of the referee is supplied by the applicant, then it is a good bet that they have chosen someone who they believe will speak highly of them and perhaps avoided those who might take a dimmer view. On the other hand, we all know that an outstanding reference for someone might be the only way a company has to get rid of him or her!

So how do psychological tests help? Firstly, they have an advantage over all these other forms of assessment in that they are standardised. In other words, the test is the same for everyone. But not only this, the methods of scoring the test and, to a large degree, the methods of interpreting the test results are also standardised. What this means is that, with most tests, any given answer sheet completed by an applicant should lead to precisely the same statements about the ability or characteristic in question, no matter who scores the test and no matter who makes the interpretation. Having said this, however, there are different levels of interpretation of test results.

A personality test might produce the result that the person scores in the top 5 per cent of the general population on characteristic X. At this level, there will be no disagreement. However, the significance of that statement in relation to job suitability is not such a clear-cut matter. Consequently, tests also have their limitations in terms of being able to contribute to uniformity of opinion about a person. But what is almost certainly the case is that, on the majority of occasions, a test can give us a surer answer than we rather more subjective, inconsistent and unreliable human beings can. It is upon this latter assumption that the use of tests in personnel selection is based.

So, what makes a test psychometric? There are various definitions that are used to describe what constitutes a psychometric test. Tests are designed to provide a partial assessment of certain human attributes. These range from intellectual ability, specific aptitudes, interests, values and personality.

The British Psychological Society has defined a psychometric test as:

A measuring instrument designed to produce a quantitative assessment of some psychological attribute or attributes;

OR

Any procedure on the basis of which inferences can be made concerning a person's capacity, propensity or liability to act, react, experience or to structure or order thought or behaviour in particular ways.

An extension of the above to include elements of a psychometric test not found in other forms of assessment might be the following. A collection of questions (or items) designed to measure a psychological attribute which are:

- Administered in a standardised manner
- Scored in a standardised way
- Interpreted according to a standardised format
- Constructed according to psychometric principles.

The crucial element in this definition is standardisation associated with the administration, scoring and interpretation of a psychometric test. According to this definition, if an assessment device is not always administered in the same manner on all occasions and respondents complete the test under different instructions and conditions, the device cannot be said to be psychometric. Similarly, if the device has no scoring key or the scoring of the device varies from situation to situation, the test cannot claim to be psychometric. Finally, if the interpretation of the results does not follow some clearly defined set of guidelines or rules and as a result the same set of scores could be interpreted differently (given all other factors being equal), we would seriously doubt whether the device was in fact psychometric.

Two of the three best techniques – structured interviews and work samples – are not psychometric assessments, although psychological principles might be used in the design. If one were to use the constructs suggested earlier in the chapter, and carefully organise and deliver recruitment interviews against those specifications, one is likely to get as good results as a personality test.

While psychometric tests might be used as comparatively simple screening tests, they are rarely used on their own. Moreover, anyone who takes them should have a follow-up session with someone who has been trained in their interpretation. Virtually all practitioners agree that the final decision about an appointment should be influenced by interview as well as psychometrics.

It should be noted that while most organisations use psychometric tests for recruitment, Rolls-Royce use them for staff development – the company can, for example, establish which employees are team players or team leaders.

Recruitment interviews

A big part of business is being able to form relationships, connect with people and build a bond of trust. Rightly or wrongly, a great deal of the interview process comes down to this sort of 'chemistry'. But there is a problem – best practice does not believe in chemistry. It requires that managers are trained not to be subjective when they recruit people. As we have seen, for a given position interviewers should have a list of the competencies required, on which they interrogate the candidates, one by one. We aim not to be swayed by gut instinct about whether an applicant will 'fit in' or not: that just results in 'cloning', because we tend to warm to people who are like ourselves. If we select on the basis of history and sameness, we reduce diversity in the organisation. We also, subconsciously or not, discriminate on the basis of background, race, gender or accent. A proper codified recruitment process rules all that out.

However, are we guilty of constructing a process that seems scrupulous just so that we avoid discrimination when it should be about recruiting the right person? Clearly, we need some rigour. It is no good saying, 'I didn't get on with that one' – we need evidence, yet gut reaction seems always to play a part. One cannot be totally scientific, and by codifying everything too much can offload responsibility. Some use it to make a safe decision and get themselves off the hook.

Unfortunately, interviewers all think they can size someone up after a few minutes, and the higher up the organisation, the greater seems to be the confidence that following hunches will work. Similarly, candidates often think that their brilliance will be obvious, without needing to have the petty details of their CV scrutinised.

When it comes to the practice of good interview techniques, there are two factors that come together to ensure success: a good structure supported by good interviewer skills. Table 1.4 outlines a few suggestions.

Occasionally, especially in the recruitment process, it is regarded as more appropriate and valuable to have a group or panel of interviewers. If the group of interviewers is well selected and prepared, group interviews can offer the following benefits:

- You can broaden the expertise available for conducting the interview to get a better assessment of the interviewee's competencies.
- You can more easily balance any biases or prejudices.
- It allows people on the panel more time for note-taking, as others are asking questions.
- There can be greater variety of style and questioning, possibly offering more interest and energy during the session.
- The interviewee can get more of an understanding of the situation or team he or she may be joining.
- The decision-making and ownership of the decision can better be shared.

On the other hand, the disadvantages are:

- A group of interviewers can be intimidating to some interviewees in some settings (the format of the interview should be explained to the interviewee prior to the interview, and time given to introducing everyone and allowing the interviewee to settle in). It can also help to have one

Table 1.4 How good structure and good interviewing skills relate to each other

Interview structure	Interview skills
Initiation	Good forward planning; the need for interview is identified, the purpose clarified, the communication process is started.
Preparation	You plan and organise according to the purpose, the time, the venue, the information, the people and yourself. The communication process ensures clarity for all and time for preparation.
Setting the scene	You make the interviewee feel welcome, and valued, you allow them time to settle in, put them at ease. You clarify the purpose of the interview, and the form and time it will take. You check out whether the interviewee needs any further information, provide it if necessary, and check they are ready to proceed.
Exchanging information	You communicate clearly and get across the information relevant to your purpose and to the interviewee's need to know. You encourage the interviewee to talk. You question skilfully to elicit the information you need about the interviewee. You listen actively; there is a flow and logic to your questions. You invite the interviewee's questions and respond accordingly. You use the time allocated, as necessary, to satisfy your own, and the interviewee's, need for all the relevant information.
Summarising outcomes	You summarise, as necessary, to draw the discussion to a close. You check out whether the interviewee needs to know anything further. You clarify what the next steps, or outcomes, of the interview will be.
Closure and follow-up	You bring the interview to a close. You thank the interviewee for their time and contribution, and close positively, again making them feel respected and valued. You note what needs to happen next as a result of the interview and ensure that it does happen.

interviewer in overall charge of the interview so that there is clear control and management of the process.

- Decision-making can be more complicated following the interview (a common method is to allow each panel member one vote; the successful candidate is the one who receives most votes). Sometimes a key person is given the power of veto, or additional votes, in recognition of their greater significance in the decision-making.

- The interviewee may gain insight into the teamworking of the people she or he will be working with, and this is not necessarily positive! The interviewee may have glimpses of any discord or negative dynamics that exist between members of the interviewing panel.
- Generally, the larger the group of interviewers the more likely the event will seem stilted, artificial and less flowing (up to six interviewers is probably manageable if well planned and led).

Finally, we have already come across the concept of offering feedback to short-listed candidates who have not been selected for the post. This is becoming increasingly common and many regard it as a mark of a quality organisation if they take the time and trouble to give feedback. It can be a very useful contribution to a person's development to give them face-to-face or telephone feedback on:

- The strengths of their application
- Ways in which it might have been stronger in terms of this job, at this time
- Ways at which the person impressed at interview
- What it might help to work on in future interviews.

Box 1.7: All these questions are indications of intended sex bias and should be avoided – they are very likely to be unlawful *per se*

What not to ask in an interview:

- What is your marital status?
- What is the number and age of your children?
- What is your husband/wife/partner's employment
- Do you live with your/parents/relatives/guardians/alone/boyfriend/girlfriend/partner/other?
- What are your parents' occupations?
- Do you have a boy/girlfriend?
- Are you in a stable relationship?

- Have you ever gone out with anyone at work?
- Are you planning to get engaged/married?
- What is your medical condition? (Women only)
- Have you had any time off owing to 'female' ailments?
- Do you suffer from period pains?
- Have you had any time off owing to period pains?
- Do you have any gynaecological abnormalities?
- Are you pregnant or do you plan to become pregnant?
- Do you intend to start a family?
- Have you ever had a baby?
- Have you ever suffered a miscarriage?

(Information provided from the Equal Opportunities Commission – www.eoc.org.uk)

Such an exchange of feedback can, of course, be two-way! It can be very valuable to know the following from the candidate:

- What did you like about our recruiting process (from advertisement through to feedback)?
- What can we do better next time?

Making the Decision and Job Offering

Input for this part of the evaluation will come from a variety of sources, depending on what is known of the candidate and where they have come from. Sources might include:

- A job application
- Résumé or CV
- A job interview
- Discussion with former employers
- Actual on-the-job observations (internal applicants)
- Discussion with peers.

Using the information obtained, an evaluation of each applicant can be performed against the job profile, factor by factor. Using a spider chart, the individual level can be annotated for each factor. If we look at the ideal person specification we developed earlier in the chapter, suppose we reviewed a couple of candidates and developed the following two profiles (Figures 1.6 and 1.7).

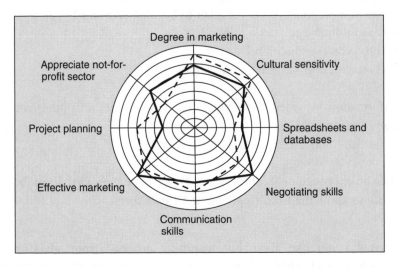

Figure 1.6 Candidate 'A' profile

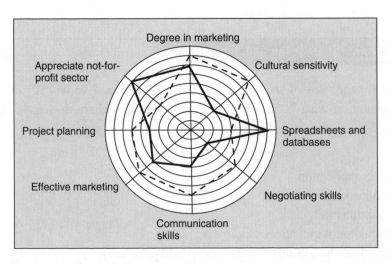

Figure 1.7 Candidate 'B' profile

It is very desirable in many jobs that claims about experience and statements about qualifications are thoroughly checked, and that applicants unfailingly complete a health questionnaire. (The health questionnaire is not necessarily limiting for applicants, as firms are required to employ a percentage of disabled people.)

Before letters of appointment are sent, any doubts about medical fitness or capacity (in employments where hygiene considerations or health risks are dominant – for example, food preparation or working in pharmacies where cytotoxic drugs are prepared) should be resolved by requiring applicants to attend a medical examination. This is especially so where, as for example in the case of apprentices, the recruitment is for a contractual period or involves the firm in significant training costs.

It is evident that the person being evaluated in Figure 1.6 is somewhat suited for the position; their project planning may have to be a development area but, other than that, their profile suggests they might be a good match for the role and the organisation.

The candidate being evaluated in Figure 1.7 has more weaknesses than the other candidate; while they may be able to develop their skills in marketing, communications and negotiating, that they scored less well on cultural sensitivity suggests that they might not be such a good fit for the organisation.

Induction Programmes

The recruitment process done properly is expensive in cash as well as resource terms; it makes good sense to help new recruits integrate promptly into their new surroundings and to become efficient and effective in their work. Failure to do so can, at the very least, lead to poor performance, with possible hidden costs such as waste of materials and loss of customers, and at worst to grievance and associated claims against the employer.

The size and type of organisation will affect the format and content of an induction programme, which will also vary according to existing knowledge, experience and seniority of the recruit. Remember, it is as essential to help the newcomer adapt to the existing culture, language and standards of the organisation as to train him or her to be effective in their particular job.

Induction should be treated as an extension of the selection process and the beginning of a continuing staff development programme. It should not be viewed in isolation. It often consists of a first stage: an organisation-wide programme, usually conducted by the human resource department. The second stage is a departmental programme, which we concentrate on here and will be of value to the more modest enterprise.

The purpose of induction is to ensure that new employees:

- Are integrated promptly into their new surroundings
- Learn relevant aspects of the organisation's goals, culture, policies, procedures and methods of working
- Become effective in their new role and well motivated
- Begin enhancing and developing their skills and knowledge needed for the job
- Understand their responsibilities.

Action for the organisation

A good induction programme will integrate new arrivals more quickly into the organisation so they become effective sooner. It is important that you value the newcomer, making them feel welcome and giving them a sound impression of the organisation. In this way, recruitment costs are seen as an investment and successful induction will be the essential first stage of the employee development programme.

Good practice will include:

1. *Planning.* Plan the induction and involve and inform others by drawing up an induction programme that should ideally be authorised by the newcomer's manager. Other staff who will be working with the new employee should be informed of the induction programme whether or not they will be involved. The induction plan should contain three stages: the first day or two should cover the bare essentials; the first three or four weeks should be learning by a mix of approaches; the three- to six-month period should gradually familiarise the newcomer with all departments.
2. *Appoint a 'buddy'.* Ask someone about the same age and grade of the newcomer to act as a friend and advisor for the first few weeks. They should be selected from the new recruit's work group and would have been involved in the induction process. Having such a person on hand will be particularly useful in a large, complex organisation or in helping to explain the myriad of detail not fully covered elsewhere. Select the person

carefully – you will want a responsible person and not the office maverick! Monitor the relationship, however, and step in if it isn't working.

3. *Start with a tidy work area.* An obvious yet often overlooked stage will be to clear and tidy the new employee's work area. Saying, '. . . this is your desk; that bloke we fired left that mess – and could you sort it out by the end of the week' is not going to be the best start! Check that all relevant stationery is to hand, where and how new resources may be obtained, and ensure equipment is in working order.

4. *On the first day.* Usually, the personnel function will inform the newcomer of housekeeping arrangements (where the toilets, coffee-making and canteen facilities are, for example) and cover issues contained in the staff handbook (such as salary payments, leave arrangements and sick pay scheme). The new employee will need copies of any necessary documentation, the organisation chart and job description, for example. An introduction to the department and team in which they will be working must also be made. Although the newcomer will be introduced to people around the organisation, a detailed look at what other departments do should follow at a later stage of the induction process.

5. *Organisational policies and procedures.* New employees must be made aware at an early stage of policies and regulations based on legislation, for example in the area of health and safety, Care of Substance Hazardous to Health (COSHH), etc. Other procedures based on national standards, such as ISO 9000, and other schemes, such as internal employee development, Investors in People or mentoring, should also be introduced.

6. *Training and development.* Decide whether training is done by the 'sitting-next-to-Nellie' approach or by professional trainers. Whatever approach is taken, a mix of explanation, observation, practice and feedback is advisable. Ensure a balanced introduction to the work and beware of information overload. The new employee should be given some real work to do to avoid boredom and to give early opportunities for achievement. This will clearly have a positive effect on their motivation.

7. *Key performance indicators.* Make the performance levels you require clear from the outset and explain how the outcomes of the job are evaluated. An employee cannot be expected to meet standards of which they are unaware.

8. *Review progress regularly.* Conduct regular progress reviews during the induction programme, for example on a weekly basis, to ensure that all the objectives and the new employee's needs are being met. The programme

may have to be adapted to match individual learning requirements and speeds. Usually, reviews will consist of informal chats but a more formal appraisal interview may take place at the end of the programme, particularly if the employee is on probation. The views of the employee on the overall induction process should be sought for the design of future programmes.

Box 1.8 provides a guide for organisations.

Action for the new recruit

New recruits should also beware of their first few days so that they too get off on the right foot. Who carries such a full load of self-certainty that the

---

Box 1.8: A guide for organisations – dos and don'ts for organisations with new recruits

Do

- Ensure all relevant staff know about and are involved as necessary in the induction process
- Review a new employee's progress regularly and be flexible enough to incorporate his or her reasonable needs into the induction programme
- Evaluate the style and content of the induction programme and improve it if necessary, taking into account the views of employees who have had recent experience of it.

Don't

- Forget that starting a new job is a stressful experience for most people
- Give the employee too much information at once
- Make assumptions about the recruit's learning speed and integration
- Forget that an induction lasts longer than one day or even one week.

(Suggestions from the Chartered Management Institute, *Management Checklists*, No. 1)

---

concept of personal inadequacy is never remotely entertained? Confident people tend to interview well, but one needs to ensure that confidence levels do not rise from the enviable to the intolerable. Business graduates with first-class degrees frequently believe themselves to be instantly qualified to take over from Lord Browne at BP.

So, consider the following if you are a new recruit:

- If you say you are charming to everyone, make sure that they don't think you are condescending.
- While you may think that you are doing right by being punctual, well turned out and very conscientious, remember your experience of your new organisation and the role is nil. You must accept this fact and behave accordingly.
- Remember, too, that play-acting will not work either. Your acceptance of your need to learn must be deeply felt and total. Any mock humility will earn you a self-induced setback – and that will not enhance your CV at all.

Box 1.9 provides a guide for new recruits to an organisation.

Box 1.9: A guide for new recruits – dos and don'ts

Ten smart things

Do

- Ensure you introduce yourself to reception and key support staff.
- Walk round the entire site and get to know where things are.
- Check that you are getting from the organisation what they offered – talk to the person that looks after personnel issues and insist on a written contract, terms, etc.
- Visit other departments, especially those that supply you internally and those you supply – agree your outputs.
- Make friends with the person that manages the office or work area.
- Introduce yourself to the managing director and their secretary.
- Learn names fast – use them too.

(*Continued*)

Box 1.9: Continued

- Insist on the right equipment from the beginning.
- Make sure you get a parking space, if appropriate.
- Make small visible achievements without boasting.

Ten dumb things

Don't

- Tell everyone how you are going to turn this place round.
- Explain how the place you have just left did things 'soooo' much better.
- Try to take on board too much information at once.
- Make assumptions about what your job is really about and how you'll look good in it.
- Forget that to be really effective takes longer than one day or even one week.
- Agree to anything in the first week.
- Treat the people that will do your photocopying as serfs.
- Buy friends.
- Think that working 15 hours a day will impress.
- Make a pass at someone.

Summary

In this chapter you have:
- Explored the main influences on today's recruitment market
- Reviewed an employer's responsibility concerning diversity and equal opportunities
- Covered a guide to writing a job description and a person specification
- Considered the various recruitment methods and the purpose and validity of each
- Reviewed best practice when making a decision and offering the job
- Learnt how to ensure induction programmes are effective.

Questions

1. Review the section on diversity and equal opportunities. Evaluate your organisation (or one with which you are familiar) and critique its policies in this area, making recommendations for any improvements you can identify.
2. Either: consider your current job description and person specification and explain whether or not it matches up to best practice. Put forward justified proposals for any improvements.
3. Or, alternatively: develop a job description and person specification for your position as a student of management.
4. Consider the selection methods used in your organisation (or place of learning). How do they compare to suggestions in the text? Give justifications for any improvements you identify.

References

Cook, P. (2004) *Professional Manager*, November, p. 21.
The Economist (2004) 'Migration Fears, Myths, and Reality', 26 February.
Equal Opportunities Commission (2004) *Who Runs Britain?*
Mackay, A. R. (2007) *Motivation, Ability and Confidence Building in People*, Butterworth-Heinemann.
Management Today (2003) April, p. 44.
Reeves, R. (2003) *Management Today*, April, p. 33.
Robertson, I. and Smith, M. (2001) *Journal of Occupational and Organisational Psychology*, Vol. 74, pp. 441–472.
The Sunday Times (2005) 16 October, p. 3.15.

Recommended Reading

Diversity

Clements, P. and Jones, J. (2002) *The Diversity Training Handbook: A Practical Guide to Understanding and Changing Attitudes*, Kogan Page.
Kirton, G. and Greene, A.-M. (2004) *The Dynamics of Managing Diversity*, Butterworth-Heinemann.

Job descriptions

Cushway, B. (2006) *Handbook of Model Job Descriptions*, Kogan Page.

Recruitment and selection

Edenborough, R. (2002) *Effective Interviewing: A Handbook of Skills and Techniques*, Kogan Page.

Edenborough, R. (2005) *Assessment Methods in Recruitment Selection and Performance: A Manager's Guide to Psychometric Testing, Interviews and Assessment Centres*, Kogan Page.

Grant, J. and Perrin, S. (2002) *Recruiting Excellence: An Insider's Guide to Sourcing Top Talent*, McGraw-Hill Education.

Roberts, G. (2005) *Recruitment and Selection*, Chartered Institute of Personnel and Development.

Management best practice

Mackay, A. R. (2007) *Motivation, Ability and Confidence Building in People*, Butterworth-Heinemann.

Part 2

Retaining People

2

Retention

There are no bad soldiers, only bad leaders.

General Ulysses S. Grant

Learning Outcomes

This chapter has been written as a general guide for managers and should not be used as a substitute for professional legal advice on these matters. It has been written to meet the needs of both the National Occupational Standards for Management and Leadership (*Unit 24*) and the Chartered Management Institute's Diploma in Management compulsory module (*Unit C45 – Managing Performance*) in as far as retention of staff is concerned. It also meets the needs of people studying the CIPD Professional Development Scheme – particularly regarding retention as part of the *People Management and Development* core module.

By the end of this chapter you will:

- Be able to devise strategies to retain your staff and help in their development for succession planning
- Guide people approaching retirement
- Know how to manage the redeployment of people
- Be able to follow the crucial steps in redundancy and removal of people.

Keeping Staff

In any organisation, perhaps 10 per cent of employees are particularly talented, 80 per cent are 'good enough' and the other 10 per cent may be authentically hopeless. Lifting the performance of the whole organisation requires a focus on the majority – the competent 80 per cent. If each of these people were to raise their performance by just a little, the cumulative effect will be enormous – so much more than fast-track programmes and special bonuses for the high-fliers. Clearly, top people are important, but if one were just to focus on them the massed ranks of the people that are delivering an acceptable level of performance may feel neglected – yet these are the very people one wants to retain. In the pursuit of the soloist, don't forget the orchestra!

Retention of good people – even moderately good – is essential for any organisation. If people leave for the competition, it sends out a clear message that there is something more attractive about the competition. If one's staff feel like that, then customers will feel the same way too, and that can quickly develop into a very corrosive cycle.

Staff retention is vital to the short- and long-term health of an organisation. There are a number of variables that influence staff retention, ranging from pay and conditions, career development prospects and the nature of relationships within the workplace. While the first two factors are largely controlled by the organisation, it is difficult to systematically control the nature of workplace relationships. It is suggested that much of the satisfaction individuals gain from their work lies in their ability to form strong and fulfilling relationships in the workplace; likewise, the reason cited by many people for leaving their job lies in the dissatisfaction and frustration caused by poorly functioning relationships.

Replacement costs usually are 2.5 times the salary of the individual, which includes lost customers, business and damaged morale. In addition are the hard costs of time spent in advertising, screening, verifying credentials, references, interviewing, hiring and training the new employee just to get back to where you started. This expenditure of time and money does nothing to give a manager or an organisation a competitive edge. However, despite these known costs and loss of productivity, many businesses do nothing to create a high-retention culture or reduce high employee turnover. The revolving door keeps moving – employees leave, managers interview and hire more workers, allowing competitors with low turnover to focus more on productivity.

The latest Recruitment Confidence Index (RCI) survey (www.rsisurvey.co.uk), a quarterly index developed by the Cranfield School of Management and *The Daily Telegraph* as a way of measuring expectations of future recruitment activity, has focused on staff retention. By measuring to what extent organisations expect to change levels of recruitment activity, the RCI forecasts changes in the recruitment climate over a six-month period. Therefore, it provides an important new dimension to current economic forecasting, as recruitment is widely regarded to be at the front end of business growth or decline.

The RCI Autumn 2004 survey reported that the Index (base 100 – Winter 1999) stands at 132 for all staff and 126 for managerial/professional staff, indicating a slight fall since last quarter. The survey also found that:

- Business confidence has risen to positive levels, meaning that more respondents are optimistic about business conditions than are pessimistic
- Recruitment difficulties are expected to be most common in engineering and logistics
- Recruitment difficulties are now expected to be highest at senior and middle management levels and have fallen at board level
- The majority of organisations expect pay increases to remain in line with inflation.

Box 2.1: RCI Staff Retention Survey, Autumn 2004

- 36 per cent of organisations have changed employee packages to include more non-financial benefits
- 49 per cent of companies surveyed use performance-related pay
- 81 per cent have a mission statement
- 66 per cent have a communications strategy
- 42 per cent of respondents thought that their employer brand was quite well defined, with 36 per cent indicating that this was very well defined and 23 per cent saying that theirs was not well defined
- 67 per cent of companies believed that their organisational values were adhered to through policies and practices
- 79 per cent of respondents provided social events for workers to encourage them to get together out of office hours.

Chart Your Course International (www.chartcourse.com) conducted a job satisfaction and retention survey in the USA in August 2004. They found that salary had become the top issue as to why people stay (55 per cent) or leave (64 per cent) their organisation for another; communication issues have increased in importance as to what causes low morale and dissatisfaction at work since their first survey in 2001. They also found that respondents suggested that their employer was not tapping into their potential, since over 70 per cent of respondents suggested that they had ideas that could improve productivity yet were largely being ignored. Further findings are summarised in Tables 2.1 and 2.2.

Table 2.1 The reasons people *stay* at their present job (all options that apply given)

Salary	55%	Good boss	33%
Interesting work	53%	Work assignments vary	30%
Benefits	52%	Feel appreciated for what I do	25%
Enjoy my co-workers	45%	Education and development	19%
Sense of purpose/mission	42%	No time to look for new job	18%
Location is convenient	40%	Career opportunities	16%
Challenging job assignments	39%	Autonomy	14%
Flexibility in work hours	38%	Perks (car, club membership, etc.)	5%

Data from Chart Your Course International.

Table 2.2 The primary reasons people would *leave* their present employer for another (all options that apply given)

Salary	64%	Low morale	27%
Career advancement	57%	Location/commute	25%
Challenging and interesting work	47%	Education and development opportunities	25%
Better managers/better managed place to work	45%	Unfair treatment	23%
Work/life balance	44%	Company in financial jeopardy	19%
Higher calling/purpose/mission	40%	More time off	19%
Better benefits	37%	Job security	17%

Data from Chart Your Course International.

Implementing retention strategies

The two surveys highlighted here suggest that staff retention is both important and that it is multi-factoral. One cannot guess at what will retain staff; perhaps a staff survey is the place to start finding out – the cost of not knowing is high (see www.daw.co.uk/audit_business.htm for a modern approach to staff surveys). Among the issues to consider when implementing retention strategies will be to:

- Monitor the market benchmark to ensure that pay rates are competitive
- Review the choice of benefits and increase the variety – for example, sabbaticals, career breaks, childcare and elderly arrangements
- Review the recruitment process and information provided on the company web pages and other literature to ensure that it gives an accurate picture of the organisation
- Review the quality of the induction procedure and training opportunities offered
- Improve the job design, job description and job evaluation process – make sure the jobholder is fully aware of all expectations required
- Introduce flexible working practices such as job sharing, flexitime and remote working, where practicable
- Check your equal opportunities policies are up to date
- Promote career progression opportunities, such as dual career ladders for technical and managerial staff
- Improve the abilities of managers and supervisors in their people-handling skills.

If you wish to review reward systems as part of your retention strategies, see Mackay (2007) – Chapter 7 looks at effort, performance and reward.

Retention and length of service

Gone, it seems, are the halcyon days of the gold watch for 25 years' service. Age regulations, referred to in Chapter 1 as they affected hiring staff, also have an affect on length of service benefits.

The regulations bring in a five-year limit on pay and benefits relating to length of service. However, it is acceptable to continue any benefits based on a length of service requirement of five years or less as these will be exempt. After five years service employers must show that there will be an advantage from rewarding loyalty, perhaps by encouraging the motivation or recognising the experience of workers by awarding benefits on the basis of length of service.

Currently, it is not easy to predict the amount or type of evidence that employers will be required to provide to prove that abolishing long-service awards will have a direct impact on business performance in order to defend their continuation; it is hoped that awards for loyalty are not simply consigned to the waste-bin as a simpler option.

Employers wanting further guidance on this issue are directed to ACAS (www.acas.org.uk), the government-appointed agency to give advice on age issues, or Age Positive (www.agepositive.gov.uk).

The Psychological Contract

During the stable 1950s, the careers enjoyed by corporate executives were built on an implicit understanding and mutual trust. Influenced by their parents' hardships in the 1930s to value job security, and by their parents' military service in WWII to be obedient to those above, the term Organisation Man or Corporate Man was invented for this generation.

Implicit to such careers was the understanding that loyalty and solid performance brought job security. This was mutually beneficial: the executive gained a respectable income and a high degree of security, the company gained loyal, hard-working executives. This unspoken pact became known as the 'psychological contract'. The originator of the phrase was the social psychologist Ed Schein of MIT. Schein's interest in the employee–employer relationship developed during the late 1950s. Schein noted the similarities between the brainwashing of POWs, which he had witnessed during the Korean War, and the corporate indoctrination carried out by the likes of General Electric and IBM.

As Schein's link with brainwashing suggests, there was more to the psychological contract than a cosy mutually beneficial deal. The bliss of stability only went so far and it raised a number of issues.

First, the psychological contract was built around loyalty. While loyalty is a positive quality, it can easily become blind. What if the corporate strategy is wrong or the company is engaged in unlawful or immoral acts?

The second issue was that of perspectives. With careers neatly mapped out, executives were not encouraged to look over the corporate parapets to seek out broader viewpoints. The corporation became a self-contained and self-perpetuating world supported by a complex array of checks, systems and hierarchies.

Clearly, such an environment was hardly conducive to fostering dynamic risk-takers. The reality was that the psychological contract placed a premium on loyalty rather than ability and allowed a great many poor performers to seek out corporate havens. It was also significant that the psychological contract was regarded as the preserve of management. Lower down the hierarchy, people were hired and fired at will. The rash of downsizing in the 1980s and 1990s marked the end of the psychological contract. Expectations have now changed on both sides. Employers no longer wish to make commitments – even implicit ones – to long-term employment. The emphasis is on flexibility. On the other side, employees are keen to develop their skills and take charge of their own careers.

Today, individuals are keen to promote their employability. The new reality of corporate life means that the traditional psychological contract between employer and employee is unlikely to return. But, in any employment arrangement, each side carries expectations, aspirations, and an understanding of the expectations and aspirations of the other side. The challenge is for both sides to make the new psychological contract an explicit arrangement.

Mental Ill-health and Employment

The cost of mental health problems to industry has increased significantly over the last decade. It has proved difficult to find a reliable method that will accurately measure mental ill-health and conditions such as stress. Some people will, for example, prefer to say that they are suffering from stress rather than disclose that they feel depressed. What one individual understands as stress, anxiety or depression may differ from how another person understands the same conditions. It is therefore interesting to note that several surveys may show similar levels for cost of mental ill-health to industry.

- Thirty-seven per cent (£11.8 billion) of the total cost of mental health problems in England is due to lost employment (Patel and Knapp, 1998).
- The number of days taken off sick due to mental ill-health has increased by 20 per cent since the 1970s (Mental Health Foundation, 1995). The

69

Department of Health found in 1995 that over 91 million working days are lost as a result of mental ill-health every year (Department of Health, 1995).

■ A study by the CBI and the Department of Health (1992) estimated that 80 million days are lost yearly due to anxiety and depression at a cost of approximately £5.3bn (1991/92 prices). A study by CBI and Percom suggests that, in a typical year, 80 million working days are lost as a result of stress-related illness.

■ In the early 1990s, half the days lost through mental illness were due to anxiety and stress-related conditions (Mental Health Foundation, 1995). By 1997, it was estimated that 12 million working days were lost from work-related illness (Health Education Authority, 1997).

Situations at work that can cause problems include:

■ Unrealistic workloads
■ Bad management
■ Role conflicts – where someone works for two bosses
■ Poor balance between effort and rewards (Mackay, 2007)
■ Other issues (summarised in Box 2.2).

Box 2.2: Causes of stress at work

■ New job
■ Overwork
■ Customer complaints
■ Anxiety – losing job
■ Change of job
■ Promotion, job move
■ Your boss!
■ A colleague
■ New boss
■ Only one of race
■ Only criticisms
■ Not enough to do
■ Unclear expectations
■ More than one manager.

Good practice to help resolve some of the problems will involve:

- Getting senior management approval
- Involve staff from across the business in the development of a mental health policy
- Educate staff about mental ill-health
- Create a supportive culture where sufferers can discuss their problems openly without fear of discrimination
- Develop a social fabric where someone with mental illness is treated in the same way as someone who has a physical illness or has broken their leg skiing
- Ensure that the organisation is not encouraging an unhealthy long-hours culture and inappropriate management behaviour.

The aim is not to turn managers into 'lay' psychiatrists but to encourage them to be sensitive to changes in people's demeanour or behaviour that might indicate there is a problem.

Typical signs of mental ill-health might include:

- Someone who is usually punctual turning into a poor timekeeper
- A usually gregarious person becoming withdrawn
- An easygoing employee suddenly becoming irritable or tearful
- Someone whose performance takes an unexpected downturn
- Other symptoms of stress (see Table 2.3).

Armed with information about the problem, the manager can look at what support they may be able to provide. While this will vary according to the individual's needs, it might mean:

- Redesigning the person's role
- Making adjustments to specific tasks
- Reducing working hours
- Changing working patterns
- Providing 'compassionate' leave – perhaps in the case of bereavement of a near relative
- Encouraging the employee to seek assistance from one of the supportive agencies.

Table 2.3 The symptoms of stress

Physical	Mental
■ Communicating less with other people ■ Feeling tired and lacking in energy ■ Being late for work etc. ■ Adding weight without meaning to ■ Eating for comfort, or not eating at all ■ Sleep disorders ■ Frequent minor ailments – colds, sore throats ■ Shortness of breath. ■ Indigestion, nausea or sickness ■ Frequent headaches	■ Feeling of boredom and apathy ■ Preoccupation with your own health ■ Constant feeling of unease and anxiety ■ Irritation with everybody ■ Fears and phobias – heights, lifts, cars ■ Feeling unable to talk to anyone ■ Reluctance to take a break or holiday ■ Inability to concentrate ■ Feeling that you aren't getting enough done ■ Fear of death – your own or other people

There is overwhelming evidence that keeping people in work if at all possible is by far the best approach. Having a job to go to helps the individual regain self-esteem and confidence and gives them a purpose – and, of course, the organisation gets to retain the services of a valuable employee. There are two caveats to this: first, the source of workplace stress needs to be addressed and, secondly, the individual must not be a cause of stress on their work colleagues. Even someone working 'below par' is better than being absent completely, where all their duties will fall to others.

Research has shown that if a person is absent from work for three months, the likelihood they will return is diminished; after six months, it is highly unlikely that they will return at all (for further information see www.mind.org.uk).

One approach that is growing in popularity is the use of mental health case workers who support both the organisation and the individual throughout the period of illness. Case workers typically facilitate communication between employer and employee on issues like adjustments to the job or time off work, and act as a central point of contact between the company and medical professionals. They can also act as an advocate for the employee within the organisation, provide training for managers and help employees ensure that they are meeting their legal obligations.

Mind provides the advice shown in Box 2.3 to guide employers on managing mental health problems at work.

Box 2.3: Better mental health at work (courtesy of Mind)

If a member of staff is showing signs of mental ill-health:

- Talk to them about it
- Make sure they know about any support the organisation offers
- Consider the need for adjustments.

If you want to develop an equal opportunity policy on mental health:

- Gain commitment at senior level in the organisation
- Review existing equal opportunities policies and procedures, and adapt them to include people with mental health problems
- Involve a range of staff in this process and consider drawing on the expertise of a mental health organisation.

If you want to promote positive mental health throughout your organisation:

- Focus on the quality of management and communication
- Consult with staff about how they rate the quality of the work environment and practices
- Carry out a stress risk assessment
- Develop an action plan
- Display and promote information that encourages employees to look after their mental well-being.

(From *Managing for Mental Health: The Mind Employers' Resource Pack*. E-mail: publications@mind.org.uk)

Speaking at a conference of the British Psychological Society in Warwick, Dr Peter Clough, of Hull University, said that employers could benefit by putting staff on 'tough Outward Bound-type courses' to help them beat stress, rather than end up sick or being moved to a different job (*The Times*, 2005). He said that researchers found that students sent up an icy mountain in −10°C temperatures and volunteers who spent days sailing a tall ship said they felt better able to deal with daily challenges. This seems to make a good case for employers helping staff manage their work/life balance.

Retention and Family Policies

Much has been said about family policies in respect of recruitment in the last chapter, but what of retention?

Suppose one of your best people has resigned because she says she can't balance childcare and work satisfactorily; at her exit interview she says that her new employer runs an on-site nursery. So, recognising that assistance with childcare might help retain other good people, what might you need to consider? The following is based on ideas from *Management Today* (May 2006, p. 22):

- *Justification.* Providing childcare can have a key influence on employee retention. Parents of either gender consider childcare a key factor in taking their job and many would turn down another job rather than lose their workplace childcare. Employers also find that staff morale and job satisfaction improve, with less absenteeism.
- *Viability.* A staff audit will find how many children are likely to use any facility and for how long (the child's age affects the duration of use of a crèche), and what parents are looking for. Many parents may have other arrangements and won't want to change.
- *Evaluate the options.* You could establish an on-site nursery, negotiate space at an existing independent nursery or offer childcare vouchers so that employees can make their own arrangements. Your own on-site nursery often offers most convenience for your people and the service can be tailored around your business – especially if shift working is used. However, voucher systems are simple to set up and allow people to choose what is best for them.
- *Consider holiday plans.* In addition to day-to-day care, 'holiday clubs' help parents during school holidays.
- *Know the law.* Childcare is highly regulated and may not be your core activity; equally, just any old building will not suffice – they have to conform to strict health and safety rules. For this reason it is probably better to bring in a specialist company such as BUPA, Bright Horizons or Asquith Nurseries.

■ *Avoid favourites.* Beware of favouring one group of employees over another as the availability of childcare places and other benefits is an emotive issue. There may be an argument to provide particular resources for strategic reasons – for example, if a particular shift is difficult to fill.

■ *Make it tax-efficient.* Employees may have up to £55 a week towards childcare that will be exempt from income tax and National Insurance.

Succession Planning

One of the key facets to retention is to ensure that organisations have considered how they will maintain a steady succession of people as others move on or move up the organisation. Not having a successor in mind may limit the desire to move a good person up – so make sure there is somebody 'waiting in the wings'. Good succession planning would involve the following considerations:

■ *Understand the context.* Good succession planning must be in the context of the organisation and the dynamics of the market in which it operates. People who might be successful in the job now might not be the right person in five years' time.

■ *Plan ahead.* One needs to take account of the broader picture, not just individual roles. When anyone leaves a post for whatever reason, there is always an opportunity to rethink how the key work processes might be apportioned among the remaining people before considering who might be best suited to take over the other effectiveness areas. There is also a need to understand the flow of critical business skills – where they are moving to, where they are coming from. If an organisation had a number of retirements coming up in the next five years with the loss of all that considerable experience, the next generation needs to be brought on now in the next two years.

■ *Include all levels.* Plans should not be limited to top-tier management, they should include all key performance areas of the organisation. Relatively junior people may hold specialist knowledge and any plan needs to take into account the transfer of that knowledge. Each department or key business process needs to formulate its own succession plan.

■ *Apply lateral thinking.* While there may not be anybody in the department just now, good managers might be in another specialist area. Moreover, the succession plan needs to be seen to take into account people from other areas or it could risk being labelled 'cronyism' or the 'old boys' network' and instil resentment to management in general and the new jobholder in particular.

- *Involve people in line.* Often, many assumptions about who wants to move into a new role are wrong. While many relish the new challenge, many quite capable people may not have the same ambitions. It is important to speak to people about their personal ambitions and commitment – in confidence, without them feeling that they are under undue pressure. Just because someone does not want the promotion just now – perhaps because they have a young family – they don't want to feel that they are going to be overlooked for ever. Ensure that those who are not chosen or don't want to be don't become disenchanted with the organisation.

- *Take action.* Once a potential successor has been identified, they need to be groomed for the challenge. Get the training in early and give them time to apply their skills. Also carry out a robust gap analysis of their skills at regular appraisals and compare them against the template for the job.

- *Don't be too prescriptive.* It is better to develop a number of people and make a final decision when you have to, provided you are open and honest with them all. In a number of years, things change and it is best to keep one's options open.

- *Monitor your plan.* Some successors may move on while others may look less promising, so keep your plans under review.

- *Do say*: 'We are developing people with the experience and contacts to be our leaders of tomorrow.'

- *Don't say*: 'This is my mate Duncan; he'll be taking over from me when I retire in 10 years time.'

Bullying in the Workplace

According to studies since the mid-1990s, bullying in the workplace has been steadily increasing, such that it was estimated in 2000 to cause between one-third and one-half of all stress-related illnesses.[1] The Health and Safety

---

[1] Dr Cary Cooper and Helge Hoel, UMIST, February 2000.

Executive announced that 'The 2004/5 Survey of Self-reported Work-related Illness Prevalence' estimate indicated that around half a million individuals in Britain believed in 2004/05 that they were experiencing work-related stress at a level that was making them ill. The Stress and Health at Work Study (SHAW) indicated that nearly one in five of all working individuals thought their job was very or extremely stressful. So, the scale of the problem is clear.

In the absence of any legal definition, bullying can be described the following way:

Offensive, intimidating, malicious or insulting behaviour, or abuse or misuse of power, which violates the dignity of, or creates a hostile environment which undermines, humiliates, denigrates or injures, the recipient.

Bullying has a detrimental effect on both individuals and organisations. It is reasonable to expect that everyone should be treated with dignity and respect at work, and it is in every employer's interest to promote a safe and fair working environment. Research published in September 2005 by the Chartered Management Institute (www.managers.org.uk/bullying) confirmed that managers in the UK support this view.

There are a number of reasons for addressing bullying:

- Concern for employee well-being
- Low employee morale – bullying not only affects the direct victims, but also those who witness it
- Management time and legal costs through compensation claims and tribunals
- Damage to the organisation's reputation
- The knock-on impact on the bottom line – falling productivity, staff turnover and absenteeism.

While managers clearly recognise the negative impact of bullying, this research investigated how managers can better deal with bullying in the workplace. Uniquely, it looked at bullying as experienced by managers at all levels of seniority. It aimed to explore the effectiveness of policies on bullying, as seen from the perspective of those managers who may be expected to implement initiatives on bullying.

CMI conclusions and recommendations

- A third of managers reported that their organisations are currently ineffective at deterring bullying, clearly suggesting that many organisations need to do more to ensure that their stance on bullying is effective.
- While implementing formal policies can play an important part in deterring bullying, within organisations only just over half of managers reported that their organisation has a formal policy on bullying.
- The organisational culture and management style should also make it clear that bullying is not tolerated, as the prevailing management style can affect the levels of bullying in an organisation.
- No single, off-the-shelf policy will suit every organisation and a variety of elements may be useful in developing an effective bullying policy. The culture of the organisation, the type of business, and the personality and management style of those in positions of authority are all factors which must be taken into consideration when developing a policy.
- Managers and staff should be involved in developing and implementing policies, and awareness of the issues should be encouraged through training and clear communications.
- There is a major gap between what managers say they would do to deal with bullying and the experience of managers when they themselves have been bullied. In the study, three-quarters of managers said their initial response would be to talk to one of the parties involved – however, less than half of those who have been bullied reported that no action was taken in their case. Since 37 per cent identified failure to address previous cases as a contributory factor to bullying, the importance of taking and communicating action is evident.

Developing a policy

To communicate a clear message that bullying is not acceptable, it is important to implement a policy. This need not be elaborate and can be included in other personnel policies. The culture of the organisation, the type of business, and the personality and management style of those in positions of authority are all factors which must be taken into consideration when developing a policy. Setting a good example is as important as having a good policy. Instances of bullying are much less likely where there is a culture of respect and tolerance.

Box 2.4: Useful organisations and support networks

- ACAS – www.acas.org.uk
- The Andrea Adams Trust – www.andreaadamstrust.org
- Chartered Institute of Personnel and Development – www.cipd.co.uk
- Commission for Racial Equality – www.cre.gov.uk
- Disability Rights Commission – www.drc.org.uk
- Equal Opportunities Commission – www.eoc.org.uk
- The Health and Safety Executive – www.hse.gov.uk
- TUC – www.tuc.org.uk
- UNISON – www.unison.org.uk

Areas to address in a policy include:

- A statement of commitment from senior management
- Examples of unacceptable behaviour
- A statement that bullying is a disciplinary offence
- Details of who to approach if victims of bullying feel unable to speak to their manager or supervisor – for example, a trained contact officer
- Confidentiality for any complainant and protection from victimisation
- An outline of the grievance procedures (formal and informal), including investigation procedures and timescales
- Responsibilities of managers and contact officers
- Counselling and support availability
- Involvement of trade union and health and safety representatives
- Availability of training for managers, health and safety representatives, and staff
- A statement on how the policy is implemented, reviewed and monitored.

For a policy to be effective and to raise awareness levels, employees should contribute to it in both the development and implementation stages. Box 2.4 provides details of some useful organisations and support networks.

Regretted and Non-regretted Staff Turnover

Retention is often seen as a key goal for Human Resources managers, but is high staff retention necessarily a good thing?

One of the crude measures of staff retention (sometimes called 'stickiness' of an organisation) is the staff turnover rate usually expressed as a percentage of employees that leave in a given year. The average for the economy as a whole is running at 15.7 per cent, so a 3 per cent figure might be considered admirable, while some organisations might lose a third of their people every year. The author was invited to assist one financial services firm that was losing 16 per cent of its staff a year, twice the sector average – in five years 80 per cent of its staff might have turned over!

There are many reasons to hold on to staff:

- The high cost of recruitment – employers are finding it harder to fill vacancies
- Leavers may have had a high cost of investment – in training and experience lost to the new employer
- Continuity problems – a particular problem in many service industries needing to maintain client relationships
- Leavers might set up in competition – especially if jilted.

However, is all retention a good thing? We may all have worked with someone that the organisation might be better off without – hence the term 'regretted' and 'non-regretted' staff turnover.

The direct cost of hiring a replacement is easy to estimate – the Chartered Institute of Personnel and Development (www.cipd.co.uk) estimate that the 2006 cost is £3950, rising to £4625 when the associated costs of labour turnover are accounted for – but the cost to a business of a person with a poor attitude and poisonous approach in place year after year is more difficult to calculate. There is also that group referred to as 'retired but not yet left' – and not limited to the older employee – of whom we have probably all met examples.

How do we recoup the loss of productivity caused by their infectious unhappiness? While the individual is not unemployable – there must be, for everyone, a job that they can enjoy – but square pegs in round holes do nothing for either such pegs or holes! Sadly, as people often lack the confidence to leave of their own volition, they stay and their effectiveness falls even lower. Interestingly, of those made redundant, two years later over a half feel that it was a good thing to have happened.

In some quarters it is suggested that, after three years in a given job, most people start to experience some drop in their enjoyment and probably their effectiveness too. While we are all different and no two jobs are exactly the same, someone having been in the same job for a decade is not always a good thing. It may be that they are fully motivated, highly effective, and a fountain of invaluable know-how and experience – or is it an indication of a loss of ambition or imagination? Perhaps their value on the open market is limited, which might raise questions about their usefulness to the organisation.

According to the CIPD research, while over 30 per cent of people leave for 'promotion outside the organisation' – probably regretted departures – is a low staff turnover symptomatic of a firm full of people that nobody in their right mind would employ?

Summary

In this chapter you have:

- Explored strategies to retain staff
- Considered issues to help in staff development for succession planning.

Questions

1. Consider the practices of your organisation, or one with which you are familiar, and consider whether they meet best practice in the retention of people. What recommendations can you make for improvement?
2. Do you have a succession plan for your position in your organisation. What are the main features to consider?

References

Confederation of British Industry and Department of Health (1992) *Promoting Mental Health at Work*, CBI/DoH, London.
Department of Health (1995) *Mental Illness: What Does it Mean?*
Health Education Authority (1997) *Workplace Health.*

Mackay, A. R. (2007) *Motivation, Ability and Confidence Building in People*, Butterworth-Heinemann.

Mental Health Foundation (1995) *Mental Health at Work – Some Facts and Figures*, MHF.

Patel, A. and Knapp, M. (1998) 'The Cost of Mental Health in England', *Mental Health Review*, No. 5, Centre for Economics and Mental Health.

The Times (2005) 14 January.

Further Reading

Back, S. (ed.) (2005) *Managing Human Resources: Personnel Management in Transition*, Blackwell Publishing.

Evans, A. (2003) *Staff Recruitment and Retention: A Guide to Effective Practice*, Spiro Press.

Mackay, A. R. (2007) *Motivation, Ability and Confidence Building in People*, Butterworth-Heinemann.

Schein, E. (1980) *Organizational Psychology*, 3rd Edition, Prentice-Hall, Englewood Cliffs, NJ.

Schein, E. (1997) *Organizational Culture and Leadership*, Jossey-Bass, San Francisco.

3

Redeployment

Learning Outcomes

This chapter has been written as a general guide for managers and should not be used as a substitute for professional legal advice on these matters. It has been written to meet the needs of both the National Occupational Standards for Management and Leadership (*Unit 24*) and the Chartered Management Institute's Diploma in Management compulsory module (*Unit C45 – Managing Performance*) in as far as redeployment of staff is concerned. It also meets the needs of people studying the CIPD Professional Development Scheme – particularly regarding redeployment as part of the *People Management and Development* core module.

By the end of this chapter you will:

- Know how to manage the redeployment of people
- Explore ideas to help in particular circumstances where redeployment is advised, including organisational changes – like new products or services – or ill-health.

Redeployment

It has been suggested that there are millions of people in jobs that they do not enjoy, are not committed to, and only realise this when they get the distance and time that a holiday provides (post-holiday blues is a recognised phenomenon). While this may form a case for redeployment, often it comes about as a result of other commercial or market forces.

Redeployment should be utilised to retain and develop experienced and skilled staff. It should help organisations modernise and adjust to changes by safeguarding the skills, experience and motivation of staff. It gives the opportunity to be innovative, making full use of the skills and experience of staff at all levels to respond to these challenges. Therefore, opportunities should also be exploited to share skills and experience across the organisation. It should be the aim of the organisation to achieve the best use of skilled staff, while offering learning opportunities for all.

Redeployment is the process of securing alternative employment for staff displaced as a result of organisational change, modernisation, capability or ill-health. The process by which staff accesses different forms of redeployment mayvary and individual staff entitlements within this may differ.

Displaced means that there is no longer a need for a substantive post, or that the particular skills or experience of a post holder are no longer required, or the employee is unable to undertake the duties of the substantive post.

To maintain security of employment within the organisation the circumstances in which redeployment should be used, in order of priority, are:

- Organisational change, where there is a change in product or service delivery which affects employment circumstances
- Displacement as a result of ill-health
- Other circumstances – for example, matters of capability, resolution of grievance or disciplinary matters, the avoidance of a TUPE[1] transfer.

General Principles of Redeployment

Redeployment requires the full cooperation of all participants, that is, managers, staff representatives and individual staff members, to be successful. Redeployment opportunities should be sought for all potentially displaced staff within an organisation. Therefore, employing organisations should work in partnership with recognised trades unions/professional organisations to develop local redeployment policies, which take account of the principles suggested here.

Displaced employees should have the right to be considered preferentially for posts and must not be unfairly denied a substantive post. Such staff may be appointed temporarily for developmental purposes or in a holding

---

[1] Transfer of Undertakings (Protection of Employment) Regulations 1987 (TUPE).

position, retaining their employment status until a substantive post becomes available. Managers who choose not to appoint a displaced employee must provide written substantiated and defensible reasons for non-appointment.

Managing Redeployment

Opportunities for training and retraining should be identified and where appropriate be accessed. Each organisation or division in a larger concern should designate a redeployment coordinator. However, during periods of substantial change this should be an explicit appointment. The redeployment coordinator should be a member of, and report to, the senior management team.

Redeployment should normally occur as locally as possible; however, it is recognised that other, perhaps national, arrangements may be required for staff in posts that have senior/particular skills/experience. Excess travel and, where appropriate, relocation expenses incurred as a result of the redeployment should be reimbursed by the redeploying organisation. Facilities should exist to enable staff to be redeployed between sites, if appropriate, throughout the organisation. Clearly, this may not be possible for more modest organisations. Where redeployment occurs between sites of larger employers, continuity of service should be unaffected in relation to terms and conditions based on service (e.g. occupational sick pay, annual leave). Statutory rights which might be affected include entitlement to claim unfair dismissal.

Successful redeployment may incur costs; however, savings can be substantial and it should be the responsibility of the redeployment coordinator to monitor costs and provide regular reports.

Specific conditions

There are certain situations where redeployment is advised and the following represents guidance for managers to assist in the redeployment of people.

Organisational change/product or service modernisation
- All staff should be entitled to protection of terms and conditions, in accordance with any existing organisational change arrangements following redeployment, except in circumstances where the terms and conditions within the 'new' post are improved.
- In such circumstances, the terms and conditions applied should be those of the 'new' post. Protection costs should be paid by the redeploying organisation.

- Redeployment negotiations or discussions should begin as early as possible following a decision that there will be a need for redeployment.
- In such circumstances, all other relevant parts of the organisation should be required to use temporary appointments to protect substantive posts for the appointment of redeployed staff.
- Excess travel and where appropriate relocation expenses incurred as a result of the redeployment should be reimbursed by the redeploying organisation.
- Senior management should identify resources to reimburse protection and meet retraining costs. This should improve the opportunities for successful redeployment.
- Trade unions/professional organisations should be involved in any organisational change process at the earliest opportunity, including the formulation of plans which could lead to organisational change. Where organisational change is agreed, trade unions/professional organisations should be involved in determining the process to be used. All staff are entitled to be represented at individual meetings, as might be agreed locally.
- The parts of the organisation are expected to identify redeployment opportunities for all staff displaced as a result of organisational change. Equally, displaced staff are expected to work with the local redeployment coordinator, their employer and trade unions/professional organisations to identify suitable redeployment opportunities and should not unreasonably refuse any appropriate opportunity.

Ill-health

Staff displaced as a result of ill-health should be dealt with in accordance with relevant guidelines. This might include the following:

- The decision regarding ill-health should be made on the advice of an Occupational Health/Medical Practitioner, taking into account all relevant medical information/records.
- Staff identified as displaced are expected to work with their employer to identify suitable redeployment opportunities and should not unreasonably refuse any opportunities.
- Staff displaced as a result of ill-health may be entitled to injury benefit as provided by the organisation's superannuation scheme – if one exists.
- Excess travel and where appropriate relocation expenses incurred as a result of the redeployment should be reimbursed by the redeploying organisation.

Other circumstances

Redeployment in other specific circumstances should be an individual decision made by agreement with the employer – for example, matters of capability, the resolution of grievance or disciplinary matters, the avoidance of a TUPE transfer.

Training issues

Employers should ensure that the relevant training needs are identified and addressed for all involved in redeployment. This may include managers involved in redeployment of staff or staff who are affected in either circumstance. In particular, employing organisations should take account of the training/retraining needs of displaced staff.

Indicators of Successful Redeployment

Evaluation of success should be integral to redeployment arrangements to determine success at individual and organisational levels. Examples of this are suggested below.

For the individual:

- Individual redeployment assessment
- Focus groups for affected staff.

For the organisation:

- Staff turnover post-redeployment compared with pre-redeployment
- Number of staff successfully redeployed.

Summary

In this chapter you have:

- Looked at issues to consider when managing the redeployment of people
- Explored what to do in particular circumstances where redeployment is advised, including organisational changes – like new products or services – or ill-health.

Questions

1. Consider the practices of your organisation, or one with which you are familiar, and consider whether they meet best practice in the redeployment of people. What recommendations can you make for improvement?
2. As a manager, what are the key issues that you will have to address when redeployment is inevitable?

Further Reading

Back, S. (ed.) (2005) *Managing Human Resources: Personnel Management in Transition*, Blackwell Publishing.

4

Women Returning to Work

Jan Mackay

Work is the price you pay for money.
From *It's a Wise Sage*, the Chartered Management Institute

Learning Outcomes

This chapter addresses the issues helping women return to work. It has been written to provide support to related elements of the National Occupational Standards for Management and Leadership: *Providing Direction – Lead People 9* and *Promoting Diversity 13*; some sections of *Working with People*; and it is a useful adjunct to some of the requirements of the Chartered Management Institute's Diploma in Management compulsory *Unit C41 – Developing your Management Style*, the compulsory *Unit C45 – Managing Performance* and the optional *Unit O42 – Developing Personnel and Personnel Performance*. It also meets the needs of people studying the CIPD Professional Development Scheme – particularly regarding women returning to work as part of the *People Management and Development* core module.

By the end of this chapter you will:

- See that an increasing number of women are returning to work after having a family
- Recognise that many of the physical hurdles are being taking away by government initiatives
- See that this sector of the workforce has been shown to be of great value to productivity

- Discover that they can be integrated back into the workplace with speed and efficiency with the correct emphasis on training and confidence building
- See that a healthy work/life balance works for both employee and employer alike.

Background

When we speak of women 'returning' to work, of course we must include in this category women who may never have worked because they started their families straight after being in full-time education or women who have not worked for reasons not related to having children.

There is also a small but growing number of men who have elected to take time away from the workplace to provide a nurturing environment for their children, and reference to 'women returning to work' should include them too.

The issue of women returning to the workplace has become increasingly recognised as being one of great importance not only to the individuals concerned, the increased productivity and effectiveness of companies, but also to the economic well-being of countries as a whole. Unemployment rates amongst women are still high compared to men, but evidence would suggest that the trend for women returning to work is a growing one.

According to the 32nd National Management Salary Survey published by the Chartered Management Institute and Remuneration Economics, it is estimated that the number of women in management roles has trebled in 10 years to 33.1 per cent. Women account for 14.4 per cent of directors (a figure which has doubled since 1999) and, at team leader level, women represent more than one-third (36.9 per cent).

Over 60 per cent of women are in employment in the UK and numbers are growing for a variety of reasons. Some seven out of 10 women claim they would want to return to work after starting a family even if they had the financial means to stay at home. Their reasons are more likely to be for social interaction and personal fulfilment. Others are in a situation where they are compelled to work for financial reasons.

Recognising the Value of Women Returners

Companies ignore the worth of women returning to work at their cost. Their abilities and energy can be a valuable resource which companies are increasingly becoming aware of and which governments are determined to see utilised on a greater scale.

When a company goes to the effort and expense of training and developing a woman to be a part of the profit-making process, it just doesn't make commercial sense to then see them disappear from the workplace to start their family without giving some thought as to how to lure them back eventually. Their skills are a valuable asset and the cost of replacing them can be high. The long-term benefits of ensuring these assets return to work outweigh the investments which may be needed on the part of the company to welcome back women returners.

Practical Considerations

Governments across the EU are developing initiatives to encourage women to return to work. In the UK, the government is keen to remove as many of the barriers women have to overcome as possible. One of the main reasons cited for not returning to work is the lack of childcare, especially for the pre-school age group.

Women returning to the workplace can find it a daunting prospect after being away from the cut and thrust of the workplace for any length of time. They may lack confidence and the skills required to operate in an ever-progressive technological environment. Will they be able to converse with adults about 'grown-up subjects' after years of talking primarily of baby issues? Will they be organised enough to deal with everything at home and get into work on time?

Considerations for an Effective Return

Women returning to work generally fall into two main categories:

1. Sequencing mothers who have planned their absence from the workplace in order to start a family and have every intention of returning at some fixed point in time.
   - Eighty-eight per cent of women who choose to return to work go back to their original employer. Just over a quarter report that employers

offer the opportunity to stay up to date during maternity leave. Three-quarters of those offered this opportunity took it up (*Survey of how parents balance work, family and home*, DTI, 2000).

- By keeping in touch with their employers by various means (regular written reports, telephone conversations, online), these women can stay up to date with policies and work in hand. Their inclusion back into the company will thus be on an informed basis, which should make the transition easier and quicker. Any continuing input from the company to keep their temporarily absent employees informed will reap the benefits when they have a valuable, skilled member of staff back in the workplace ready and able to increase productivity.

- This approach is particularly valuable in maintaining a woman's level of confidence in her ability to perform tasks at work which she may well have taken for granted before embarking on a period of absence, but could easily lose in the environment outside of work.

2. Women who for financial or personal reasons have made a decision to return to the workplace after a period of time away or, indeed, have never been to work.

- Women returning to or starting out in the world of work face many of the same problems as sequencing mothers, but without the benefit of continued support from past employers. Their skill levels may be so low as to necessitate accessing training initiatives such as Learndirect (www.learndirect.co.uk) to brush up on basic skills before applying for vacant positions. This would certainly indicate a level of commitment and the ability to take on new challenges to any potential employer, and also give the participant a greater sense of confidence in their abilities.

Childcare provision

Childcare has been cited by over 30 per cent of unemployed women as being the reason they are not able to return to work. Government initiatives have increased the number of childcare places available in recognition of this fact. The ideal situation is if the company is able to offer in-house childcare, but this is rarely available.

Nursery costs can be high for employees and it may be a worthwhile incentive for employers to offer to subsidise these costs.

Once a child reaches the age of four, it is entitled to a free part-time place in a school nursery, playgroup or day nursery.

Childcare Link (0800 0960296) is a freephone information line for England and Scotland providing information on childcare provision and local Children's Information Services – or visit the Childcare website.

Flexible working environment

The Work and Families Bill was published in October 2005 and is expected to become law in April 2007. One of the significant provisions of this Bill will be to extend the right of carers to request flexible working arrangements. This can go a long way towards making it easier for the employee to return to work, whilst at the same time being available to look after a family. As a manager, however, care must be taken to ensure other team members are not inconvenienced by these arrangements.

Offering job share schemes or allowing employees to work from home are a developing trend in many organisations, but they do require the right sort of organisational culture for the scheme to work – as well as a good working relationship between the job sharers and the supervising manager.

Companies have already recognised that by taking a flexible approach which helps employees balance work and family life it can lead to improved staff morale and productivity that translates to increased effectiveness and efficiency. More on flexible working will be discussed in Chapter 12.

Skill realisation/awareness

One of the hurdles some women face is that they just cannot see how they can be of any value to a potential employer. Because they have been 'at home with the children' or have not been in the work environment for a number of years they assume their abilities have been diminished and they have very little to offer. Employers too can miss out on the possibilities by not recognising how some of the activities these women have been engaged in while bringing up a family and running a home may be adapted to the workplace. For instance, Table 4.1 outlines some of the tasks a mother/home provider has to undertake and the skills required to perform them.

A great many of the skills required to take an active part in running a home and/or bringing up a family can be transferred and developed to the benefit of an employer.

93

Table 4.1 The skill sets of running a home that have application in the workplace

Task	Skill set
Shopping	Budgeting, planning
Arranging birthday parties	Organisation, planning, dealing with sensitive situations
School runs	Time management
Preparation of meals	Planning, budgeting, decision-making, project management
Doctors, dentists	Time management, communication, planning
Child development	Communication, mentoring
Involvement in school and societies	Communication, planning, organisation, team building
Making a home, decorating, cleaning	Learning new skills, planning, budgeting
Home maintenance utilising specialist firms	Planning, budgeting and cost control, dealing with suppliers

Training

As with any other employee, a woman returning to work will benefit enormously from a good training programme. Identifying areas where skills need to be improved to perform effectively gives the opportunity to grow not only in ability, but also in confidence. An input by the company into providing training will be an indication of how much importance is placed on the continuing development of its employees.

Confidence building

A recognition of potential shortfalls in skills when delegating tasks should help avoid morale-crushing episodes where the employee is overwhelmed by their workload.

A healthy appraisal system within the company (see Chapter 6) will ensure any training issues that need to be addressed are dealt with promptly. The ability to perform a task with all the necessary skills will be a major confidence boost, but it must be remembered that these employees may not have the where-withal to come forward and point out where they need some help. They may be afraid of appearing inadequate. It is the manager's responsibility to keep appraised of their abilities and progress and suggest ways to go forward.

Having a sympathetic colleague to talk to can be helpful in offloading small fears and worries – many mothers will feel a sense of guilt for leaving their children with carers which can quickly paralyse their concentration. Providing a new employee with a non-judgemental mentor or buddy to steer them through these initial barriers will free up time and energy to get on with important skills development.

Women returning to work may need more frequent assurances that the work they are doing is to the right standard. A manager's feedback is important for any employee, but will be vital in helping to build up the confidence of a 'returner'.

Summary

In this chapter you have:

- Seen that an increasing number of women are returning to work after having a family
- Recognised that many of the physical hurdles are being taking away by government initiatives
- Seen that this sector of the workforce has been shown to be of great value to productivity
- Discovered that they can be integrated back into the workplace with speed and efficiency with the correct emphasis on training and confidence building
- Seen that a healthy work/life balance works for both employee and employer alike.

Questions

Imagine that you were chatting to a friend who wanted to return to work after 15 years raising a family. She has good keyboard skills and Pitman Shorthand. She is applying for an administrative/clerical function in your organisation and you have been asked to help guide her. Drawing on your reading from this chapter – and being mindful of Chapter 1:

1. Outline her possible CV.
2. Write some notes to help her prepare for an interview with another manager in your organisation.

Further Reading

Longson, S. (2004) *Returning to Work: A Guide to Re-Entering the Job Market*, How To Books.
Wolfin, D. and Foreman, S. (2004) *Back to Work: A Guide for Women Returners*, Robson Books.
Mackay, A. R. (2007) *Motivation, Ability and Confidence Building in People*, Butterworth-Heinemann.

5

Job Evaluation Schemes

It is people, not jobs, who create value ...

A. R. Mackay

Learning Outcomes

This chapter outlines various approaches and considerations in the development and implementation of a job evaluation scheme (JES). It may prove particularly useful to both employers and employees to assist in their mutual understanding of the process and to facilitate internal communications.

Modern organisations have come to realise that it is *people*, not *jobs*, who create value; that multi-skilled, multi-functional work teams are a key to success; that during a year, an individual can play many roles; and that we must all seek the continuous development and growth of all people as we genuinely devolve responsibility in our flatter, leaner organisations.

By the end of this chapter you will:

- Realise the purpose of running job evaluation schemes
- Evaluate the various schemes in use today
- Know how to weight various factors in jobs
- Run a professional job evaluation scheme

- Understand the link between job evaluation and pay and rewards
- Recognise best practice in job evaluation.

The Purpose of Job Evaluation Schemes

Job evaluation (JE) can help to overcome difficulties in managing internal relatives between different people and different jobs and maintaining an equitable and competitive pay structure. It can address grading issues logically and systematically, and it can reduce the subjectivity to value judgements that many people make about job worth. However, it is not scientific, not fully objective and certainly not a panacea.

JE is, however, based on systematic analysis and can provide a framework within which judgements can be made. It can help to produce order out of the chaos that exists in organisations that have allowed pay decisions to be made in an entirely *ad hoc* and subjective manner (Armstrong and Baron, 1995, p. 20).

The aims of a JES are to provide a systematic, rational and consistent approach to defining the relative worth of jobs within an organisation. It is a system for comparing different jobs in order to provide the basis for an equitable and defensible pay structure. Most organisations introduce job evaluation to help manage the complexities of determining equal pay for work of equal value (The Industrial Society, 1996).

It can be argued that some traditional JESs can fail to produce a return in terms of increased organisational effectiveness, competitive advantage and high levels of stakeholder value to justify the considerable investment in time and money that a full and formal JE process demands.

The skill is to choose a JES that matches the organisation's system and culture, and to introduce it in a way that carries employees along with the process (Incomes Data Services Ltd, 2003, p. 3).

Equal pay

The Equal Pay (Amendment) Regulations (1983) provide for a woman to seek equal pay with a named male comparator on the grounds that the work done, although different, is of equal value in terms of the demands it makes. Equal value claims can be set aside if employers can show that their job evaluation scheme is analytical in nature and free from sex bias in design and implementation.

Types of Schemes in Practice

JESs fall into two main categories – non-analytical and analytical schemes:

- *Non-analytical schemes* are characterised by making comparisons on a whole job basis. They are not usually accepted in equal value cases and are generally seen as less objective and consistent.
- *Analytical schemes* rely on splitting the job up into a number of different aspects and measuring each of these separately. The main types of analytical schemes are:
  - *Factor comparisons.* Benchmark jobs are chosen and evaluated against common factors. The scores are directly converted into money.
  - *Point-factor rating.* Factors that are important to the jobs and distinguish between them are identified. Levels within these factors are identified and a point score allocated to each level. Jobs are assessed against these factors and a total score is given. (This is the basis of many JESs in both the public and private sectors.)
  - *Competency-based schemes.* Appropriate competencies are identified and used as factors in a similar way to the point-factor schemes.

Because they give close attention to a detailed analysis of the job and measure across a range of factors, analytical schemes produce more consistent results and are generally better accepted by employees, as well as being appropriate measures for equal value.

The case of Bromley and Others vs H. J. Quick is significant. The Court of Appeal ruled that a JES must be analytical if it is to succeed as a defence to an equal value claim (ACAS, 1997).

However, JESs that claim to measure the size of jobs by attaching point scores to them are, in a sense, using points as a means of indicating intrinsic value. They appear to state that a job is 'worth' so many points. But the points have no meaning in themselves. They are simply ordinal numbers – i.e. they define the position of a job or factor in a series; they do not represent any unit of measurement such as output, sales, pay or hours.

Organisational Culture

Because JE attempts to measure the value that the organisation places on jobs, and the factors that are considered to be worth rewarding, it is an articulation of the culture of the organisation. JE is sometimes criticised for being too rigid, particularly when schemes are based on factors that are no longer important to the organisation. There is a tendency for schemes to reflect the status quo and not encourage change. However, many organisations have successfully developed schemes that are more flexible and, by emphasising new values, have become drivers of change.

Choice of Factors in Job Evaluation Schemes

The choice of factors is crucial, as these determine how jobs will be rated and compared. The factors are perhaps the most easily identifiable aspects of the JE process and send a clear message to staff about which elements the organisation considers most valuable and deserving of recognition. They can also be the basis for determining whether a scheme can be held to be discriminatory.

Factors used in organisations studied fell into four general categories:

- Inputs – what employees contribute to jobs
- Processes – how jobs are done
- Accountabilities – to whom or for what the job is responsible
- Impact – the job's overall effects or influence on the organisation.

The number of factors applied varied but is typically between five and 10. Most often broad categories of factors are chosen and then broken down into components or sub-factors. For example, in the UK, Medway Council measures jobs against 13 factors that fall under four broad headings: knowledge and skills; effort demands; responsibilities; and environmental demands. The Police Consortium JES used by Derbyshire Constabulary is based on seven generic factors, below which are further sub-factors designed to take into account police-specific criteria.

Whatever factors are chosen, they need to fulfil the following criteria (Incomes Data Services Ltd, 2003, p. 9):

- Be measurable
- Differentiate between jobs to an acceptable degree
- Be comprehensive
- Be non-discriminatory and unbiased
- Be factors for which the organisation is willing to pay
- Be balanced across the job population covered.

The Weightings of Factors in Job Evaluation

Factors can be weighted to ensure that the overall scoring reflects those that the company feels are the most important. Factors might include 'knowledge', 'initiative and independence', 'working conditions', 'mental demands' and 'emotional demands' – or any others that are specific to the organisation. This provides the opportunity for further tailoring of a scheme to meet the values of a particular organisation.

As with the selection of factors themselves, the weightings may be determined by working parties including representatives from key stakeholder groups.

Factor weightings are usually expressed as percentages. These can then be used as multipliers so that the value the organisation associates with each factor is represented in the total points score of each job.

The Evaluation Process

Completing the actual evaluations involves gathering evidence about jobs and undertaking role analysis. Not all organisations evaluate every job. The selection of which jobs to evaluate aims to ensure:

- Employee confidence in the overall credibility of the scheme
- A fair range of jobs has been selected to avoid any gender bias.

In practice, it also depends on how many jobs there are to evaluate and what investment an organisation is willing to make in the JES. In the literature, it appears that most organisations have chosen to evaluate all their discrete roles to provide greater transparency. Medway Council evaluated every distinct role; Derbyshire Constabulary identified 340 discrete roles in preference to selecting a sample of benchmark roles, while East Midlands Electricity initially aimed to evaluate 25 per cent of jobs but ended up evaluating all job types across the company.

Preparing for full evaluation

Some companies run a pilot scheme to establish logistical effectiveness and to provide benchmark evaluations to act as a reference for the wider JE process. This may be run by the project team (Sainsbury's), through sample interviews (Derbyshire Constabulary), or through benchmark roles (Prudential) prior to a roll-out across the whole organisation.

In all examples reviewed, it was considered important to maintain a consistent approach and regular meetings of the job evaluation team were arranged.

Role analysis

When an analytical point-factor methodology has been followed, the most common way to evaluate each job is to explore their content, factor by factor. Using the information that is provided about each job from a role profile, analysts select the most appropriate answers from a series of questions under each factor heading. The overall score for each role can then be used to provide a rank order of jobs from which a grading structure can be modelled.

Role analysis should cover a logical sequence to ensure that all factors and sub-factors are covered. The analysis should cover what people actually do and atypical instances should be avoided, as should imprecise or inflated descriptions of their work. Questions should not be leading, yet ample opportunity should be given for individuals to give a full account of their role.

While individual interviews are favoured, in large JESs structured written questionnaires are most often used (Armstrong and Baron, 1995, p. 137). Questionnaires covering the above points can be completed by individuals and approved by their line managers before submission to the JE panel.

Realignments

An inevitable outcome from a JE exercise is that some roles are assigned values that place them in a different position in the pecking order than before. Thus, there are likely to be some employees' jobs that are either underpaid or overpaid. Some organisations try to make the impact on the pay-bill cost neutral by setting the length of the pay bands to accommodate as many winners and losers as possible. Other organisations alter their bonus structure to offset the cost of the realignments.

Where JESs have shown some jobs to be underpaid relative to others, common practice is to move the job into the pay band applicable to its evaluation score, but on the minimum point of the scale.

At the other end of the scale, when it has been shown that some jobs have been overpaid in the light of a JE review, the job's salaries are 'red circled' while the jobs are placed in the pay band appropriate to their new ranking. Typically, their pay is frozen at its existing level until the pay band catches up with it, at which point they become eligible for any annual pay rises, increments or performance-related increases associated with the new band. Firms vary in the length of time a job's salary is red circled; the length of protection is chosen to ensure that it does not infringe equal-value considerations.

Occasionally, some jobs will be found to have a salary applied, often by a manager trying to recruit for a new post or to fill a vacancy quickly, without reference to any benchmark. Here, the jobholder will have enjoyed a period of an inflated salary relative to other equivalent-value job roles in the organisation. Realignment will cause the most grief, particularly for the jobholder, who will naturally feel hard done by.

Any case involving a salary freeze or reduction needs an appropriate system for appeals.

Appeals

All organisations reviewed have a formal appeals system to investigate grading or banding decisions. The right to appeal may be restricted to certain grounds. Common examples include situations where the jobholder feels that the information upon which an employee's job has been analysed is wrong, or because the JES has been implemented unfairly. A deadline is invariably set by which time appeals may be lodged.

The first stage of the appeals process is typically a relatively informal meeting with the line manager and an HR representative. If the issue cannot be dealt with promptly, the appeal may then escalate to an appeals panel, usually chaired by an independent manager. To guard against any subjectivity, employees may ask for their job to be reviewed again by a different analyst (Derbyshire Constabulary). While the result of this new evaluation was final, it did have the possibility that a job may be evaluated even lower.

Job Evaluation and Link to Pay and Rewards

It is most often the case that employers use the results of a job evaluation exercise as the basis for devising equitable pay and grading structures. While this is often the case, JE data may also be used for other purposes. For example:

- Performance appraisal
- Employee training and development programmes
- The redesign of poor-quality jobs.

However, there is an intrinsic link between JE and the introduction of new pay and grading structures. While the results of a job evaluation exercise suggest a hierarchy for a new grading structure, many other elements must be taken into account when determining grade boundaries and associated salary scales. Employers are likely to take into account:

- Cost/budget considerations
- The potential increase in the pay bill
- The range of scores shown in the evaluation
- The overall pay spread desired
- The number of employees in each job
- The number of pay bands that is manageable or desirable given the size of the organisation
- What employees feel is fair – so-called 'felt fair' considerations
- How employees will progress through the new bands

- Promotion policy
- The need to strike a balance between external competitiveness and internal equity.

Establishing grade boundaries

Where a point-factor method is used, the distribution of scores from the JE provides the basis from which a grading structure can be defined. It is common for a number of jobs to cluster around certain point scores. These clusters provide a good indication as to where grade breaks could be set. Organisations often look at a job's score against certain key factors to determine the exact position of the boundaries.

Many organisations have moved towards broad-banding arrangements underpinned by JE. This can be an efficient way of reflecting the ranking outcomes without creating an overly bureaucratic and complex hierarchy of jobs. Having extended pay ranges means a move away from promotion as the only way of progressing, with the expectation that lateral movement between functions may become more common.

The effect of changing scales and weighting parameters

In a study of five JESs, the effects of three manipulations on total job value scores and pay grade classifications were investigated (Sliedregt et al., 2001). The manipulations were: omitting certain scale anchors, changing scale weights and reducing the number of JE characteristics.

For example, if a factor were based on lifting heavy objects, then this can be shown to have a male sex bias and would be inappropriate. Equally, if a weighting were changed to favour manual dexterity, then it may be argued as being less relevant for an office-based job role while favouring a manual assembly line.

The results of the study revealed that the various manipulations hardly affected the relative total job values. The researchers concluded that 'JE instruments perform very well in assessing relative job worth – that is, ranking jobs according to their total worth'. Perhaps not surprisingly, they found that these manipulations did affect pay grade classifications to varying degrees. It is obvious that if the weightings are changed then many jobs in an organisation will also change their pay grade – hence the importance in ensuring that the factors and the weightings reflect organisational culture and the true demands placed on jobholders.

Overview of Job Evaluation Best Practice

Limitation of job evaluation schemes

While JESs aim to provide a systematic, rational and consistent approach to defining the relative worth of jobs within an organisation, they are neither completely objective nor scientific. However, this method is concerned with comparisons, both between jobs and against defined standards. As with any other management system, it must be matched to the needs of the business.

- *Job descriptions.* According to advice from the ACAS (1997) advisory booklet on JE, job descriptions need accurate formulation. They need to be written in a standard format to enable valid comparisons between jobs and complete coverage of all tasks and responsibilities. Their style and content should be appropriate for interdepartmental use and cover the whole range of factors for the chosen job. Finally, they need to be checked and agreed by the jobholder and their line manager.
- *Choice of systems.* Overall, analytical systems are favoured over non-analytical, as they provide a rational basis for evaluation, provide a defence of an equal-value claim and are less subjective. In particular, it is crucial to avoid discrimination in the selection and weighting of the factors.

Implementation of schemes

The following is a distillation of activity given as best practice:

- *Steering committee.* One should be set up to oversee and manage the JE project. It should allow independence of the JE panel.
- *Job evaluation panel.* A JE panel should report to the steering group and be responsible for organising job analysis, selecting benchmark jobs and evaluating jobs. If a home-grown scheme is being introduced, the panel should be involved in its design. The composition of the panel is crucial, as the credibility of the scheme often rests with the credibility of the

individuals concerned. Use a 'diagonal slice' of the organisation to ensure a representation of views from all sections and levels of the hierarchy.

- *Benchmark jobs.* Select benchmark jobs that are truly representative of the organisation and ensure information on jobs is of consistent quality.
- *Consider anomalies.* Think through any likely anomalies before implementing the scheme in full and decide how underrated and overrated jobs are going to be dealt with.
- *Agree an appeals process.* Plan and agree an appeals process before launching the scheme. Line managers of individuals making appeals should be involved in the process. An appeals panel should be separate and independent from the JE panel. Decide how jobs might be 'red circled' and for how long. Consider how overpaid jobs might be handled fairly and objectively, including how assistance to individual jobholders might be made within organisational constraints.
- *Questionnaire development.* If written questionnaires are being used, the guidelines suggested earlier should be followed.
- *Communications strategy.* The development of a comprehensive and sensitive communication strategy is essential. Mixed messages and inaccurate information can lead to the rejection of the JES by some quarters. 'Road shows' by the steering committee or the JE panel have proved to be effective as part of this process.
- *Maintenance.* All schemes need regular maintenance to guard against 'grade drift' and to ensure that the JES is still matching the organisation's needs. A sample of jobs must be evaluated on a regular basis to check that the JES is operating effectively, especially in times of rapid organisational change.

Summary

In this chapter you have:

- Reviewed the purpose of running job evaluation schemes
- Explored and are able to critique the various schemes in use today
- Looked briefly at how to weight various factors in jobs
- Explored how to run a professional job evaluation scheme
- Looked at the link between job evaluation and pay and rewards
- Uncovered best practice in job evaluation.

Questions

1. Make a case to senior management for a job evaluation scheme in your organisation. Which scheme would be most appropriate? Explain your reasons.
2. Consider what the weighting factors might be for your organisation. Assign a percentage value to reflect their importance in the organisation.
3. Imagine that your senior management team wish to introduce a job evaluation scheme in your firm and you have been asked to contract an external consultancy to run it for you. What criteria would you use to assess the appropriateness of the firm you employ?
4. How would you break the news to your department that a scheme is going to be introduced? Write some notes covering what you would need to say.

References

ACAS (1997) *Job Evaluation – An Introduction*, Revised Edition, Advisory Conciliation and Arbitration Service, London.

Armstrong, M. and Baron, A. (1995) *The Job Evaluation Handbook*, IPD.

The Industrial Society (1996) 'Job Evaluations', *Managing Best Practice*, No. 28, October.

Incomes Data Services Ltd (2003) *Job Evaluation Studies*, No. 754, Summer.

Sliedregt, T et al. (2001) 'Job Evaluation Systems and Pay Grade Structures – Do They Match?', *International Journal of HR Management*, Vol. 12, No. 8, December.

6

A Goals-orientated Approach to Appraisals

He is a modest man – who has a good deal to be modest about.

Sir Winston Churchill on Clement Attlee

Learning Outcomes

Why do staff generally dread appraisals? This chapter is designed to help. It has been written to provide support to key elements of the National Occupational Standards for Management and Leadership: *Working with People – Units 26 and 27,* and it meets many of the requirements of the Chartered Management Institute's Diploma in Management compulsory *Unit C45 – Managing Performance* and much of the optional *Unit O42 – Developing Personnel and Personnel Performance.* It also meets the needs of people studying the CIPD Professional Development Scheme – particularly regarding how to run appraisal as part of the *People Management and Development* core module.

By the end of this chapter you will:

- Understand a 'goals-orientated approach' focuses on the real needs of the business and the individual's job
- See that, for effectiveness, managers must concentrate on Key Result Areas
- Know how to set goals professionally so that they are clear to both parties

- Understand the importance of continuous performance review, with regular feedback throughout the year
- Know the importance of encouraging self-assessment of performance
- Learn how to guide detailed preparation by both parties – an essential process before the performance discussion
- Explore performance discussions as a two-way communication process
- Know why performance discussions are separate in time from any salary review.

Improving Performance

Most organisations are being pressured for improved performance and managers are being asked to get more from fewer resources. At the same time, employees in many organisations are asking for better and more direct feedback on their performance. So, together, the performance of an organisation will depend directly on the performance of both its managers and staff. Obviously, improved performances will not just happen, they must be managed!

Helping senior managers and their subordinates to focus on priorities within their jobs is the first step to managing performance. Therefore, most progressive organisations have, or are implementing, a system of performance appraisal – the most effective is a goals-orientated system. Any performance appraisal system should allow an individual manager to achieve clarity with his or her member of staff about their precise job, and the goals they should be achieving within it. This is a fundamental way of doing things – a culture.

So, how do managers achieve high-performance cultures? Organisations aspiring towards high-performance cultures are strong on three things:

- Clarity about objectives and goals
- Continuous assessment of performance and feedback
- Recognition for performance.

This is a basic part of the managerial function of all line managers and optimum performance is best achieved by addressing the above three steps.

The Goals-orientated Approach

It is usually a motivating experience for employees to see clearly achievable goals in front of them and to be recognised by management when they achieve these goals.

The overall objective of a performance appraisal system may differ from one organisation to another, where the specific objectives will depend on the needs of the organisation at a particular time. In general, any system of appraisal or review is likely to include a number of major objectives:

- *Improvement of individual performance.* Management should not be afraid to state clearly that improving individual performance comes first. Departmental and organisational performance should improve as a consequence.
- *Personal development of the employee.* It is important that employees are able to see some benefit to them from a performance appraisal system. Adopting the personal development of the employee as a key objective will demonstrate this. In which case, management must ensure delivery of this development.
- *Deeper understanding of the job.* Very often, managers and their staff, always under pressure from lack of time, do not fully understand the key elements of one another's jobs.

  A successfully operated performance appraisal system greatly facilitates this understanding:
  - It institutes direct dialogue on a regular basis
  - The focus is on the job itself
  - The focus is on the performance of the individual within the job.
- *Focus on the real needs of the company.* A key element within a performance appraisal system that is goals orientated is that it focuses on the needs of the company and not on esoteric values unrelated to pressures within the business. This clearly benefits line managers, when company-wide and/or departmental goals can be adapted to form part of an individual's goals.
- *Improved communications.* In a busy, over-pressured working environment, managers frequently fail to allow time to communicate adequately with their staff. A goals-orientated system facilitates communication about the really important issues concerning achievement in a particular job.

Typically, the quality of this communication is better and deeper than normal day-to-day discussions.

The Goals-orientated Approach follows five straightforward steps, each requiring particular issues to be addressed to ensure success. Let us take each in turn.

Stage 1: Clarity about the Job

The first stage in any system of performance appraisal must be to identify and understand:

- The job objective
- The Key Result Areas (KRAs).

Job objective

This must be achieved before setting job goals of any sort. Many managers take it for granted that the objective of a job is obvious and clearly understood. This is an unsafe assumption.

Try this test – you and one of your staff sit down in separate rooms and each writes down the job objective for both of your jobs.

The resulting misunderstandings may surprise you! Clarifying the job objective also clarifies the context for Key Result Areas and goal setting.

Key Result Areas

Key Result Areas are those aspects of a job in which it is critical to achieve success, if the overall job objective is to be achieved. Key Result Areas:

- Identify the vital elements of the job
- Contribute to effectiveness – by helping us 'to do the right things'
- Focus on results rather than activities.

Manager and subordinate should together identify all the Key Result Areas for the job in question. In most management jobs these will number between six and 10. Examples of KRA can be found in Table 6.1.

Table 6.1 Examples of Key Result Areas

Output	Technical knowledge	Career development
Client service	Recovery	Time management
Fees	Delegation	Profitability
Quality	Business development	Teamwork
Budget control	Performance management	Personal development

It is difficult to conceive of any managerial job that does not have the Key Result Areas of quality, performance management and teamwork.

- *Focus on key values.* The management team may use the performance appraisal system to spread through the organisation values that are deemed important at any point in time. For example, Key Result Areas could be established for all managers in any one area of client service, total quality or productivity/efficiency of, say, case management systems. Use the performance appraisal system to reinforce other important programmes or emphases in the organisation.

Stage 2: Setting Goals

Agreeing the job objective establishes *why* a job is done, identifying Key Result Areas establishes *what* has to be done, goal or objective setting further establishes *what* has to be done and begins to look also at *how*.

Skilful goal setting focuses attention on the important targets to be achieved within each Key Result Area. This helps employees to see clearly what they should be focusing on, in the period ahead.

Goal setting is a joint exercise carried out between the reviewer and the employee being reviewed; goals are not handed down as tablets of stone by an aloof manager. The whole thrust of a goals-orientated performance management system will wither and die if all managers do not fully involve their subordinates in this goal-setting exercise.

Following goal setting, both parties should be clear about what is expected of the job incumbent. These goals can then be the basis on which performance will be assessed at the end of the review period.

113

Qualities of goals

To be useful during and at the end of the review period, goals should be:

- *Specific and measurable.* Goals must not be couched in vague terms. If they are to be useful at the point of performance then they must be as measurable as possible. This is done by making these goals as quantifiable as possible. The measurement of goals is improved by being quite specific and also by using a time frame within which the goal must be achieved. Some examples of poor and good goals can be found in Table 6.2.
- *Achievable.* Goals that are agreed with subordinates should be achievable. If an employee perceives a goal as unattainable then they may well become demotivated. When agreeing goals with subordinates, take great care that both parties see them as attainable.
- *Challenging and stretching.* There is little point in agreeing with an employee any goals that do not challenge them or stretch them to further improved performance.

  As the reviewing manager, therefore, you must ensure:

- That the goals being set are a challenge to the individual
- That they also stretch what already may be very good performance.

  The manager should look for a little extra without bringing the employee to breaking point – and that little bit extra should not just be in the number of hours worked!

- *Jointly agreed.* It is important that goals are jointly agreed. Individuals will feel far greater ownership of goals when they've played a part in setting

Table 6.2 Examples of poor and good goals

Poor goals	Good goals
Improve fees in the organisation	Increase fee income from our private clients by 5% over the next three months
Improve staff relations in the department	Reduce by 25% the number of within-the-department occasions when grievances go for resolution to the level above the first-line manager; reduce by 25% the total number of grievances within the department

them. This greatly facilitates their commitment to enhanced achievement. There may be occasions when a manager must, to some degree, impose a goal – for example, when they are unable to bring the employee to the desired level of enhanced performance. However, managers should be able to achieve the required 'jointness' of approach in the vast majority of situations. Inability to do so, in even a significant minority of occasions, would indicate a lack of skill in the manager.

- *Time bound*. Valuable for job holder to monitor progress towards goals; also useful for problems to surface earlier rather than when it is too late to resolve.

Structure of goals

Two factors make goal setting difficult for managers:

- A lack of previous experience
- Failure to take a structured approach.

Managers can set better goals by providing each goal with a structure that gives the goal a beginning, middle and end. Examples of this simple structure are shown below.

As can be seen (Table 6.3), the period for which the goals are set may vary. One to four goals should be set in each Key Result Area.

Table 6.3 Examples of the three-part structure of goals

Beginning (use an active verb)	Middle (state what is to be achieved)	End (end with a measure, e.g. quantity, quality or time)
Reduce	Debtors	By 7.5% over previous year
Delegate	All analyses of time reports	Before end of first quarter
Increase	Private client income	By 15% over previous year
Review	Development needs of direct reports	Prior to end of next quarter
Broaden	Commercial base of the service	By adding 10 new clients

Stage 3: Reviewing Performance in the Job

Ideally, this should be a continuous process, yet many organisations, if they bother to appraise at all, reduce performance appraisal to, at best, a once-a-year chore. Then often a one-sided discussion takes place, supposedly focusing on performance over the previous year. However, the task of reviewing performance is too important to leave to a once-a-year event; it must be a continuous process. Reviewing performance on a regular basis is a sure way of securing the benefits outlined earlier for performance appraisal and management.

Regular appraisal or review of performance should have a beneficial effect on employee motivation. People who are accustomed to regular reviews and feedback will usually be better motivated and the organisation develops an achievement culture.

In a dynamic organisation the goals themselves may well need to be modified during the review period. Events within the organisation or in the external environment may require that this be done. For example, within the financial services sector, a shift in interest rates could radically alter the attainability of a particular goal; for firms of solicitors, legal aid regulations have experienced many changes of late so organisations need to keep their goals under review from time to time – often more than annually. Without a regular review, you risk approaching the year end with outdated goals. This makes accurate assessment of performance impossible.

A word of warning – avoid generating unwieldy forms. Many attempts at performance appraisal fail on the basis of placing too much emphasis on the forms that go with it. Beware, the boredom that goes with '*Oh no, not another form*' is infectious – it transmits from manager to employee.

The more organisations can reduce emphasis on the form-filling of their review systems, the better will be the focus on the individual's job. It should, in fact, be possible to complete the framework for performance appraisal using a blank page. An example of a relatively simple form is shown in Figure 6.1. Make one to suit your department.

The performance of individuals should be reviewed against the goals that you set earlier in the process. This ensures that performance will be evaluated against the criteria for success within a particular job. Find out, before you begin, whether any external issues or events have affected the likelihood of the goals being achieved. In the example given in Figure 6.1, two other people who directly reported to the reviewee were on sick leave,

Performance Review		
Name: *Jenny Dixon*	Job Title: *Junior Associate*	Date: *6th December 2006*
Job Objective / Purpose: *Develop the Commercial Department of Duncan Alexander & Wilmshurst*		

Key Result Areas	Goals	Achievement
	Beginning (Active verb) *Middle* (Whatever it is you want to achieve) *End* (Measure)	*Progress / Non-Progress Attainment / Non-Attainment*
Debtors	*Reduce debtors by 7.5% over previous year*	*Good progress: debtors down to 45 days from 62 days average in 2005*
Delegation	*Delegate all analyses of time reports before end of 1st quarter*	*Time reports late from one report (AJM) due to sick leave – well done with others*
Staff	*Define development needs of direct reports prior to end of next quarter*	*All reviews completed save one (DEM) owing to his sick leave – due Jan 07*
Business development	*Increase private client income by 15% over previous year*	*Private client income up 12.5% - what needs to be done to achieve goal?*
Business development	*Broaden commercial base of the service by adding 10 new clients by year end*	*Attendance at 5 seminars brought in 6 clients – why some success; where now?*

Agreed Development / Training Needs

Jenny has done well achieving her administration and staff delegation / development goals but agrees she needs guidance on marketing and business development initiatives.
Agreed to attend 'Networking Skills' and 'Tactical Business Development' workshops before end March 2007.

Additional Comments

Jenny has also made progress on dealing with inter-department conflict solving potential problems with confidence; shows enthusiasm in her business development role and will achieve goals with improved skills

Signature: *Jenny Dixon*   Signature *Mac Mackay*   Date *6th December 2006*

(Reviewee)   (Reveiwer)

Figure 6.1   Example of a simple appraisal form

preventing the achievement of two of the goals; what has been achieved was acknowledged.

The manager alone should not undertake the evaluation of performance. It is consistent with best practice in industry and commerce that the reviewee is *also* asked to form a judgement as to how he or she believes they have performed during the previous period. This, in fact, is a maturing process

---

Box 6.1: A summary of Stage 3

- Must be a continuous process
- Regular reviewing of performance motivates employees
- Reduce emphasis on forms
- Review performance against goals
- Encourage self-assessment
- Value the feedback process.

---

for the person concerned. To assist in this endeavour, give a copy of the KRAs and goals to the reviewee a few days in advance of the appraisal. Ask the reviewee to prepare an outline view of their performance in advance of the discussion.

Many people can remember being told at appraisal time of 'incidents' that had in fact taken place several weeks/months earlier. So, give immediate feedback – quick response after incidents (see Chapter 18 of Mackay, 2007, on how to give constructive feedback). Feedback should be given as close as possible to the event, rather than stored up for some rainy day. This achieves maximum benefit in situations where:

- Change is required in the event of poor performance
- Positive reinforcement is required for good performance.

Such continuous feedback will ensure that there are no surprises at the end of the review period. Stage 3 is summarised in Box 6.1.

Stage 4: Preparing for the Discussion

To prepare satisfactorily for a performance discussion, managers must consider:

- Assessing the individual's performance in the job
- Preparing the structure of the discussion
- Preparing the reviewee prior to the meeting
- Helping the reviewee to understand the system
- Developing skills for the reviewee

- Planning for a good use of time
- Job focus – not a 'systems' focus.

Assessing individual performance

The first stage in your preparation is to examine performance in the job:

- Are the existing Key Result Areas and goals still relevant?
- Have the goals set for the period been achieved?
- If not, were the reasons within the individual's control?
- What specific behaviours helped or hindered attainment of the goals? (Knowing this will help with the exchanges during the discussion.)

Make sure that the review is in the context of the whole period, not just focused on recent events.

Plan the appraisal structure

It will be helpful to prepare an overall plan of how time will be used during the discussion; this permits you to emphasise one issue over another by ensuring through your plan that this issue gets more time.

You should also plan for the specific ways in which you will involve the reviewee. An appraisal is supposed to be a two-way process – it is all too easy for the reviewer to spend far too much time talking.

A structure some find helpful is to plan the appraisal discussion so that it has a beginning, middle and an end. A sample preparation outline using this approach is shown below.

Beginning
- Opening – establish rapport
- Give brief overview of performance management system
- Give overview of process for this discussion, emphasising joint collaboration, and request feedback on own performance
- Request reviewee's view of their own overall performance.

Middle
In preparation, it will be important not only to look at the Key Result Areas, but also the manager should give some thought to specific ways that the reviewee might be involved – perhaps in finding out more information or

Table 6.4 An example of the structure of the middle of an appraisal discussion

Key Result Area	Specific ways to involve reviewee
■ Recoverable fee output Fees billed and recovered in first quarter were 7% up on previous year	How achieved? Can growth be maintained?
■ Client care The number of clients that had cause to complain increased by 14% last period	Why? Warning signs missed? What corrective action to be taken?
■ Teamwork Support staff pulling together much better this year	How did you improve team spirit?
■ Staff development One member of staff not as involved as others	Why? Was this person involved in the client complaints? What action to be taken?

thinking through how they might deal with any issues. An example of the structure of the middle part of the appraisal discussion is shown in Table 6.4 using different KRAs than earlier examples.

At the end of the discussion on each KRA, summarise briefly and refer to next year's goals.

End

In the overall summary it is important to request feedback from the reviewer on ways that he or she may be helping or hindering their own performance – do they have the confidence to open up about how they can control their achievement in work?

Remember to say thanks!

What should the reviewee prepare?

A successful appraisal system relies on reviewee involvement and two-way discussion. To achieve this, the reviewee needs to have spent time preparing for the interview. To this end, encourage the individual to:

- Review his/her performance against the agreed goals
- Produce data on which performance will be reviewed.

Good preparation will pave the way for detailed discussion that focuses on the job done. Two areas are worth addressing:

- *Help for reviewee*. Many organisations approach performance appraisal without providing any help for employees on how they should cope with the overall system and, in particular, with the performance discussion. It greatly facilitates the smooth running of performance discussions if adequate preparatory work is done. Initially, such help can be provided by clearly explaining the system's objectives, principal elements and values to all staff who will be affected by the system.
- *Skills for reviewee*. If the reviewee feels defensive it is difficult to continue a constructive two-way performance discussion. It is worth arranging coaching in ways to increase openness and to encourage individuals away from over-defensive behaviour. Any line manager involving small groups of direct reports should be able to undertake such coaching. If the individual manager is capable of clearly demonstrating their own openness and ability to avoid becoming defensive in the face of feedback, the development of these skills in subordinates is greatly enhanced.

Plan good use of time

One aspect of preparation work is critical and requires detailed planning. You must have a clear vision of the state of mind you want your staff member to be in at the end of the discussion.

You must plan the amounts of time you need to spend on separate parts of the discussion in order to achieve this state of mind.

Failure to plan can lead you into the trap of spending too much time on one or two negative aspects within a generally positive performance. This leaves the employee with a very negative view of their overall performance, which may not have been your intention.

On being critical

If adverse criticism needs making, do not be afraid of it. However, if handled correctly it can be of benefit to both manager and employee. Do remember that not many people like criticism but most will welcome constructive feedback. Again, while a review of Chapter 18 in Mackay (2007) is worth considering, there are five fundamental rules to follow:

1. Do not allow the negative aspects to monopolise all the airtime available.
2. The overall concentration of time for the discussion should, in the vast majority of cases, be on strengths and thereby highlight and reinforce positive performance.
3. Plan to start and end on a positive note.
4. Focus on the act not the individual.
5. Remember to link positive activity with 'and' not 'but' (see Tables 6.1 and 6.2).

Focus on job, not salary

Money is important to individuals and needs ultimately to be linked with performance management. However, the discussion of performance should be separated from any discussion concerning salary by as much time as possible. This allows:

- Full concentration on job performance and what will enhance it
- No distraction for the appraisee of waiting to hear, at the end of the discussion, what adjustment will be made to their salary
- No clouding of a positive appraisal by pay gripes.

Discussions concerning salary, when they take place later, will obviously have to refer to performance, but the two discussions should be as separate in time as possible.

Stage 5: Conducting the Discussion

This stage concerns the attitude of a manager approaching the event that can make or break an appraisal system in one fell swoop: the face-to-face discussion between manager and subordinate. It is crucial that the manager gives the discussion the attention it deserves. Failure to treat the meeting with respect will deliver the clear message that the system itself is held in contempt, by you or even by the whole organisation.

There are a number of fundamental issues that need to be addressed when conducting the discussion.

Preparation

The most important element within appraisal discussions is the level of preparation that is put into them. Building on the preparation 'beginning–middle–end' model discussed earlier, you need to structure each interview at preparation stage so that it is quite clear what will be happening at the beginning, middle and end of the discussion. When using a blank page for this preparation, much of what goes into the box at the beginning and at the end will be reasonably similar from one interview to the next; it is the middle portion that will require the major part of planning for each separate discussion.

Meeting arrangements

The manager is responsible for arranging:

- A suitable time during which there will be no interruptions
- Adequate advance notice of the meeting to allow the appraisee to prepare
- Cover for phone calls
- Understanding from all other staff/colleagues that no interruptions are acceptable
- A location that preferably will not require either party to sit behind a desk
- As relaxed an atmosphere as possible – consider the use of some ice-breakers.

Full involvement of reviewee

It is critical that the person being reviewed is involved and feels involved in the performance appraisal discussion. A discussion is a two-way inter-change! The reviewing manager should be quite clear before starting the interview on the value of involving the employee, and plan specific issues/incidents on which he/she wants to hear the employee's view. Failure to make performance review discussions a fully two-way process will greatly limit, if not totally eliminate, the benefits of such discussions.

Reviewee's evaluation

The appraisal discussion is not an opportunity for the manager alone to comment on the performance of the reviewee. It is an opportunity also for:

- The individual to evaluate their own performance
- The manager and reviewee to come to a common understanding of the level of performance during the period under review.

A few days in advance of the discussion, give the individual the current copy of Key Result Areas and goals, and ask him or her to 'pencil in' their view of their own performance. Once you have done likewise the discussion can focus on merging these views.

Active listening

Most managers believe that they are good listeners. In fact, the evidence points in the opposite direction. This belief on the part of managers more often than not masks the necessity to improve listening skills. Well-honed listening skills are critical to appraisal discussions. Without them, the reviewee will have the clear impression that the manager is not interested in their views; such a conclusion will again limit the benefits of a performance review.

Good listening is particularly important when the reviewee has evaluated their own performance more highly than has the reviewer. In such situations, reviewers who listen well can usually better influence a reviewee to achieve a more realistic view of performance, if that is necessary.

Promote individual development

A key objective for the system of performance appraisal is the development of employees' motivation, ability and confidence. Thus, due attention should be given in these discussions to finding agreed ways in which an individual employee can be further developed. This will benefit both individual and organisation. Failure to deliver on this aspect of performance management, particularly if it has been a stated objective, will bring the system very quickly into disrepute.

Honour commitments

Managers often shoot themselves in the foot by not honouring commitments that they give during appraisal discussions. If managers give a commitment on personal development or any other issue during the course of the appraisal, it is imperative that they ensure this is honoured in full. Failure to do so seriously affects the personal relationship between reviewer and reviewee and, in addition, has negative kickbacks for the company.

Agree future goals

As well as reviewing past performance, appraisal discussions must also either finalise or prepare the way for agreement on goals for the forthcoming period. It is advisable, as you conclude each Key Result Area, to outline fairly briefly what could be the goal for the forthcoming period and test how the reviewee responds to that. This then leaves you in a position where it is a relatively quick exercise to dictate the future goals and pass them to the person for agreement.

Do not discuss salary

Even though the performance appraisal system and the salary system must have consistent outcomes, it is of great importance that there is no discussion of salary during the appraisal discussion.

The major requirement during the discussion is for the employee to focus on performance and how that may be improved.

If a salary increase is also going to be discussed at the end of the interview, then the focus of their attention will be on that throughout the discussion and not on those elements of performance that can be improved.

Keep a record

Successful appraisal systems are about sharing thoughts concerning performance. They are not about filling in forms. However, it is helpful to keep some limited notes and this can be done either on a blank page or on simple forms. The appraisee should be given the opportunity to review any written record and comment on it. Notes on forms such as shown earlier are only 'for the record'; the real emphasis is on the sharing of views.

Follow-up

To ensure that commitments are honoured and that performance is reviewed regularly, managers need to ensure adequate follow-up procedures. This can be as simple as making a diary note to come back to issues that require a later response within a specific time period. With such planning, you should get to the following review having completed all the items you had undertaken in the previous one.

Essential Requirements of the System

Continually improving performance won't just happen – it has to be managed. Managed, that is, by the overall management team and also on a personal level by each manager. It is essential that the following features of effective systems be incorporated into a company-wide approach.

Strong commitment from the management team

None of the benefits described will be fully realised unless the management team takes a very active interest in the process of performance appraisal and management. Their commitment to this is vital. The management team must be fully committed to all elements of a performance appraisal system.

Commitment is a set of behaviours, not just an e-mail, memo or staff brochure showing support. Each manager, particularly senior management, must therefore question themselves about the specific behaviours that they will engage in to demonstrate commitment.

Commitment behaviours required are as follows:

- Promote the system actively by regularly talking formally and informally with people at all levels.
- Ensure that performance management is a Key Result Area for each manager.
- Check regularly on the manner in which the performance management system is being carried out by his/her subordinates. More emphasis here should be placed on the quality of the reviews than whether or not they were completed on time.

High level of subordinate participation

Successful performance appraisal systems are highly participative. Within a goals-orientated system, all employees should be involved in the process of setting the goals for their future performance and in reviewing that performance. Many earlier systems failed on the issue of lack of subordinate participation.

The benefits that can be derived from such a high level of participation are:

- Increased reviewee commitment to the agreed goals
- Substantially improved communication between boss and subordinate.

Adequate training fully supported by the organisation

Many organisations introduce a performance management system without providing any training for managers who are to implement the system. Without such training the system will almost certainly fail. The specific skills required by managers are discussed below.

Skills for managers

Managers require two types of skill. These skills can be very adequately developed in a short training course:

- *Goal setting* – experience shows that most managers do need help with setting goals, which have the degree of clarity and measurability necessary.
- *Coaching and counselling* – managers need these skills for the interactive side of performance review, to help with conducting the appraisal discussions.

Undertaking this training also provides opportunity for overcoming some of the fears that a manager might have concerning an appraisal system.

Training of reviewees

Training for those who will be reviewed is often overlooked. These employees also have fears about the system. It is useful to conduct a short workshop where employees can discuss the system and understand and develop some of the skills it will require. Such training could be described as the missing link for an organisation that does almost everything right, but then leaves out adequate communication and skill development. Organisations that invest time in training their managers and employees reap the benefit during the implementation phase of a performance appraisal system.

Consistency of application

Consistent application of a performance appraisal system across the organisation is a must. You cannot do without it. Failure to manage this adequately will result in discontented employees at various locations in the organisation. Consistency is best achieved by making performance management a Key Result Area for all managers.

Senior management must keep a very close eye on the management of this, and check up on one another to ensure consistency across departments throughout the organisation.

Strong line commitment to regular recognition of good performance

Good performance must be regularly recognised, although not necessarily in a monetary manner. Managers in general do not take sufficient opportunity to celebrate or make a fuss about good achievement. We need to pay more attention to recognition and regularly compliment employees where good performance is evident.

Managers who do this regularly derive all the benefits of having motivated, able and confident staff.

Outcomes from performance review match reward systems

The performance management and reward systems must be linked, though separated in time. In other words, discussion about money should be separated from discussion about performance, but the outcomes should be similar: if you tell someone that their performance is very good, they should see a reflection of this in their salary.

It may take some time (up to a year or two) for an organisation to manage this linkage correctly. This is particularly so if the organisation is introducing a performance appraisal system for the first time. Appraisal skills have to be mastered before approaching full integration with the salary system.

Conclusions for successful application of a goals-orientated appraisal system are summarised in Box 6.2.

Box 6.2: Conclusions for successful application of a goals-orientated appraisal system

- A successfully operated system of performance appraisal is of benefit to both individuals and the organisation they work for.
- Organisations intent on achieving success need to create a culture that will value achievement: an appraisal or review system that is results orientated helps to create and maintain such a culture.
- Achievement of success in running such a system demands commitment and hard work by the management team.
- Reviewing performance is a core system within management.
- It brings about individual performance improvement and development of the individual.

Summary

In this chapter you have:

- Seen the value of the focus of the system being on the real needs of the business and the individual's job
- Recognised that, for effectiveness, managers must concentrate on Key Result Areas
- Explored how to write goals that are specific, measurable, attainable, stretching and jointly agreed
- Seen the importance of reviewing performance continuously, with regular feedback throughout the year
- Recognised the value of encouraging the self-assessment of performance
- Seen that detailed preparation by both parties is essential before the performance discussion
- Explored performance discussions as a two-way communication process
- Seen the value of keeping the performance discussion separate in time from any review of salary.

Questions

1. Write a concise proposal to senior management making your case for a goals-orientated approach to appraisals for all staff in an organisation that to date has no formal appraisal system.
2. Compare and contrast your current appraisal system with the one proposed and summarise how you would make any refinements.
3. Revisit your goals for the next year and assess whether they are in the same format as in Stage 2 above, redrafting them as appropriate.
4. Imagine that you have been asked to outline how two senior partners in a consultancy practice (law, accounts, engineering, etc.) might appraise each other. What advice would you give?

Reference

Mackay, A. R. (2007) *Motivation, Ability and Confidence Building in People*, Butterworth-Heinemann.

Further Reading

Bacal, R. (2003) *The Managers' Guide to Performance Reviews*, McGraw-Hill Education.
Maddox, R. B. (2000) *Effective Performance Appraisals*, Crisp Publications.
Sandler, C. and Keefe, J. (2006) *Performance Appraisals That Work: Features 150 Samples for Every Situation*, Adams Media Corporation, USA.
Scott-Lennon, F. (2004) *The Appraisals Pocketbook*, Management Pocketbooks.

7

A Manager's 'BARC'

Experience is what you got by not having it when you most needed it.
From *It's a Wise Sage*, Chartered Institute of Management

Learning Outcomes

The successful manager is able to manage one-to-one interactions with staff in order to get the best from them and ensure their continued motivation within the organisation. This chapter and the companion web pages look at the key skills of *Briefing* staff clearly, *Assessing* the work appropriately, *Reinforcing* good activities and recognising a *Coaching* need where improvement is required. It has been written to cover elements of the National Occupational Standards for Management and Leadership (*Managing Self and Personal Skills – Unit 3*; *Providing Direction – Unit 11*; *Working with People – Units 21 and 28*; and *Achieving Results – Unit 50*), and it covers some of the requirements of the Chartered Management Institute's Diploma in Management compulsory *Unit C45 – Managing Performance* and most of the optional *Unit O42 – Developing Personnel and Personnel Performance*. It also meets the needs of people studying the CIPD Professional Development Scheme – particularly regarding the *Leadership and Management* module as a core module leading to Graduate Membership of the CIPD.

By the end of this chapter you will:

- Understand the communication skills needed to develop people most effectively
- Know how to use those skills to greatest effect
- Appreciate the value of briefing, assessing, reinforcing and coaching.

BARC Overview

The BARC® Management Process will help develop the specific communication skills managers need to develop the people that work in their organisation most effectively. These skills are briefing, assessing, reinforcing and coaching. A manager's active use of the processes involved will encourage them to use effective behaviours again and again in similar situations.

Using the BARC Management Process, therefore, will enable individuals to have the most positive impact on all their people, especially new recruits.

Briefing, assessing, reinforcing and coaching are very specific skills that will be discussed in detail in this chapter. However, as a preface, there are four key areas that contribute to the most appropriate environment in which to use the BARC skills, as illustrated in Figure 7.1. They will be described below for the practitioner.

- *Management by example.* This means being a 'do as I do' manager, demonstrating these skills and treating people who report to you in the

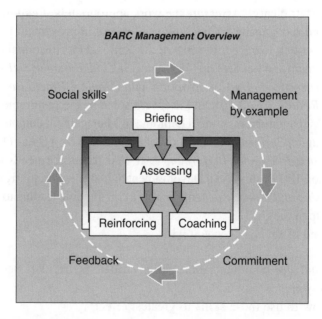

Figure 7.1 The 'BARC' Management Process shown in overview

same way as you would want to be treated yourself. The people who report to you will look to you as their model. What you do and say helps to show them 'what to do' and 'how to do it' when they in turn deal with others. Therefore, the way you use effective communication skills in your daily dealings with people will send a clear message to them that these skills are important and that you expect them to use the skills themselves.

You should always ensure that your team is kept fully informed of what is happening around them, what is required of them (this is particularly important for new recruits) and the way that they will accomplish this. You will achieve this by regularly briefing people to maintain their involvement and motivation and increase their effectiveness.

- *Commitment – to joint aims.* To allow you and your team to measure effectiveness and improvements you need regular review meetings to assess progress in achieving your joint agreed plans. This assessing process will allow you to make the best possible decisions to maintain and improve standards and involve your team in ongoing development.
- *Feedback.* When you recognise that a member of your group has really tried to improve the way he or she handles a situation, you should reinforce the effort (even if everything has not been perfectly right). Prompt reinforcement will encourage people to continue doing the things you praise. It is not always easy to try new ways of doing things and it may take time for some people to achieve change. People are more likely to keep working at these new methods if they receive praise for using them.
- *Social skills.* These are fundamental. Finally, you will be able to interact with people on a mutually appropriate level. This has long been recognised as another very important management skill and one that is often talked about, but little used. It does not mean talking down to people – it means having a mutually satisfying conversation. It also involves skills such as coaching. Effective coaching on your part really encourages learning to be put into practice. When you find uncertainty, you will be able to coach people, according to their individual needs, through any problems that they meet, in order to build their skills and confidence.

Throughout all these interactions you will be continuously giving and receiving feedback.

The BARC Management Process has, at its heart, the three Key Principles:

1. Maintain or improve self-esteem of the people that work with you.
2. Listen and show you understand those people around you.
3. Ask for ideas or offer suggestions by involving those people around you.

Remember – the main aim of briefing, assessing, reinforcing and coaching (BARC) should not be to penalise or soul search about the past, but to endeavour to solve problems and build positively for the future. Reviewing the BARC Management Process in the online pages is a first step in understanding the use of these skills; attending a BARC Management Workshop will give you a sound practical basis for these activities.

In summary, then, as a manager you can:

- Model – by demonstrating effective interpersonal skills yourself when you deal with your own people
- *Brief* – by keeping your people informed of what is wanted and how they can achieve it
- *Appraise* – by regularly discussing plans to monitor progress and ensure positive development
- *Reinforce* – by positively recognising and acknowledging those skills people need to use so as to encourage their repetition
- *Coach* – by working with others to give them a better understanding of how to develop and apply the best possible skills in their particular circumstances
- Feedback – by giving and receiving feedback effectively so as to assist in improving skills and behaviours.

Briefing Effectively

Why brief?

You need to keep your team fully informed of what is happening around them and what is expected of them (this is particularly important for new entrants). By briefing people you can help them to achieve targets set or gain most benefit from training. When people are fully briefed they are more likely to understand where they should be going and better equipped to achieve success.

What is briefing?

Briefing is not simply a case of telling or informing. You will need to listen to ideas and suggestions to become cognisant with the situation in order to be able to assess the required steps to take. It is an exchange of information and ideas from which a framework of objectives can be developed to achieve an operational reality.

How to brief effectively

A number of issues need to be thought about before giving a briefing:

- What information do you need to provide to give a clear picture?
- What questions may you be asked?
- What may already be known?
- Do you brief in groups or individually?
- What is the best time and place for you and your team?

A well-planned briefing will give you the confidence to take your team forward. If you have spent the time and trouble to be well informed you are demonstrating the value of the exercise and your commitment to it.

To get the most out of a briefing it is helpful to follow the guidelines outlined below.

Explain the reason for the briefing and give your support
Begin by explaining the need for the briefing and giving some relevant background. Focus the group or individual on how they will benefit from any developments while at the same time recognising efforts already made and praising skills and abilities already shown. It is vitally important to begin proceedings from a spirit of positive cooperation from all involved and avoid at all costs a position of confrontation.

Explain what is involved and what is expected of the individual or group
By giving specific details about the situation and the targets that need to be reached you will be giving reassurance to your audience that you understand the issues involved, while at the same time giving them the framework on which they can confidently offer their ideas for progress. Remember

to use the SMART acronym when setting objectives (see Chapter 4 of Mackay, 2007).

Are there any questions?

Encourage them to ask questions at every stage, but particularly at this stage when they will have taken on board a lot of information. This may be a point where a number of questions may indicate a lack of understanding by the group, which may need to be addressed before proceeding. If you ask the question 'Do you understand?', you put your follower under pressure. Any doubt they have about the information you've given will have to be expressed as an admission of poor learning ability on their part; asked like this, they may just say 'yes' so as not to appear stupid and then worry about it later.

As the provider of information, it is your job to be understood, to be clear, not their job to understand. So, when checking whether the message is getting across and being received as intended, ask 'Have I explained that clearly?'

Listen and respond honestly to questions, comments or concerns and concentrate on addressing the issues raised rather than the person raising them. It is important to minimise any dissatisfaction due to perceived criticism.

Ask for cooperation in achieving success

Without your team being 'on board' the chances of reaching the desired goals are very small. Asking for their ideas is not an indication of weakness on your part. They will feel a sense of ownership of the project and be more inclined to give of their best.

Express confidence and agree a review date

Set a date for a review of progress so that the value of the exercise can be noted. By expressing your confidence in an individual or group they will feel more positive in their approach to the project.

Assessing the Work Done

Why assess?

Just try driving a car without looking through the windscreen. A manager needs to be constantly aware of the progress their team is making. If you don't assess progress, how can you know if you are going in the right direction? Just as importantly, the act of assessing tells your team you are taking an active interest in their progress and also gives them the opportunity to discuss their work and maybe make suggestions for improvements.

It is especially important when an individual has just completed training or is in a new job. By being open and honest with them you help to maintain their self-esteem and encourage open discussion which can identify new ways forward or the start of a problem that can be solved before developing into a trauma.

What is assessing?

Assessing gives an opportunity for looking back over an agreed action plan and the progress made against specified targets, and also seeing that the aims are still appropriate. It is a non-judgemental exercise that should inform all parties as to progress so far and give opportunities for the inclusion of new factors that may be relevant, such as recent training. It should be an opportunity for discussion and should occur on a regular basis as a matter of course, and not as a one-off interrogation or just part of a formal annual appraisal procedure.

How to assess effectively

Outline the purpose and importance of the discussion
Create the right environment to encourage the maximum contribution from all your team. Be positive, friendly and non-threatening. Outline the purpose of the meeting and indicate how important the meeting is to you as well as to other participants. The aim is to convey that you are generally interested in their development. Evidence your commitment by picking out relevant points from previous discussions.

Ask for details of the progress made
When you are given details, make sure you note them down both to equip yourself with information for a summary and to emphasise the importance of the discussion to you. It is important to recognise that individuals may have differing abilities to give you the information you need, so help the

discussion along by asking general questions like 'How did you get on with the training last week?' or 'Has this procedure made any difference to your work?' Always bear in mind the agreed targets from your briefings and see how the progress made is following the projected course.

Check for understanding

Go over what you have understood to be the case in order to give the person an opportunity to clarify or amend any of the details in your summary. From this point you'll be able to decide on the next course of action; make sure this is linked to what has gone before.

Be ready to give positive actions and further development suggestions once you have updated your knowledge of progress to date. Whatever course of action is suggested, remember to acknowledge the value of achievements so far and express your confidence in future development.

Only when you have assessed effectively will you be able to judge whether to reinforce specific behaviours or whether the individual or team needs to be coached to improve that effectiveness in a particular area.

Reinforcing Successfully

Why reinforce?

By reinforcing their effective behaviours you can provide the encouragement people need to continually try to improve their level of performance. They respect your opinions and look to you for approval and support. When they perform well, recognition from you, in the form of praise, will encourage them to continue that good performance.

What is reinforcing?

Reinforcing is a deliberate or conscious effort on your part to praise or support the use of specific behaviours and/or achievements.

Praise and support are powerful tools that can be used to develop your people and motivate them to continue using effective behaviours. We all want to repeat actions or behaviours that are rewarded by someone we respect. Your reinforcement is especially important after you have coached a person on how or when to use a specific skill. New employees may need more reinforcing to give them confidence to try out different actions and skills, and naturally your own judgement will decide how often to reinforce each member of your team.

Coaching and reinforcing are interrelated skills. Think of reinforcement as the 'glue' that makes coaching 'stick'. Reinforcement will make any behaviour 'stick' whether you've coached it or not, so be aware of only reinforcing behaviours you want to see repeated.

How to reinforce effectively

Be specific

It is vital that your support or praise is specific. A general 'pat on the back' may boost their self-esteem for a moment but it doesn't identify what skills are specifically creditworthy and worth repeating. 'You did a good job with that customer' will mean different things to different people and can involve many different behaviours. '*I liked the way you handled that conversation, you stayed calm and showed the person you understood their feelings when you said to them – I can see why you're upset, nobody likes to receive incorrect information. Well done*' gives a much clearer idea of the behaviours you want to see repeated.

By focusing on specific behaviours used you can point out how using their skills enabled them to be effective. In some cases, even the best use of their skills will not result in a fully satisfactory outcome. It is particularly important to reinforce people in these circumstances as this will maintain or improve their self-esteem and encourage their continued efforts.

Be sincere

Your praise must also be sincere. Keep your comments short and to the point, bearing in mind there may be some awkwardness or embarrassment on the part of the person being praised. Let the person enjoy this moment of positive reinforcement, while you show them sincerely that you support their efforts.

If you praise, then 'ask for more', your reinforcement may appear as an insincere sweetener. Make it clear that the main object of the current discussion is to compliment their use of appropriate skills and not to pick out any shortcomings you may have noticed. However, if an individual wants to discuss problems they encountered, listen and show you understand. Suggesting another time in the near future to explore these in a coaching discussion will be supportive without devaluing your praise.

Be timely

Praise people as soon as possible after they have demonstrated the specific skill or behaviour. This resulting awareness of the link between their actions and your praise will make the reinforcement more effective.

End the conversation with an expression of confidence. This will improve the other person's self-esteem. By encouraging them to continue using specific appropriate skills and being concise you will avoid embarrassment and provide a natural ending for the discussion.

Coaching Better Performance

Why coach?

As a manager, one of your most important tasks is to coach your people. Proper and timely coaching helps ensure that your people perform as effectively as possible. When they perform well they work well within the team.

Coaching is particularly important when individuals are using new skills at work or managing change in their jobs. Your coaching can provide the confidence and build the appropriate new skills if required. When you coach you will be demonstrating your belief that you value people.

Basically, you will call on your coaching skills in four situations:

- When there is a problem to be resolved. An individual is about to face (or has faced) a particularly difficult situation.
- When there is an opportunity for action. You see that a situation can be handled more smoothly using specific skills.
- When someone comes to you. One of your team may want to discuss a problem or perhaps talk about their ideas on how to handle a particular situation.
- After training. When a member of your team has just undergone some training and you want to ensure these new skills are used in their job.

What is coaching?

Put simply, coaching is the process of instructing, guiding or prompting someone to use specific skills to work towards a desired outcome.

You may ask, 'What is the difference between *instructing*, *guiding* and *prompting*?' Well, think of a sports coach. The amount and type of coaching given depends on the level of skill of the athlete involved. A novice needs more frequent coaching and would need to be *instructed* on the proper techniques and when to use them. An athlete with some experience probably has the basic skills but may need to work on some of the finer points as well as when to use them. In this case the coach would be *guiding*. Finally, the experienced athlete with good technique may become a bit complacent at times and will require some *prompting* to keep their performance at its peak.

How to coach effectively

Part of the working relationship

Coaching should be a normal, integral part of the working relationship with your team. It's not something a manager does only when one of the team is incompetent or performing poorly. Experienced people also need coaching to improve and maintain their skills. As a manager, you are responsible for seeing that your unit works as effectively and efficiently as possible. Coaching is a valuable tool to help you achieve this. Indeed, it's likely to be your coaching that determines whether or not your people use their many skills well and continue using them.

Seeking and telling

The key to effective coaching is to strike a balance between 'seeking' and 'telling'. Seeking builds commitment by drawing on the other person's ideas and leading them to consider what skills might be appropriate in a given situation. Too much telling, on the other hand, can invite resistance, especially if the other person feels that they are being threatened or that their ideas are being ignored.

There is, however, a place for telling in a coaching discussion. As a manager, you are likely to have additional information and insights. You should be able to provide guidance and advise people on how to identify potential problem areas and deal effectively with work situations.

Outline the situation and its importance

Open the discussion in a positive, friendly and non-threatening way. Be specific about the situation you want to discuss and what you hope to achieve. Refer to any data or information you have to support what you are saying. If the person has come to you, summarise their description of the situation and check that your understanding is correct. Focus on the problem and the opportunity to use appropriate skills (rather than on the individual concerned) and set the scene for an open, productive discussion.

Explaining the importance of the discussion will also maintain or improve self-esteem. Give the other person every indication that you know they want to do a good job or improve their skills and that you value their efforts.

Discuss and clarify the details

This is the 'fact-finding' part of the discussion. The more information and facts that you gather at this time, the easier and more effective your coaching will be. Here are two useful ways to bring out as much information as you can about a situation:

- *Seek the person's input.* The individual will know the key details of the situation. Use questions like 'Who', 'What', 'When', 'How', etc. to bring out all these details. When possible, take notes and highlight important points. This will indicate to them that you value their input. Where they have already used a particular skill effectively, make a point to praise them and recognise their efforts. This will improve the person's self-esteem and avoid any defensiveness.
- *Clarify information.* From your experience and knowledge of the situation, you may be able to provide details or make suggestions of which the individual isn't aware. It's important at this point to identify and discuss any limitations (your business's policies, particular procedures like COSHH regulations, cost and resource constraints) that may affect how the person could handle, or has handled, the particular situation.

If the person voices concern or feelings about the situation, listen and show them you understand. This will encourage open communication. Be careful not to judge the actions or show disapproval at this point, as doing this will hinder a positive discussion.

People who are new to your business or new to a particular job will probably need more detailed help than experienced members of the team. Be supportive and set the tone of your approach to suit the person with whom you are dealing.

Summarise details and agree on outcomes

Both of you need to be clear about what has been discussed. Recap on the main details to make sure all the relevant facts have been identified, and that you both understand the situation. Based on this understanding, you are ready to agree on what the outcome of the discussion could be. It is important at this point to call on the other person's experience and seek their ideas. This will help build their commitment to the outcome agreed.

Discuss the alternative(s)

This step is the 'heart' of the coaching process. You will need to review the situation with the person and discuss possible strategies, anticipate problems and identify alternatives to achieve the desired outcome.

When discussing alternatives, run through with the person what they might do or say at specific points. If possible, look at a number of different behaviours that could be used. When you are doing this, seek their ideas to build their commitment to the behaviours they are going to use. To gain their active participation, ask questions like these:

- How do you plan to handle. . .?
- What will you do if. . .?
- How do you think we should proceed if. . .?
- What were you planning to do about. . .?
- What reaction might you expect if. . .?

Discuss the pros and cons of each idea. Maintain the person's self-esteem by recognising and building on their good ideas. If they offer a suggestion that doesn't seem workable, look at it closely to see if some parts of it can be built on. If they voice concerns, listen and show you understand. Your input based on your own experience is valuable at this point. If your ideas build on those already suggested, so much the better, as the other person will be receptive to such suggestions.

Develop and agree on a plan of action

Now that you have identified possible ways of addressing the situation, you should encourage the individual to develop an appropriate plan of action. Use as many of the other person's ideas as possible. This will build their self-esteem and commitment to carrying out the actions. During your discussion you will have covered many issues. Summarise the behaviours that you have agreed will be used.

Express confidence and agree a review date

End the discussion on a positive note. Let the person know you think they can handle these (or future similar) situations. This will build their self-esteem and confidence. Set and agree two follow-up dates to review progress. In doing so, you will also show that you are available, and willing, to provide support. This is particularly important with new people or someone having difficulties.

Summary

In this chapter and the online material you have:

- Been introduced to the notion of four key skills when managing people and how to create the right environment for them to best work in
- Seen that professional briefing gives people the best chance to get the job right first time!
- Seen that assessing is more than just asking, 'Well, how did you get on?' – setting the scene ensures that you get good feedback from others in an environment of mutual trust
- Learnt that reinforcing good behaviours is just as important as spotting what went wrong
- Recognised that when something was not achieved, it may have been something to do with the briefing process you initiated
- Explored a stepwise approach to professional coaching of people in the workplace.

Questions

1. What are the issues that a manager would need to consider before deciding whether to brief individuals of a workgroup or the whole team together?
2. Why is it important to 'set the scene' before assessing work done?
3. What is the value in finding something to reinforce even when the major objectives of a brief have not been achieved?
4. Consider a situation that you have experienced where you felt that it would have been more helpful to have had some coaching from the 'leader'. How, in the light of the BARC Management Process, should they have handled the situation?

References

Mackay, A. R. (2007) *Motivation, Ability and Confidence Building in People,* Butterworth-Heinemann.
To explore your own BARC Management Programme, contact the author (www.daw.co.uk).
Want to become an accredited coach? Contact the School of Coaching: http://www.theschoolofcoaching.com.

Further Reading

Antonakis, J. (2004) *The Nature of Leadership,* Sage Publications.
Bacal, R. (2003) *The Manager's Guide to Performance Reviews,* McGraw-Hill Education.
Downey, M. (2003) *Effective Coaching: Lessons from the Coachers' Coach,* Texere Publishing, USA.
Mackay, A. R. (2007) *Motivation, Ability and Confidence Building in People,* Butterworth-Heinemann.

8

Discipline and Grievance

The average company spends almost 4500 hours – or the equivalent of two full-time managers' time – resolving workplace grievance each year.
Chartered Institute of Personnel and Development (*Financial Times*, 20 November 2004)

Learning Outcomes

This chapter has been written as a general guide for managers and should not be used as a substitute for professional legal advice on these matters. It has been written to cover key elements of the National Occupational Standards for Management and Leadership (*Unit 24*) and covers the requirements of the Chartered Management Institute's Diploma in Management compulsory module (*Unit C45 – Managing Performance*) and components of the CIPD Professional Development Scheme in as far as how disciplinary and grievance procedures should be managed as part of these programmes of study.

By the end of this chapter you will:

- Be aware of the changing legislation in this important area
- Have gained an overview of the legal requirements of employers to follow a defined process in managing disciplinary and grievance matters
- Be able to reconsider a number of working practices that affect people at work, including bullying, working hours and sexual harassment
- Have reviewed a range of causes of absenteeism and know where to get further advice on such matters.

The Changing Legislative Landscape

From 1 October 2004, new three-stage notification and consultation procedures came into force to settle disputes before a case goes to trial. Failure by either party to follow these rules means that they automatically lose any resulting employment tribunal. If the company is at fault, it can be forced to pay up to 50 per cent more than would have been the case if it had followed the rules.

The Chartered Institute of Personnel and Development (www.cipd.co.uk) conducted research into grievance and discovered that about 60 per cent of the 1200 employers approached in the study said that they did not believe the new regulations would reduce the number of employment tribunals. The report said that companies do not invest enough time in resolving disputes before they escalate into formal disciplinary procedures. Those that provide mediation training are likely to have significantly fewer disciplinary procedures, averaging 22 cases per year compared to 49 among organisations that do not provide such training, according to the Institute. However, one-third of respondents said they did not train their managers in dispute resolution.

Almost seven in 10 employers say the number of tribunal claims is on the rise, according to the employment trends survey from the CBI employers' organisation (www.cbi.org.uk) published in September 2004. The number of employment tribunal applications had jumped by 17 per cent to 115 042 during the previous year, although this was down from a peak of 130 408 in the 12 months from 2000 to 2001. There has since been a sharp drop in people taking their employers to a tribunal, although the amounts of compensation paid have risen, giving an average of £16 276.

It is estimated (*Professional Manager*, 2003) that there are around 800 000 employers in the UK who do not have adequate dispute resolution procedures – and that 97 per cent of firms have less than 20 employees. It is suggested that small to medium-sized enterprises (SMEs) are often so focused on trying to make a success of their business that the intricacies of employment law simply pass them by. Even the larger companies who are aware of the rules often fall foul of the law; although they have the procedures in place, their managers simply do not follow them. Managers often cannot be bothered to invest the time in doing it right at the outset, not realising how much time it will take – and cost – to sort out the tribunal case at the end.

The reluctance of managers to deal with disciplinary matters or tackle poor performance may be a symptom of the last decade of delayering. In the slim, supposedly fitter organisations of today, managers have increased spans of responsibility, often coming from a technical rather than a management background, and they simply do not know how to deal with people effectively.

Blogging – a new phenomenon

From Samuel Pepys to Adrian Mole, we have heard of famous diaries. Many people keep one, either to record their thoughts or to remind themselves of what they have been doing. But would you like to see your diary published and read by thousands of people? It seems that several million 'bloggers' are more than happy to do so.

'Blogs' – or 'weblogs', to give them their full name – are a type of online journal or diary. Those who maintain blogs, known as 'bloggers', do so for various reasons: some have strong opinions, some have professional advice to impart, others are simply keen to share their lives online.

The weblog began as exactly that – a log of links published on personal websites. The links, which anyone could click on and view, gave people an easy way to access these little nuggets. From this, the idea of the weblog grew as people started adding comments to the items they published, or 'posted', on the Internet. After just a short time, today many blogs do not follow the original definition – in fact, they do not contain links at all – and are much more like online diaries.

It is very easy to set up a blog, and most are hosted by one of the many free 'blogging' services such as TypePad or Blogger. Blogging software takes the hard work out of web publishing and makes it simple to create and update online content.

However, employees using Internet blogs and podcasts to talk about their employers increasingly face dismissal. Ellen Simonetti, a former Delta Airlines hostess, developed considerable notoriety when she was dismissed on 1 November 2004.

The risk of bloggers being fired is rising rapidly as companies clamp down on leaks of commercially confidential information. It is worth noting that few companies have written policies that include references to employees' blogs and podcasts,[1] but this does not prevent employees from being dismissed for telling the Internet world what is on their minds or divulging company data. Employees can have a false sense of security when it comes to postings; they mistakenly believe that if they shroud the blog or podcast with anonymity, they are immune from the consequences.

Over in the USA, however, in most states employment is 'at will', meaning that employers can fire an employee without cause. Learning that an employee is disloyal to the company may be all an employer requires to exercise its option to terminate the person's employment.

In the UK, it may not be so clear-cut but it is recommended that companies incorporate blogging and podcasting policies into existing guidelines on confidential information, trade secrets and use of company electronic resources. The policy should also warn blog authors that using company time or computers to update their sites may be in violation of company policy. And blogging at home about one's employer, even on personal time, can in some circumstances result in dismissal.

If an employer is discontented with an employee's blog, the employee's removal of the inappropriate content or the entire site may not even be enough to remedy the harm.

As soon as the information is made public by Internet posting, the content can be copied and posted to other sites without the original writer's knowledge or permission. Once the horse has bolted, it may be difficult to capture it again.

---

[1] *Podcasting* is the method of distributing multimedia files, such as audio programs or music videos, over the Internet for playback on mobile devices (like mobile phones, iPods and MP3 players) and personal computers. The term *podcast*, like 'radio', can mean both the content and the method of delivery. The host or author of a podcast is often referred to as a 'podcaster'. Podcasters' websites may also offer direct download or streaming of their files; however, a podcast is distinguished by its ability to be downloaded automatically using software capable of reading particular feeds.

Usually, the podcast features one type of 'show', with new episodes either sporadically or at planned intervals, such as daily or weekly. In addition to this, there are podcast networks that feature multiple shows on the same feed.

Podcasting's essence is about creating content (audio or video) for an audience that wants to listen or watch when they want, where they want and how they want.

Disciplinary and Dismissal Procedures

Important note for employers

On 1 October 2004, the Employment Act 2002 (Dispute Resolution) Regulations 2004 came into force. They lay down disciplinary, dismissal and grievance procedures that provide a framework for discussing problems at work. This section explains the procedures in outline only. It is primarily intended for managers in small firms. Separate guidance is available for employees from the Department of Trade and Industry (www.dti.gov.uk/resolvingdisputes).

This section gives general guidance only. It has no legal force and cannot cover every point and situation. If an organisation would like advice on a particular situation, they are advised to contact 'ACAS' for more details (www.acas.org.uk; helpline 08457 47 47 47). It is important to note that the Regulations aim to set a minimum standard and are not intended to replace existing best practice. The new procedures should complement a firm's existing disciplinary and grievance procedures, not replace them. The company's disciplinary and grievance procedures must be set out in writing (see the following sections for more details).

If anyone needs more advice, ACAS offers many services to help, from good practice on setting up procedures to seeking a resolution if an employee applies to a tribunal. Equally, there is no substitute for professional advice from an employment lawyer, and in England and Wales the Law Society will provide appropriate direction (www.lawsociety.org.uk) or www.lawscot.org.uk for Scotland.

Implementing disciplinary and dismissal procedures

This section sets out the steps an employer needs to take when considering dismissal or disciplinary action. Generally, the aim should be to resolve the problem while keeping the employee on. That may not be possible, but the employer must follow the procedures outlined below. Failure to do so may result in a tribunal case that goes against the firm. As stated above, this is no substitute for professional advice.

Communicating disciplinary and grievance procedures
From 1 October 2004, all employers are required to issue a written document that sets out their disciplinary rules and the new minimum procedures.

This will only affect an organisation if they have not already made this information available to their staff or if their procedures change as a result of the new procedures. This information can either be communicated in the employee's contract, his or her written particulars of employment, or the letter sent when offering the employee a job. Alternatively, employers could set out the details in a statement of change. Guidance on producing this statement is available from the DTI and ACAS. (DTI guidance on producing a written statement of employment particulars can be downloaded from www.dti.gov.uk/er/individual/statementpl700.htm or a sample written statement can be obtained from www.dti.gov.uk/er/individual/example-pl700a.htm. ACAS guidance can be accessed at www.acas.org.uk/publications/g01.html.)

If an employer does not issue this statement to their staff, and one of them takes an employment tribunal case against them and wins, the employer will be liable for an additional fine of up to four weeks' wages.

Informal warning

When someone is not performing satisfactorily or is misbehaving at work, an employer's first priority should be to help them to improve. Their line manager should have an informal discussion of the problem with them. They need to understand what they are doing wrong and what they have to do to come up to standard. The manager needs to make a brief note of the date on which the issue was discussed and what action was agreed, copying the same to the employee.

Formal warning

If the issue isn't resolved or the matter is very serious, the manager should tackle the matter more formally. The employee should be invited to a meeting for a formal discussion, where the employee has the right to be accompanied by a colleague or trade union representative. If the manager is not satisfied with the employee's explanation they should write the employee a letter setting out the problem, what they expect him or her to do about it, when they expect to see an improvement and what they will do if there is no improvement.

Where the employee's poor performance or misconduct is sufficiently serious, for example because it is having a serious harmful effect on the business, it may be appropriate to issue a final written warning. For example, an employee in a small shop is responsible for unlocking the premises every morning, but arrives unacceptably late. If informal discussions do not resolve the issue and the employee does not give a reasonable explanation, the employer could issue a final written warning, after holding a formal meeting. The final written warning could state that if the employee is late at any time during the next six months, he or she would be subject to dismissal procedures.

A final written warning should give details of and the grounds for the complaint. It should warn the employee that failure to improve or modify behaviour may lead to dismissal, and it should refer to the right of appeal. A tribunal is unlikely to find a dismissal to be fair unless the employer gave a final written warning (except in cases of gross misconduct).

If the situation still does not improve and the manager feels further action against the employee is necessary, then the manager should start the standard procedure.

Standard procedure

This is a three-step disciplinary and dismissal procedure that applies to:

- All dismissals except:
  - 'Collective' or constructive dismissals and dismissals where employment cannot continue for reasons beyond anyone's control (such as a factory fire)
  - A very small subset of gross misconduct dismissals.
- All disciplinary action, such as demotion or reduction of pay, except action which is part of a workplace procedure, i.e. warnings (oral or written) and suspension on full pay.

Note that the standard procedure applies to the case of an employee on a fixed term contract of a year or more which is not renewed. It also applies when someone is dismissed on grounds of age and has not reached the age of 65 or whatever is the normal retirement age in the company, or when someone is dismissed for health reasons. Note that part-time employees must be treated in the same way as full-time ones. Employers should also use the standard procedure when they are making someone redundant. Failure to use the standard procedure in such cases may result in the employer losing a tribunal case.

The three steps are:

1. The written statement.
2. The hearing.
3. The appeal meeting.

The written statement

Employers must prepare a statement setting out what the employee has done, or failed to do, that may result in disciplinary action or dismissal. In the case of redundancy, retirement on health grounds or the end of a fixed-term contract, the statement should set out the circumstances which led the employer to take the decision to end the person's employment. A copy of this statement must be sent to the employee and the employer must arrange a meeting to discuss the matter.

The employer does not have to put all the details of the employee's conduct in the written statement. But if they don't, the details must be explained to the employee before the meeting, so there is time for him or her to consider a response. The law does not allow the employer only to present this information at the meeting.

The hearing

When arranging the meeting, employers should bear in mind that:

- The meeting should be far enough ahead that the employee has had time to think about the written statement, but it should not be delayed for too long. The employee has a duty to take all reasonable steps to attend.
- The employee has a statutory right to be accompanied to the meeting by a workmate or a trade union representative.
- The meeting must be at a reasonable time and in a convenient location. If the employee or person accompanying them is disabled the employer must take this into account and make reasonable provision to ensure that they can participate fully.
- If they haven't already done so before writing, the employer must ensure they have carried out a thorough investigation of all the relevant circumstances of the case and communicate them to the individual before the meeting.

After the meeting the manager should decide what to do and tell the employee what their decision is. At the same time the manager must offer the employee the opportunity to appeal against that decision if it goes against him or her. The employer must set a time limit for the appeal (the ACAS Code recommends five days).

The appeal meeting

If the employee wants to appeal he or she must inform their employer, who should then arrange a meeting to hear the appeal. The same rules apply to this meeting as to the hearing. If possible, a manager more senior than the manager who held the disciplinary hearing should hold the appeal meeting. If the size of the firm makes this impossible they will need to make an extra effort to deal with the matter impartially. Following the appeal meeting, after due consideration, managers must inform the employee, in writing, of their decision, making clear that it is final.

Instant dismissal

This is a special case. It is almost always unfair to dismiss an employee without first making any investigation of the circumstances. However, in very rare cases it has been known for tribunals to rule that an instant dismissal was fair because the circumstances made an investigation unnecessary. For example, an employee who engaged in serious misconduct in front of witnesses and there was no likely explanation or mitigating circumstances. In these rare circumstances, the Regulations allow an employer to move directly from the written statement to the appeal without having to hold a hearing. Thus, it is a two-step procedure and employers must follow these two steps or the dismissal is automatically unfair:

- *The written statement.* Employers must set out what the employee has done, or failed to do, that resulted in their dismissal. It should also mention that the employee has the right of appeal against this decision. A copy of this statement must be sent to the employee.
- *The appeal meeting.* If the employee wants to appeal he or she must inform their employer, who should then arrange a meeting to hear the appeal. Following the appeal meeting the employer must inform the employee of their decision, making clear that it is final. Employers should regard the modified procedure as a safeguard rather than a viable option.

Employment tribunals

If the grievance, disciplinary or dismissal procedures are not completed when the case goes to a tribunal, the tribunal will decide whether that is the fault of the employee or employer. If it is the fault of the employer the compensation payable will be increased by at least 10 per cent and possibly up to 50 per cent. If it is the employee's fault the compensation will be decreased in the same way. If there is no award, there is no additional penalty.

Note that a tribunal can rule that a dismissal is unfair or that a grievance is justified even though the employer has stuck to the letter of the procedures. The tribunal must be satisfied that the employer acted reasonably in the circumstances (taking into account the size and resources of the organisation). As a guide for employers, see Box 8.1 for principles of reasonable behaviour.

Box 8.1: Principles of reasonable behaviour – from ACAS

- Procedures should be used to encourage employees to improve, where possible, rather than just as a way of imposing a punishment.
- You must inform the employee about the complaint against him or her; the employee should be given an opportunity to state his or her case before decisions are reached.
- The employee is entitled to be accompanied at disciplinary meetings.
- You should not take disciplinary action until the facts of the case have been established.
- You should never dismiss an employee for a first disciplinary offence, unless it is a case of gross misconduct.
- You should always give the employee an explanation for any disciplinary action taken and make sure the employee knows what improvement is expected.
- You must give the employee an opportunity to appeal.
- You should act consistently.

Note that an employee cannot take a case of unfair dismissal against you until he or she has been employed by you for a year or more. There are some important exceptions to this rule. Some dismissals are automatically unfair whenever they occur. In particular, you cannot fairly dismiss a woman for becoming pregnant or a trade union official or health and safety officer for carrying out legitimate duties.

(Drawn from the ACAS Code of Practice on Disciplinary and Grievance Procedures for Employers)

Grievance Procedures – A Guide for Employees

A grievance is defined as some action that the employer or a colleague has taken or proposes to take which affects him or her, and which the employee considers has been taken for some reason that is not connected with the way he or she is doing the job. Employees should be encouraged to raise these issues informally. This may solve the problem quickly and protect good working relations. However, if this informal approach does not work, then the employee must formally raise the grievance. Employees are required to participate in the subsequent procedure.

An employee cannot take an employer to an employment tribunal unless he or she has written to them about the grievance and waited 28 days (although there are some exceptions to this). The 28-day period is to allow employers to respond, but they should not wait that long if they can help it. If employers fail to complete their side of the procedures, any award made in a tribunal case could be increased by 10 per cent and maybe up to 50 per cent. But if the employee starts the procedures but doesn't complete them, his or her award could be reduced by 10 per cent and maybe up to 50 per cent. If there is no award, there is no additional penalty.

The standard procedure is a three-step grievance procedure that applies to almost all grievances (see below for exceptions).

Actions which are part of normal workplace procedures, such as warnings and paid suspensions, can be the subject of grievance procedures, as can behaviour by colleagues. Dismissal, however, cannot be the subject of a grievance – an employee must deal with this as explained earlier in the chapter. There are a few exceptions to the standard procedure (see 'When the procedures do not apply').

The three steps are:

1. The written statement.
2. The meeting.
3. The appeal.

Written statement

The employee must set out his or her grievance in writing and send a copy to their employer.

Meeting

The employer must invite the employee to a meeting to discuss the grievance. They should not delay the meeting unreasonably but give themselves time to look into the background to the grievance and check what action has been taken in similar cases.

The organisation and running of these meetings should follow procedures outlined for meetings and hearings above.

After the meeting, and after due consideration, the employer must inform the employee of their decision in writing and offer an appeal meeting if the decision goes against him or her.

Appeal

These are used if the employee is still dissatisfied, and he or she should tell the employer that he or she wishes to appeal against the decision or lack of one. The employer must arrange a meeting to discuss the appeal. Again, the organisation and running of appeals should follow procedures outlined for appeals above.

Modified procedure

In general, the standard grievance procedure will apply even after the employee has left the organisation. However, there is a shorter procedure that can be used when the aggrieved employee is no longer working for the employer and:

- Both parties agree in writing that it should apply; or
- It is not reasonably practicable for one or other party to carry out the standard procedure – for example, if one of them has left the country for an extended period.

The two steps are:

- The ex-employee sends a written statement of grievance to his former employer
- The employer writes back to the ex-employee giving his response to the points raised.

The procedures do not apply

They do not apply if the grievance is of a 'collective' nature. The grievance is counted as collective if it is raised by a recognised trade union or a workplace representative on behalf of two or more employees.

The procedures will not apply when one party behaves in such a violent and unreasonable manner that the other party could not be expected to sit down with them and go through the procedures.

Finally, there will be circumstances when factors beyond the control of either party mean that it is effectively impossible for the procedure to be gone through, for example if one of the parties concerned leaves the country or becomes seriously ill.

Bullying at Work

Bullying is clearly an important issue and a factor for many workplace grievances. The Department of Trade and Industry sponsored the trade union Amicus to front a £1.8m initiative that will investigate the causes of workplace bullying and seek solutions. The three-year *Dignity at Work Partnership* is the most ambitious research project of its kind. It was officially launched at the Houses of Parliament on 27 October 2004, Ban Bullying Day, with industry leaders such as BT, Legal & General, and Royal Mail signing up as partners.

They will be drawing up a Dignity at Work charter and training employers and union representatives to learn how to deal with workplace bullies. They want to make sure that the policies are implemented properly and advertised throughout an organisation, so that people know where to go and are no longer scared to talk about bullying.

Every day the Andrea Adams Trust (www.andreaadamstrust.org.uk), a charity set up to campaign against bullying in the workplace, receives about 85 calls and more than 60 e-mails from targets of workplace abuse. Victims suffer relentless psychological intimidation and are sometimes even driven to suicide.

Bullying hides behind a plethora of euphemisms, with phrases such as 'strong management' frequently used to excuse intimidating behaviour. However, if one's management style makes someone feel hurt, demeaned or inadequate in any way, the manager is guilty of bullying.

One of the areas that the Dignity at Work Partnership will be investigating is the effectiveness of anti-bullying legislation in countries such as Sweden, where it has already been introduced. While legislation may be one approach, the Andrea Adams Trust Chief Executive, Lyn Witheridge, suggested that, '. . . what is needed is a fundamental change in thinking and in culture. I don't think that people that have lost their self-esteem should be taken through the courts' (*Financial Times*, 2004).

With bullying having such an effect on self-esteem, a guide to reducing bullying in the workplace was dealt with in Chapter 2. It also features in another text by the same author in a section that focuses on maintaining self-esteem (Mackay, 2007).

Working Hours

There are defined regulations about working conditions, not least some discussions on what should be an appropriate number of working hours. Both managers and employees need to be aware of the issues, and also consider options for alternative working hours to develop more harmonious approaches to the world of work and to reduce grievances.

Working Time Regulations 1998

This regulation states that workers have a right to:

- A limit of an average of 48 hours a week which a worker can be required to work (though workers can choose to work more if they want to)
- A limit of an average of eight hours work in 24 which night-workers can be required to work
- Eleven hours rest a day
- A day off each week
- An in-work rest break if the working day is longer than six hours
- Four weeks paid leave per year.

Setting the duration of working time remains a fundamental issue in industrial relations. While major general cuts in weekly working hours have been rare for some years (with the most notable exception being the introduction of a statutory 35-hour week in France), they remain on the agenda of many trade unions and some governments. Furthermore, less dramatically, smaller working time reductions continue to be negotiated, often as a quid pro quo for workers in exchange for forms of flexibility sought by employers. The EU's 2002 Employment Guidelines (see www.europa.eu.int/comm) invite the social partners 'to negotiate and implement at all appropriate levels agreements to modernise the organisation of work, including flexible working arrangements, with the aim of making undertakings productive, competitive and adaptable to industrial change, achieving the required balance between flexibility and security, and increasing the quality of jobs'. Subjects to be covered may, for example, include '... working time issues such as the expression of working time as an annual figure, the reduction of working hours, the reduction of overtime, the development of part-time working, access to career breaks, and associated job security issues'.

Achieving further reductions in working time is still a central demand for the trade union movement across Europe. The European Trade Union Confederation (ETUC) adopted a resolution (see http//:www.etcu.org) at its 1999 congress which included a commitment to continue campaigning for a 35-hour week and all other forms of reduction and reorganisation of working time through collective bargaining 'combined, where necessary, in an appropriate fashion with legislative initiatives'. At European sectoral level, the European Metalworkers' Federation (EMF) adopted in 1998 a working time charter which: 'set a target of a 35-hour working week with no loss of pay; rejected all demands for an extension of working time; and laid down a European minimum standard of 1750 hours maximum contractual working time per year' (which translates as a 38-hour week). Another example is that the European Federation of Public Service Unions (EPSU) adopted a policy statement at its 2000 general assembly which sets the 35-hour working week as a 'priority demand' for its affiliates.

In 2004 the European Commission launched a consultation exercise on the working time directive. While there is an opt-out provision allowing workers to agree to working longer than 48 hours a week, only the UK makes extensive use of it. Where one-third are said to have signed an opt-out, Britain is the only EU country where working hours have increased in the past decade, and while the Commission aims to 'improve the balance between work and family life', it is unlikely to happen without tougher EU legislation.

Alternative working hours

In the past, those who secured full-time permanent positions usually worked a contractual 35- to 40-hour working week, working five days per week between the hours of 9 a.m. and 5 p.m. Now, more flexible working styles are varying, restructuring and reducing the hours we work.

Variable hours

- *Flexitime* allows workers some flexibility in the number of hours they work each day, whilst stipulating the total number of hours they must work across the week. The most common method is to establish core hours (e.g. 10 a.m.–4 p.m.) that must be worked, and for employees to make the time up to their contractual hours at either end of the day. In some cases they may take time off in lieu for any additional time over and above their normal working hours. Flexitime arrangements allow employees to achieve a work/life balance that meets their individual needs.
- *Annual hours contracts* are a relatively new development and calculate contracted hours over the course of a full year. For example, an average 37.5-hour week becomes 1702.5 hours over the course of a year after deducting typical vacation entitlements and discretionary bank holiday leave. Such schemes are designed to create flexibility for the employer by allowing work levels to be varied over the year to meet peaks and troughs in demand without incurring overtime payments – they are currently popular in the financial services industry, particularly in call-centre operations.
- *Time accounts* are a formalised way of compensating workers for working additional hours. Common in continental Europe, most time accounts stipulate a period during which the accounts have to 'balance' to prevent huge holidays building up or periods of excessive work. Time accounts can also be tied in to other employee benefit schemes.
- *Voluntary reduced work time* (*V-time*) brings a new level of flexibility to the security of a full-time job. An idea more popular in the United States, V-time involves an agreement with the employer that an employee will work fewer hours for a certain period of time. The employee retains his/her rights as a full-time worker (with *pro rata* benefits) and, at the end of the V-time agreement, reverts to the original working arrangement.

Restructured hours

- *Shift work* is commonplace in a number of industries and professions where the nature of the work does not allow for a complete break, particularly those related to manufacturing and production, nursing and medicine, the media, and the caring and protection services, to name a few well-known examples. It usually takes the form of employees working timed shifts on a rota basis over a period of weeks.

- *Compressed working weeks* represent an increasingly popular option which offers employees the opportunity to work full-time hours in a limited time frame. One of the most common options is the four-day week, whereby staff work four 10-hour days with the fifth day off. The other is the nine-day fortnight, whereby staff work four nine-hour days, and on the fifth work either eight hours or (on alternate weeks) take the day off.

Reduced hours

- *Part-time work* is commonplace in most organisations in the UK, and is now the most popular form of flexible working. Part-time workers are entitled, under the Part-time Workers Regulations (2000), to the same rates of pay as full-time workers doing the same kind of work, and have a right to holidays, training and benefits on a *pro rata* basis. Part-time work offers those with caring responsibilities the opportunity to work fewer hours, but can also assist those who want to pursue other goals, such as further education, training or voluntary work. It is a popular option for many women returning from maternity leave, but can also reduce stress at work and result in greater job satisfaction for those seeking a more balanced lifestyle.

- *Term-time/school hours* contracts are usually only found in the education sector and do not require employees to work during school, college or university vacation periods.

- *Job sharing* is still comparatively rare, and involves two people sharing the responsibilities of one, usually full-time, post, dividing the pay, holidays and other benefits between them according to the number of hours they each work. This is, for many, an attractive idea and could be a way of working reduced hours at a senior or professional level not traditionally open to part-time workers. Job sharing can give you a greater flexibility to pursue other interests or to work freelance in your own time, and can be a way of balancing work and family life without having to sacrifice the quality of either. The success of any job-sharing arrangement will largely rest on the relationship that one develops with a co-worker to ensure that the pair works effectively, and fairly, together.

A worker's right to opt out

While the European Directive 1998 stipulates a maximum 48-hour week, *Management Today* (2004) reported that the UK government is signing up to the limit. However, both unions and some politicians are calling for the UK to maintain its opt-out as it infringes individual liberty.

Writing in the same journal, Richard Reeves said:

If I chose to work more than 48 hours a week, what right has the government to instruct me otherwise? Maybe I'm getting the overtime to pay for a family holiday; perhaps I'm running a business during a critical period; perhaps – shock-horror thought – I'm doing more than 48 hours of work a week because I like it!

The first head of department that the author had to work for, David Warring, said on my first day in Beecham Pharmaceuticals:

We expect you to put in the necessary hours but if you are working longer hours it tells me one of two things: we are either making so much profit that we can afford to employ an assistant for you, or you are ineffective; just let me know which one it is!

The competitiveness that comes from working long hours is worth nothing if the people are doing so miserably against their own will or instincts. What employers must do is to improve the quality of working life and then leave it to individuals to decide for themselves what the right work/life balance is going to be.

Absenteeism

In 2003/04 an estimated 39 million working days were lost overall, 30 million due to work-related ill-health and 9 million due to workplace injury. Moreover, in the same period, an estimated 2.2 million people in Great

Britain were suffering from an illness which they believed was caused or made worse by their current or past work (figures from www.hse.gov.uk).

More worryingly, there were 235 fatal injuries to workers in 2003/04, a rate of 0.81 per 100 000 workers. In 2003/04, employers reported 159 809 other injuries, a rate of 629.1 per 100 000 employees (0.63 per cent).

Good health is good for business – and it needs to be at the top of every manager's agenda. Not only in the cause of reducing grievance, but simply in terms of enabling people to be as effective and as efficient as possible in any job role.

If bad job design or huge workloads are putting employees under stress, if managers are tired and irritable because they have constant back pain, neither will be able to perform to the best of their ability.

The following sections review some common causes of absenteeism and grievance, and also deal with a range of work-related health issues that employers have a role to play in their management. It is not intended to substitute professional advice and any employer is encouraged to seek appropriate guidance. The information has been provided courtesy of the Health and Safety Executive, BUPA, Wellness and the Trade Union Congress (TUC).

Stress

As we saw in Chapter 2, included under the heading of mental ill-health, too many people took time off for stress. Figures from a recent survey (Smith et al., 2000) provided an estimate of 13.4 million working days lost in Britain each year due to stress, depression or anxiety. This survey estimated that, on average, each sufferer took 29 days off work because of their complaint. This compares with 6.5 million working days lost and average days lost of 16 per affected person estimated from similar studies (Health and Safety Statistics Highlights, 2001/02).

Calculations based on an HSE report (2002) estimated that for work-related stress the cost to employers was about £353–381 million (1995/96 prices) and to society about £3.7–3.8 billion. It should be noted that since these calculations were done, the estimated number of days lost due to stress has more than doubled.

HSE's key messages on stress are:

- Work-related stress is a serious problem for organisations. Tackling it effectively can result in significant benefits for organisations.

- There are things organisations can do to prevent and control work-related stress.
- The law requires organisations to take action.

See also the websites of the International Stress Management Association (www.isma.org.uk) and the Mental Health Foundation (www.mental-health.org.uk).

Figure 8.1 (see page 166) shows an adaptation of the HSE recommended approach to the process of doing a risk assessment for stress.

Musculoskeletal disorders

These events (largely back pain and upper limb problems) affect an estimated 1.1 million people each year according to the HSE and result in the loss of 12.3 million working days. Poor work habits have a lot to answer for. Incorrect lifting techniques, repetitive tasks and uncomfortable working positions are rife in the workplace.

Employers have a legal obligation to ensure that their people are aware of safe practices and are not being injured by work. Often, the problem is that people don't appreciate the importance of the advice they are given and carry on with their old bad habits.

Useful contacts include www.backpain.org.uk.

Alcohol

Alcohol does not improve the performance of anything.

Anon

Alcohol abuse affects many people – one in 13 is reported to be dependent on alcohol, and alcohol is behind 3–5 per cent of all absences from work. An employee under the influence of alcohol cannot perform at their peak – and certainly will not be fit to carry out any job that involves driving or operating machinery.

An employee whose work is suffering because of a drink-related problem is entitled to confidentiality and support. A clear organisational policy on alcohol will help managers ensure that they deal with any problems in an appropriate way (a guidance leaflet is available from the Chartered Management Institute – www.managers.org.uk/drugs).

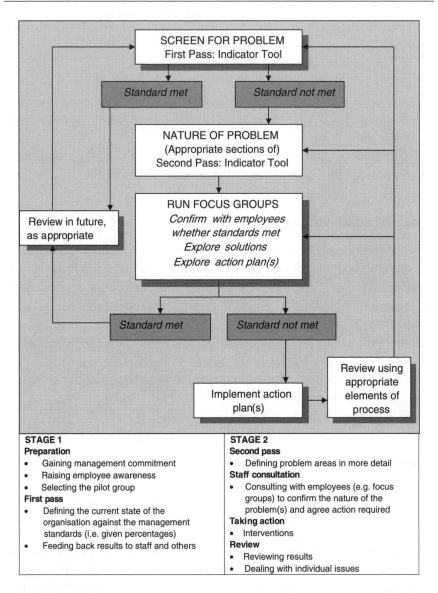

Figure 8.1 An adaptation of the HSE process of doing a risk assessment for stress

Employers should be aware of some alarming trends in young people. In 1996/97 admission rates for mental and behavioural disorders due to alcohol in under-14s were 18.7 per 100 000 of the population per year (Williams et al., 2005). By 2002/03 this figure had increased by 24 per cent to 23.2 admissions per 100 000 people. Admissions for the same problems in women aged 15–24 also rose by 9 per cent from 38 per 100 000 in 1996/97 to 41.5 in 2002/03. The researchers noted that around 5.9 million people in England and Wales drank twice the recommended weekly amount of alcohol.

While it is reported (Knoops et al., 2004) that moderate consumption – two or three standard glasses of red wine or a couple of pints of beer – keeps the arteries to the heart muscle open and preserves the flow of oxygenated blood to the brain, staff should be encouraged to consume in moderation after work, not before and not during!

Drugs

Drug misuse is a serious problem not only for the individual, but also for the business where they work. Drugs affect the way a person thinks, perceives and feels, leading to impaired judgement and concentration. Someone who is using drugs may put themselves and their colleagues' safety at risk.

Managers need training to help them deal with the problem in a confidential and supportive manner.

Useful contacts include NHS Direct (www.nhsdirect.nhs.uk) and the Institute for Occupational Safety and Health (www.iosh.co.uk).

Heart disease

It is estimated that one in every four men will have a heart attack before the age of 65; coronary disease is also on the increase in women. There is good news for the individual as there is much they can do to reduce the risks. Smoking, poor diet, obesity, high cholesterol and lack of physical activity are among the key risk factors.

The British Heart Foundation provides a Workplace Health Activity toolkit, with information, practical ideas and materials to help employers encourage their staff to lead healthier lifestyles.

Useful contacts include the British Heart Foundation (www.bhf.org.uk).

Smoking

It is estimated that, at any one time, around 8 million smokers in the UK are trying to give up their addiction. Helping employees give up their habit is in the interest of business, since smoking contributes to higher sickness rates and increased levels of early retirement due to ill-health.

In the UK, three people die each year from passive smoking at work, according to the Health and Safety Commission – small wonder trade unions and pressure groups such as Action on Smoking and Health (ASH), the anti-smoking charity, take action. It may be that employers not introducing their own policy to control smoking in the workplace risk leaving the floodgates open to a tide of compensation claims from employees past and present.

Employers must ensure as far as reasonably practicable the health, safety and welfare at work of all their employees under section 2 of the Health and Safety at Work Act 1974. This means that if a risk can be demonstrated from working in a smoky environment, the employer must take action. Under the Workplace (Health, Safety and Welfare) Regulations 1992, employers also have to ensure that there are arrangements to protect non-smokers from discomfort caused by cigarette smoke in rest areas.

It is important that businesses negotiate with their employees to agree a policy on smoking in the workplace which will not only protect non-smoking workers, but should also guard against possible compensation claims.

Businesses not having a policy on smoking in operation risk costly court cases. Civil claims for compensation arising from passive smoking in the workplace have been successfully pursued. Introducing a complete ban on smoking overnight is equally risky for employers, as this action could infringe employment rights. Employers should always consult their employees before introducing a policy and give plenty of notice before it comes into force.

As smoke-free is not the same as risk-free, Box 8.2 is a suggested outline guide to introducing controls to smoking in the workplace.

New anti-smoking legislation came into force in Italy in January 2005 amid an outcry from business owners (*The Times*, 2005). Smoking was banned in public places, including shops, hotels, bars, restaurants and theatres, unless they had separate areas for smokers. Any such areas must be well ventilated and equipped with automatic doors. Not only must staff at such venues ban smoking indoors, but they must also call the police if anyone refuses to comply. Failure to do so could cost the business owner a fine of €2000 (approximately £1414) and even their licence. The maximum fine for the smoker will be €250. While a number of the organisations that represent business owners in Italy are against the measures, a survey of the public showed 80 per cent were in favour.

Box 8.2: A guide to introducing controls to smoking in the workplace

1. *Inform staff.* Employers should take time to develop their smoking policy, giving a minimum period of three months' notice, as suddenly imposing a smoking ban could infringe employment rights.
2. *Consult.* Employers should consult employees and their representatives on the appropriate smoking policy to suit the particular workplace. Consider a vote on smoking restrictions.
3. *Ban it.* A complete ban may be justified for safety reasons, for example where there is a risk of fire or explosion. Make sure you have 'no smoking' signs prominently placed in designated no smoking areas.
4. *Police it.* Introduce a specific policy on smoking in the workplace. The policy should give priority to the needs of non-smokers who do not wish to breathe cigarette smoke. This policy should be written down and easily available to all staff, and included with information when a job offer is made.
5. *Enforce it.* Make staff aware of the details of the policy and what will happen to those employees who do not abide by it. Any smoking policy should be made part of all employees' contracts or terms and conditions of employment, so that breaches of the policy can be subject to normal disciplinary and grievance procedures.

In England and Wales, new legislation is scheduled for 2007 to ban smoking in all pubs and clubs – including private clubs. BT also banned smoking in all of its offices and service vehicles in February 2006.

Diabetes

About 3 per cent of the UK population have diabetes and there could be another million or so people where the disease is undetected according to the charity Diabetes UK (see wwwdiabetes.org.uk). There are two types:

- Type 1 is an auto-immune condition which usually appears in people under the age of 40, often in childhood.

- Type 2 develops when the body can still produce some insulin, although insufficient for its needs. This type usually appears in the over-forties and is associated with obesity and inactivity. It also tends to run in families.

The main symptoms are increased thirst, the need to urinate frequently, extreme tiredness, weight loss and blurred vision.

Employers should give some thought to how to deal with hypoglycaemic shock (where individuals do not have enough sugar in their blood) and a quiet private place where an individual who is insulin-dependent might inject themselves. Diabetics do not want to use the toilets nor be accused of being a Class A 'drug' user!

Asthma

Occupational asthma costs society up to £1.1 billion a year; it is estimated that there are 1500–3000 new cases each year. The condition can be caused by exposure to a variety of substances that are used in the workplace – latex and solder, wood dust, and some glues and resins. The main symptoms are wheezing, chest tightness and breathlessness.

Employers are required by law to assess risks to their employees and to prevent or control exposure. If someone is – or thinks they are – suffering, fast action is required. Early removal from exposure can lead to a complete recovery, but once the condition is established, exposure to any airborne irritant can trigger an attack.

Dermatitis

Occupational dermatitis affects virtually all industry and business sectors and results in around half a million lost working days a year. The vast majority of cases are caused by the exposure to chemical agents – some of which may appear to be quite innocuous.

The signs include redness, itching, scaling and blistering of the skin; if the condition worsens the skin can crack and bleed. Dermatitis can spread over the whole body.

If it is spotted early and appropriate precautions taken, most people will make a full recovery. Managers need to make sure that they know what products their staff are using, and if necessary look for safer alternatives or find different ways of doing the job.

Sexual Harassment

The Equal Opportunities Commission (see www.eoc.org.uk/EOCeng/ EOCcs/Advice/sexual_harassment_rights.asp) defines sexual harassment as any unwelcome physical, verbal or non-verbal conduct of a sexual nature. These are liable to civil claims in the employment tribunal. Examples of sexual harassment at work include:

- Comments about the way you look which you find demeaning
- Indecent remarks
- Questions about your sex life
- Sexual demands by a member of your own or the opposite sex
- Any conduct of a sexual nature which creates an intimidating, hostile or humiliating working environment for you.

It should be recognised that incidents involving touching and other physical threats are criminal offences and should be reported to the police, since sexual harassment is against the law.

Women and men have an equal right not to be subjected to sexual harassment at work.

The Sex Discrimination Act (SDA) 1975 makes it unlawful for employers in Great Britain to treat a woman less favourably than a man (or vice versa) in similar circumstances by subjecting her, or him, to a detriment. It is also unlawful to discriminate against an individual undergoing gender reassignment.

The SDA applies not only in circumstances where you are a company employee, but also to a wide range of other employment situations. These include if you are:

- Working in a partnership
- A member of a trade union

- A member of a professional body
- A member of an institution which issues qualifications that are required to carry out a particular trade or profession.

The SDA applies regardless of length of service or number of hours worked and to a number of employment situations, including the recruitment process.

Sexual harassment itself can amount to less favourable treatment, but in many instances it will be accompanied by other forms of unfavourable treatment, such as not being recruited, criticism of work, lack of promotion, enforced transfer and ill-health or dismissal.

You can only make a claim of sexual harassment under the SDA if the sexual harassment you are complaining of took place in work or at a work-related function. This means that the harassment has to happen during what is known as 'the course of employment'.

Depending on the facts of your case, you may be able to claim under other legislation in addition to the SDA. Again, whether you are an employer or an individual, there is no substitute for professional advice from a qualified solicitor and in England and Wales the Law Society will provide the appropriate direction (www.lawsociety.org.uk) or www.lawscot.org.uk in Scotland.

Summary

In this chapter you have:

- Reviewed the changing legislation in this important area
- Taken an overview of the legal requirements of employers and seen how following a defined process in managing disciplinary and grievance matters can reduce the need for employers to defend themselves in industrial tribunals
- Looked at a number of working practices that affect people at work, including bullying, working hours and sexual harassment, and identified ways to reduce problems at work
- Seen how important stress management is to staff and explored ways to audit and reduce workplace stress
- Reviewed a range of causes of absenteeism and uncovered where to get further advice on such matters.

Questions

1. Does the organisation where you work or study have a properly documented disciplinary and grievance procedure, and is it known to all its employees? What recommendations would you make to improve practices?
2. Consider stress in your place of work or study. Using the HSE first-pass audit tool (Figure 8.1), what recommendations would you make to reduce stress in the workplace? Identify any resource implications for your suggestions.
3. Imagine a colleague at work confides in you that another member of staff has made inappropriate and unwarranted sexual advances towards them. What action would you recommend they follow? What would you do?

References

Financial Times (2004) 28 October.

Health and Safety Statistics Highlights (2001/02) Available at: http://www.hse.gov.uk/statistics/overall/hssh0102.pdf, with supporting material available from links within this document and via the HSE statistics web page (www.hse.gov.uk/statistics/index.htm).

HSE (2002) 'Economic Impact: Revised Data from the Self-reported Work-related Illness Survey in 1995 (SWI95)', HSE Information Sheet 2/99/EMSU. Available at http://www.hse.gov.uk/statistics/2002/ecimpact.pdf.

Knoops, K. T. B. et al. 'Mediterranean Diet, Lifestyle Factors, and 10-Year Mortality in Elderly European Men and Women', *Journal of the American Medical Association*, Vol. 292, pp. 1433–1439.

Mackay, A. R. (2007) *Motivation, Ability and Confidence Building in People*, Butterworth-Heinemann.

Management Today (2004) September, p. 31.

Professional Manager (2003) November, p. 23.

Smith, A., Brice, C., Collins, A., Matthews, V. and McNamara, R. (2000) *The Scale of Occupational Stress: A Further Analysis of the Impact of Demographic Factors and Type of Job*, HSE Books,

CRR 311/2000, ISBN 071761910 9. Available at: http://www.hse. gov.uk/research/crr_pdf/2000/crr00311.pdf.

The Times (2005) 2 January.

Williams, S. et al. (2005) 'Hospital Admissions for Drug and Alcohol Use in People Aged Under 45', *British Medical Journal*, Vol. 330, January, p. 115.

Further Reading

Daniels, K. (2004) *Employment Law for HR and Business Students*, Chartered Institute of Personnel and Development.

Disciplinary and Grievance Procedures: ACAS Code of Practice 1 (2004) Stationery Office Books.

Lockton, D. (2003) *Employment Law*, 3rd Edition, Lexis Nexus UK.

Mackay, A. R. (2007) *Motivation, Ability and Confidence Building in People*, Butterworth-Heinemann.

Peyton, P. R. (2003) *Dignity at Work: Eliminate Bullying and Create a Positive Working Environment*, Brunner-Routledge.

Slocombe, M. (2005) *Employment Law Guide*, 8th Edition, Lawpack Publishing.

Part 3
Releasing People

Part 3

Releasing People

9

Retirement

Luckily, life is not so easy as all that; otherwise we should get to the end too quickly.

Sir Winston Churchill *My Early Life* (1930)

Learning Outcomes

This chapter has been written as a general guide for managers and should not be used as a substitute for professional legal advice on these matters. It has been written to meet the needs of both the National Occupational Standards for Management and Leadership (*Unit 24*), the Chartered Management Institute's Diploma in Management compulsory module (*Unit C45 – Managing Performance*) and the CIPD Professional Development Scheme in as far as retirement of staff is concerned. It also gives managers ideas to help pass on to the retiree who may need guidance to help plan for retirement.

By the end of this chapter you will:

- Be able to devise strategies to retire your staff and follow recent guidelines in managing the process appropriately
- Guide people approaching retirement
- Know how to manage the retirement of people.

Retirement

When one looks at the Internet to review material on retirement, the vast majority of advice is centred on financial planning. Recent research in 2004 from Prudential reveals that around 4 million people aged 55 and over have less disposable income than they did one year ago. The Prudential 'Mood of the Nation Index' confirms that many of these have fallen further into debt and a large number are pessimistic about the chances of their financial situation improving.

In the previous 12 months, says the report, 2 million people aged 65 and over have seen their disposable income fall – the same number as in the 55–64 age bracket who are still mainly in the workforce. One of the effects of this is that just over a quarter of a million people aged 55 and over have had to take on more debt and may have been forced to raid their savings.

The consequence of this is that more than 2 million people currently continue to work in retirement and pension companies expect this number to grow – especially as the UK population overall has over £1 trillion in unsecured debt to service.

The same Prudential research revealed that 33 per cent of British workers aged 45–55 admit to feeling nervous or depressed about retiring; 27 per cent of those 55–64 feel the same way too. The result is reluctance in some to retire and a growing tide of pensioners moving back to the workforce. The research shows that over 775 000 retirees want to return to the workforce but are not being employed because of their age. Moreover, it was discovered that 72 per cent of those retiring in 2003 did not seek any financial advice before doing so, with 85 per cent of women admitting they did not seek any advice to plan ahead.

New age discrimination legislation comes in to force on 1 October 2006, whence employers will not be able to retire employees below the age of 65 or the employer's normal retirement age. If the normal retirement age is below 65, this will have to be objectively justified. In practice, this new default retirement age leaves employees over the age of 65 largely unprotected by the new regulations. The government has also indicated that this default age will be reviewed in five years' time and could possibly mean that it could be raised to 70. Naturally, this gradualist approach to raising the retirement age will create more uncertainty and the possibility of yet more reviews or procedures and employment practices.

For retirees, opinion is that many people could improve their financial well-being through better planning. The larger pension planning companies offer a series of free planning guides which help people plan for the future and manage their day-to-day finances; employers are encouraged to direct their staff to seek professional advice (see www.50connect.co.uk).

However, as with other situations when someone is leaving the organisation, there is much that managers can do to limit the negative impact that the change can have on the organisation. The retiring person may have skills and insights that have value to the organisation and wise managers should endeavour to retain the best for the mutual benefit of both parties. The retiring person may benefit from the extra cash and the self-esteem that comes from maintaining some sort of work, while the employees may value a mentor or counsellor – provided that that person has the necessary skills and aptitude. Part-time working, short-term contracts, flexible working and remote working all have their part to play in assisting the transition.

An employee's guide to planning for retirement

In the UK, as an employee you are under no obligation to retire at the state retirement age. If you want you can delay the drawing of your state pension. During the period that you defer receiving your state pension it will be increased, so that once your pension is started the weekly payment will be higher than would have been the case at the usual state pension age.

The start date of receiving benefits from private pensions cannot normally be extended beyond age 75. Whether a delay in the start of your private pension payments will result in a higher income being paid to you will depend on the terms of your particular pension plan. Talk to your Independent Financial Advisor or pension provider for information.

Whatever your financial situation, many retirees feel a sense of loss after they have left their colleagues and sold their briefcase on eBay. They have been saving and investing for decades for the 'big day' only to ask soon thereafter, 'Is this all there is?' Some report that they feel a kind of nothingness, a drift to retirement – it can be a vacuum. Many people get their identity from their jobs, from their accomplishments.

Many may count themselves among the working hardliners who might find this ambivalence about retirement hard to believe. What many wouldn't give for a break from long commutes, tedious meetings, office politics, having to climb into workclothes each day!

Sadly, the frustration of the recently retired is real. One former colleague said, 'Retirement left a greater void in my life than I expected.' Another said, 'I can fill the time, but at the end of the day, what have I really done with it?'

Consider what would you do with 24/7 free time! By the time you reach your sixties, you will have spent decades on your career. You met many, if not most, of your friends – quite possibly your partner – through your job. A sizeable chunk of your self-worth and sense of usefulness comes from how you have earned a salary. Is it possible that you would be lost – at least for a while – after you have given it all up?

While working forever is no solution, some retirees design self-sustaining portfolios and craft-fulfilling lives, usually through a mixture of travel, family and challenging ventures (sometimes for pay, sometimes not). However, creating such a retirement doesn't just happen. It takes planning, which is best done long before the retirement party.

Box 9.1 should give you a guide as an employee (and others who may be called upon to advise a potential retiree) in thinking about this next stage in your career plan.

While most people may not want to be employed full-time forever, many want to be of service, of use – valued as individuals and by others. Considering how to spend the time in retirement is as crucial to any retirement plan as calculating how to spend the retirement money.

Box 9.1: Things to consider when embarking on retirement

Begin the process through various self-assessments, review case studies and talk with those who have already been there. Consider:

- Do you mean to fully 'retire' or just change occupation and move to a more part-time occupation?
- How much annual income will you need from your pension?
- Will you want to relocate in retirement. If so, how far from where you live now? The country cottage may become boring, the Spanish villa lonely.
- How will family – children, grandchildren or elderly parents – feature in your plans?
- How will you structure your time once you are freed from nine-to-five commitments?

Will you try a new career – or some other rewarding, new endeavour? (You may be looking for a way to contribute, to be productive and to have an impact – but not a job as such.)

So, how can you start planning the rest of your life? The following are some possibilities to consider:

- Begin a 'rehearsal retirement' by visiting new locations and trying new activities without making too great a financial commitment. Borrow some golf clubs to see if you like the game. Charter a boat before setting off to the Boat Show. If you can arrange it, consider the concept of the 'gap year' – taking time off, especially in between big transitions, to audition a different life.
- Discuss a 'phased retirement' with your employer, allowing a transition time between full-time work and full-time free time. Consider training as a coach or mentor – older people with a positive attitude have much to offer.
- If you think you'll want to continue to work part-time, seek out employers known for valuing older workers, such as some of the retail chains, for example.
- Perhaps your skills might lend themselves to running your own self-employed business – you don't have to build a whole empire and there are (still) some useful tax advantages.
- Don't wait until retirement to begin your philanthropic pursuits. Start now, working with organisations that support the causes you care about.

If you're married or in a long-term relationship, don't keep all your dreams and anxieties to yourself. No plan will work until both parties agree on it.

An Employer's Guide to Retiring Employees

While not a substitute for proper legal advice, it is worth appreciating that there are two fundamental regulations affecting employers that came into force on 1 October 2006, namely:

- There will be a national default retirement age of 65, making compulsory retirement below 65 unlawful unless objectively justified.

- Employees will have the right to request to work beyond 65 or any other retirement age set by the company. The employer has a duty to consider such requests.

The new regulations set a default retirement age of 65 (to be reviewed in 2011). This means employers can retire employees or set retirement ages within their company at or above 65 years of age. Retirements or retirement ages below the default retirement age will need to satisfy the test of what is called 'objective justification' (see www.acas.org.uk).

However, employers do not have to have a fixed retirement age. Indeed, as the guidelines from ACAS suggest, there are many business benefits to adopting a flexible approach to the employment and work patterns of older workers.

Employees will have the right to request to continue working beyond their retirement date and employers have a duty to give consideration to such requests. Each request must be thought about on an individual basis – taking into account opportunities to vary the employee's hours or the duties they perform. However, employers are under no obligation to agree to such requests – provided they can show that they have taken careful consideration in each case.

Fair retirement

So what constitutes fair treatment? Potentially a minefield of regulation, the following is an attempt to clarify the steps that an employer must take. A fair retirement is one:

- That takes effect on or after the default retirement age (or on or after the employer's normal retirement age – if there is one)
- Where the employer has given the employee written notice of the date of their intended retirement and told them about their right to request to continue working (see below for the timing requirements of this notice).

If the employer's normal retirement age is below the age of 65, it must be objectively justified. For the retirement to be classed as 'fair', employers need to have informed the employee in writing of their intended retirement date and of their right to make a request to work beyond retirement age at least six months in advance (but no more than 12 months before the intended date).

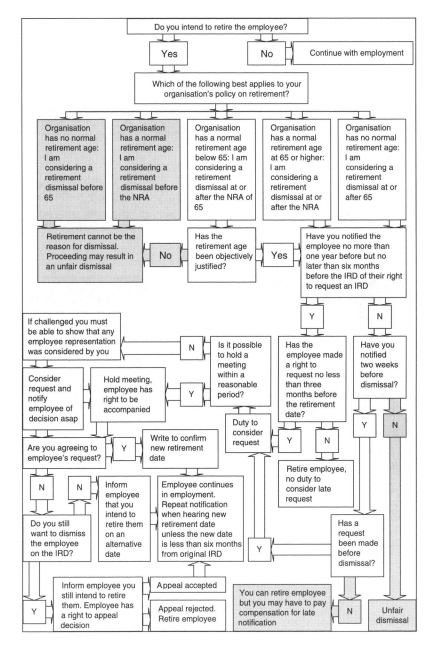

Figure 9.1 Fair retirement flow chart (NRA = normal retirement age; IRD = intended retirement date). Adapted from ACAS.

If employees do make such a request, employers must have followed the correct procedure for dealing with it. Figure 9.1, adapted from the government agency ACAS's free booklet 'Age and the Workplace', sets out a guidance flow chart for fair retirements.

Summary

In this chapter you have:

■ Considered a guide for people approaching retirement
■ Looked at issues to consider when managing the retirement of people
■ Reviewed the crucial steps in dismissal of people through retirement.

Questions

1. Consider the practices of your organisation, or one with which you are familiar, and consider whether they meet best practice in the retirement of people. What recommendations can you make for improvement?
2. Do you have a succession plan for your position in your organisation (assuming you were to retire in six months' time). What are the main issues to consider?
3. With an ever-increasing number of people reaching retirement – and the government increasing statutory pension age – what are the options for older workers? Critique your organisation on its policies for managing such people.
4. As a manager, what are the key issues that you will have to address when redundancies are inevitable?

Further Reading

Back, S. (ed.) (2005) *Managing Human Resources: Personnel Management in Transition*, Blackwell Publishing.

Jay, L. (1999) *Retirement Redundancy Removal*, Croner's Guide to Managing Redundancy, Croner.

10

Redundancy

You're a lightweight – you're fired.

Alan Sugar on how not to do it!

Learning Outcomes

This chapter has been written as a general guide for managers and should not be used as a substitute for professional legal advice on managing redundancy matters. It has been written to meet the needs of both the National Occupational Standards for Management and Leadership (*Unit 24*), the Chartered Management Institute's Diploma in Management compulsory module (*Unit C45 – Managing Performance*) and components of the CIPD Professional Development Scheme in as far as the redundancy of staff is concerned. It also gives managers ideas to help their staff directly when facing redundancy.

By the end of this chapter you will:

- Be able to devise strategies to organise a redundancy programme
- Guide people approaching redundancy
- Be able to follow the crucial steps in redundancy and removal of people.

A Blessing or Curse?

It has been suggested that many – as much as half – of those people who have been made redundant look back and consider that it was a blessing in disguise because it forced them to look hard at what they wanted to do. The redundancy payment often allowed some time for setting a new direction too, without having to worry unduly over how they were going to make ends meet. The author has been made redundant on three successive occasions from industry; each time it was traumatic but each time it lead to better things – it just takes a while to reorganise and do a little careful planning.

However, being made redundant is not without risk. There are, of course, significant financial risks; there may be a gap before finding new paid employment and the new chosen career may be less lucrative.

The growth of British industry requires constant review of products and methods of work, and the successful application of new technology. Industry's ability to maintain competitiveness in world markets depends on this. However, it is inevitable that redeployment of labour and redundancies will sometimes be necessary. A poorly thought out approach to change can result in a level of uncertainty that damages company performance and, should redundancies be unavoidable, may lead to financial and emotional costs to the individuals affected.

Redundancy has two different meanings for the purposes of UK employment law: one to establish entitlement to redundancy payments and one for the right to be consulted.

For entitlement to redundancy payments, under the Employment Rights Act 1996, redundancy arises when employees are dismissed because:

- The employer has ceased, or intends to cease, to carry on the business for the purposes of which the employee was so employed
- The employer has ceased, or intends to cease, to carry on the business in the place where the employee was so employed
- The requirements of the business for employees to carry out work of a particular kind has ceased or diminished or are expected to cease or diminish
- The requirements of the business for the employees to carry out work of a particular kind, in the place where they were so employed, has ceased or diminished or are expected to cease or diminish.

Dismissal Not Related to the Individual

For the purposes of the right to be consulted, which applies when an employer proposes to make 20 or more employees redundant over 90 days or less, the law defines redundancy as:

Dismissal for a reason not related to the individual concerned or for a number of reasons all of which are not so related.

This definition might include, for example, a situation where dismissals are not related to the conduct or capability of the individuals, but are part of a reorganisation where there is no reduction in the overall numbers employed because the employer has recruited new staff.

If an employer is thinking of dismissing an employee on the grounds of redundancy they must follow a standard dismissal procedure. This involves: writing to the employee, setting out the reasons for the dismissal; meeting with the employee to discuss the dismissal; and, where necessary, holding an appeal. The procedure does not apply to some collective redundancies.

Thus, redundancy usually means that an employer has needed to reduce their workforce. This may either be because the place of work is closing down or because there is no longer the need (or no longer expected to be the need) for people to carry out the particular kind of work that they do. Normally, a job must have disappeared. It is not a plausible redundancy if an employer immediately takes on a direct replacement. It does not matter, however, if an employer is recruiting more workers for work of a different kind or in another location (unless the individual were required by contract to move to the new location).

If an individual were dismissed because of a need to reduce the workforce, and one of the remaining employees moves into their job, the departing person will still qualify for a redundancy payment so long as no vacancy exists in the area (type of work and location) where they worked.

From 1 October 2006, when new age discrimination legislation comes into force, there will be a ban on most forms of age discrimination in the workplace. While it sets a national default retirement age of 65 and gives employees the legal right to work beyond 65 if they wish, the legislation includes a series of exemptions and tests that could catch employers out. Uncertainty also remains over the final rules governing redundancy payments.

Information for both the employee and employer covering the wide gamut of legislation is available online and useful resources include Redundancy Help (see www.redundancyhelp.co.uk) and government-specific sites (see www.dti.gov.uk/er/redundancy.htm); also visit the Department of Trade and Industry website (www.dti.gov.uk/er).

Organising a Redundancy Programme – An Employer's Guide

You have just heard from the CEO that next year is going to be a 'year of downsizing'. The payroll is going to have to shrink with some operations shut down, others moved. Either way, there will be some redundancies. The following represents 10 things to consider:

- *Plan ahead.* Think carefully about what your people requirements might be as an ongoing process. Consider natural wastage (where people leave of their own volition), retrain people or put a hold on recruitment to diminish the workforce.
- *Demonstrate selectivity.* Compile a list of selection criteria that reflects the attributes, skills and experience that the employer needs in the organisation. A sound job evaluation scheme is useful here (see Chapter 5). Score each person likely to be considered for redundancy and thus the choice is made. It is important that redundancies are seen objectively to be fair.
- *Listen to staff.* It is a legal requirement that if 20 or more people are being made redundant in a 90-day period, a trade union or employee representative must be consulted. And it is a consultation, not a negotiation. Employers must show that they have considered what they say in good faith.
- *It is not personal.* The whole basis of redundancy is that it is related to the position, not a reflection of the jobholder as an individual, their performance or their worth.
- *Communicate.* Let people know the honest view: 'As part of our restructuring/business planning/gearing to face the future, unfortunately a number of positions will be lost. Sadly, those people in those posts will no longer be needed but they will be offered the best support we can provide.'
- *Consider the pros and cons of volunteers.* While voluntary redundancy might make life easier for you in the short term, you risk losing people you might want to keep. Moreover, they may be unhappy if they apply and are turned down.
- *Make it face to face.* Do not text (ur p45 is w8ng @ HR) or e-mail in any circumstances. Tell people individually face-to-face and plan to ensure that all concerned will be available at the right time. You need to manage the bad news.
- *Do the decent things.* Don't settle on the legal minimum, it is a false economy. Offer those you are dismissing help and support, and help them

to get a new job. You may ask people to waive their rights in return for more generous redundancy terms. You also need to be seen as reasonable and fair by those that remain.

■ *Deal with low self-esteem.* Those who leave may certainly have it, so help them audit their strengths, rewrite their CV and prepare for new recruitment interviews. Those who remain may fear they are next, so it is crucial to let people know how well they are doing and set clear, achievable goals for their work.

■ *Follow them up.* A personal phone call to make a genuine enquiry a couple of weeks after redundancy does no end of good to the displaced individual – and reaps exceptional PR for the organisation if handled professionally.

Your Rights in Redundancy – A Guide for Employees

So, you are an employee facing redundancy – what are your rights? The following are some suggested ideas. As mentioned, the new age discrimination legislation coming into force on 1 October 2006 has clouded the area of redundancy payments; the following is a general guide but not a substitute for proper legal advice.

Payments

If all usual procedures appear to have been followed and your dismissal seems to be as a result of a genuine redundancy, you will be entitled to a statutory redundancy payment as long as you have been employed more than two years. The statutory redundancy payment is based upon your age, gross weekly salary and length of service. There is a top limit of £260 a week when calculating your gross weekly salary and the total maximum statutory payment is capped at £7800. Often, however, your contract of employment may provide for a more generous redundancy payment, and even if it does not, it may be the custom and practice of your employer to pay an enhanced redundancy. If this is the case, the higher redundancy payment should be made, rather than the statutory amount.

Often, it is possible to negotiate a global severance payment in any event with your employer, especially where there are question marks over the validity of the redundancy. Employers are usually keen to settle where this is the case. Professional advice should always be sought in connection with such negotiations, and is essential where you are asked to sign a Compromise Agreement setting out the terms of settlement.

Notice period

Your notice period is normally governed by contract, but in any event, all employees are entitled to the statutory minimum of one week's notice for up to two years service, and then two weeks for every two years worked, three weeks for every three years etc., up to 12 weeks for 12 full years worked. Often, employers make a payment in lieu of notice as part of the severance package. This can be negotiated to be paid without deduction of tax (currently only up to £30 000), as long as the contract does not make a provision for your employer to make a payment in lieu of notice. If there was such a provision in the contract, the tax must be deducted on such payment in the normal way.

Bonus payments

There are many different types of bonus schemes: some are commission related, which are based upon specific contractual formula, and others purely on the basis of performance, at the discretion of the employer. Often, in this latter type of arrangement, employees are not even aware of the basis of the calculation upon which the bonus is paid. The actual discretion may link to individual performances, the company's performance as a whole or simply give the employee the right to a discretionary bonus 'on terms to be notified to the employee from time to time', with a separate document listing criteria or a specific formula.

If the bonus is expressed to be contractual, then it should still be paid to you notwithstanding the actual date of dismissal (*pro rata* if the dismissal falls before the year end).

If the bonus is discretionary, the position is more difficult. Certainly, if your employer has by custom and practice paid bonuses to employees where they have left employment before the year-end bonus has been determined, then you should also be paid such a bonus in line with this practice. Recent cases have shown that employers may not have as much unfettered discretion as they think. In the case of Clark vs. Nomura, the employee's bonus was discretionary. It was not guaranteed in any way, being based upon individual performance. That performance was good. The employee was nevertheless dismissed shortly after the year end with no bonus having been paid. The courts awarded the employee substantial damages, largely reflecting the bonus that would have been paid, holding that 'an employer would be in breach of contract in relation to an unfettered discretion if no reasonable employer would have acted in that way'.

It should be noted that where a general discretion is stated in your contract, and your employer seeks to withdraw the scheme during the bonus period (especially where redundancies are being planned), this is likely to be a breach of contract. If there is to be a withdrawal or amendment, this should take place at the end of the bonus year and only apply to future entitlement.

Individuals should always seek professional advice from an employment lawyer.

Summary

In this chapter you have:

- Looked at issues to consider when organising a redundancy programme
- Explored strategies to help staff facing redundancies
- Reviewed the crucial steps in redundancy and removal of people.

Questions

1. Consider the practices of your organisation, or one with which you are familiar, and consider whether they meet best practice in how they manage the redundancy of people. What recommendations can you make for improvement?
2. As a manager, what are the key issues that you will have to address when redundancies are inevitable?
3. One of your staff has been with the firm for several years and is being made redundant. They come to you for ideas on where to go for advice on what to do next. Write a list of factors that you would have to consider about the person before giving such advice and compile a comprehensive list of possible sources of information for them.

Further Reading

Back, S. (ed.) (2005) *Managing Human Resources: Personnel Management in Transition*, Blackwell Publishing.

Fowler, A. (1999) *Managing Redundancy*, Chartered Institute of Personnel and Development.

Jay, L. (1999) *Retirement Redundancy Removal*, Croner's Guide to Managing Redundancy, Croner.

11

Removal – Leaving Work

Governments... can print money. You can too, in effect, through the process called downsizing.

Scott Adams, *Dogbert's Management Handbook*, from the author of
The Dilbert Principle

Learning Outcomes

This chapter has been written as a general guide for managers and should not be used as a substitute for professional legal advice on these matters. It has also been written with the employee in mind; while a useful series of ideas for employees, it aims to give managers a wider perspective of how to assist their staff when leaving work for short or extended periods, or permanently.

It has been written to meet the needs of both the National Occupational Standards for Management and Leadership (*Unit 24*), the Chartered Management Institute's Diploma in Management compulsory module (*Unit C45 – Managing Performance*) and the CIPD Professional Development Scheme in as far as the removal of staff is concerned.

By the end of this chapter you will:

- Be able to approach the removal of people from your organisation more confidently
- Know how to assist employees when leaving the organisation – or manage your own departure
- Know how to guide them on how to leave an organisation on a high – or manage your own departure

- Understand the role that outplacement consultancies can offer
- Know how to manage exit interviews
- Be able to follow the crucial steps in the removal of people.

'We're Going to Have to Let You Go...'

It is not uncommon for employers to pay off a member of staff without following formal procedures and keeping within employment law. Increasingly common today is the 'agreed' or 'assisted' departure. Typically, the employee is called in for a 'chat' and presented with a choice, either:

- Go through the formal redundancy or performance process that could lead to dismissal (the financial consequences being explained), or
- Agree to a more generous lump sum pay-off in return for signing a binding compromise agreement.

While many employees may feel that they have Hobson's choice – the threat of being dismissed for performance-related reasons (whether justified or not) is usually enough to coerce someone who is concerned about the long-term implications for their career into accepting whatever offer is made.

One option for employees in this position is to walk out and claim constructive dismissal, where they would have to show that the employer's behaviour breached its implied duty of trust and confidence. An employee can say that their dismissal breached their employment contract (known as 'wrongful' dismissal) or, if they have at least a year's service, they can bring a statutory claim for 'unfair' dismissal on the basis that their employer acted unreasonably. The Court of Appeal has decided that tribunals can compensate employees for 'real injury to self-respect' arising from the way that they were sacked.

If an employer was to invite an employee to a 'without prejudice' meeting to discuss their future (or rather a lack of one!) with the company, merely saying 'without prejudice' does not mean that the contents of the meeting are off the record or 'privileged'. This tactic will work only if the discussions are aimed at settling an existing dispute between the parties, rather than one arising from the meeting itself. Even the fact that the employee has raised a grievance may not be enough to trigger the 'without prejudice' protection. While the courts will not prevent employers from throwing money at employees to persuade them to go quietly, employers need to be more circumspect about what they say in severance negotiations.

Employers need to guard against discrimination claims when removing staff. Running roughshod over good practice can leave an employer exposed to inferences of unlawful bias on grounds of sex, race, disability, sexual orientation and so on, which can be very expensive in compensation and damage to reputation. From 1 October 2006, when age discrimination legislation comes into force, it will be even trickier to remove staff. Approaches such as 'last in, first out' and length of service criteria will be banned. Younger staff could even bring discrimination claims if the boss disciplines them for poor performance and then turns a blind eye to a similar performance by an employee nearing retirement. Secondly, employees who remain will closely observe the way the employer treats those leaving. Declining staff morale could lead to the loss of the people the employer really wants to keep.

On Leaving Work – An Employee's Perspective

We all do it – leave work! Even the most diligent people stop at some time and go off and do something else. This section looks at the ways in which we leave work but does not look at leaving *for* work or being *asked to* leave work. There are three ways in which we leave work, outlined below.

Leave at the end of the day

We often don't stop to think about this activity, treating it as pretty routine, but there are ways in which we can improve the way we approach it. There are three approaches, depending on the duration of time away from work:

- *Returning to work tomorrow.* This is the most frequent way of 'leaving', where the aim is to have the happy prospect of a drudgery-free evening, possibly with people whose company we enjoy, and have some overnight or between-shift rehabilitation. However, in order to make the prospect of returning soon afterwards appealing, get into the habit of identifying a pleasurable task to do immediately on your return. Some might advocate a first task as 'BANJO' – an acronym for Bang A Nasty Job Off – to not have that onerous task hanging over us throughout the next day. While good practice, as these jobs are often not as challenging as we feared, they may make the prospect of returning to work less pleasant than it might be – and we start the next day with a gloomy outlook.

- *Leaving work for the weekend/a bank holiday/or a day off.* This is particularly important for us, but one that needs even more of the sort of planning mentioned above. Don't let last-minute crises take hold and eat into that time off – schedule properly in advance and put in the extra hours over the days before if need be and gain agreement on deadlines after your return. Having a positive attitude to returning will be especially important, so plan accordingly and the break will be that much more refreshing.

- *Leaving for an extended holiday break.* Here there are freedom tokens to spend during the break with the prospect of going back again eventually. If you've ever felt that it has taken the first half of the week off to get over the week before you left – or the trepidations of returning takes the shine off the half week prior to getting back – you need to reappraise your situation. Read Chapter 12 for some ideas!

Official departure

This is where you know that you have a new destination in life: a new job, a vocation, some extended study leave, to raise children, or a move to retirement, all without the desire to return to that organisation. The best of these depends on your individual circumstances, but all are especially good when *no reference is required*! While the period before departure may be as short as a week, it may be a month or even three; the time is technically referred to as *Leaving Utopia Limbo* or *LUL*. There is a temptation to exhibit the following behaviours:

- Have a slapdash approach to work
- Take on no new projects
- Take no orders
- Disregard punctuality
- Indulge in a little espionage
- Practice a little product or stationery theft.

The golden rule is *don't*. Read the next section for a guide on leaving professionally.

Walking out!

All people whinge about work from time to time: about the boss (and they about themselves, too), about colleagues (and they about themselves, too) and about staff (and they about themselves, too). Some people just 'talk the talk', others 'walk the walk' and actually do it! While there is no chance of a reference, no chance of walking back and no security, it seldom disappoints in the short term – sadly only a few hours.

While leaving work is a powerful tool – use it wisely!

An Employee's Guide to Leaving on a High

If you are leaving an organisation yourself, or need to advise others on how to leave gracefully, the following are 10 top tips:

- *Don't burn bridges.* Rather than use the departure as an opportunity to let off steam about everything that annoys you about the organisation, your boss or that miserable so-and-so in accounts, however tempting that might be, be gracious. Focus on the good memories and be remembered for all the right reasons.
- *Maintain your professionalism.* Make sure that, if the opportunity arises, you give a full and clear handover of your work to whomever remains. Your reputation is still being made long after you have moved on to your next venture and any bad taste you leave may come back to haunt you.
- *Plan your succession.* Even if you are being made redundant, minimise kickback from your former boss, colleagues, clients or suppliers by emphasising that they are losing a key figure – someone you respect may be losing a mentor, however informal. Again, any negative feelings others have about you may come back to haunt you in a later venture.
- *Nostalgia is not what it once was.* Naturally, things will change when you have gone. Of course, your replacement will do things differently – just as you would if you were taking over from them. Don't let it bother you that what you built up will change – look forward to the new venture and how you'll make a positive impact, wherever that may be!

- *Don't let it get personal.* Different people will react to you in different ways. Some individuals may dismiss you as no longer relevant, others may feel they are able to speak more openly and some confidences may be shared like never before. Be ready to respond to their different reactions sensitively and with discretion.
- *Invest time with others.* It is a very small world and your colleagues today may become your clients tomorrow, or a handy new supplier – some even your new boss!
- *Get your story straight.* You must be consistent and ensure that your reasons for leaving and your plans for the future should be the same for all you tell.
- *Don't give too great a gloss.* Keep a balance when defining your future – make it bright enough so that people understand why you are leaving and want to wish you well, yet not so glorious that they resent your opportunity, feel rejected and dissatisfied that they are staying.
- *Lifelong learning.* Take time to reflect on what new skills, attitudes and ideas you take with you on to your next venture, especially retirement.
- *Keep in touch.* Yesterday's colleagues are tomorrow's network. Who knows, you might be invited back one day – naturally into a more senior role!

Taking a Career Break – An Employee's Guide

A career break is just that, leaving paid work to have a child, look after a family, or to undertake some further study or voluntary work, amongst other reasons.

Most commonly, it is women who take such breaks. In fact, a pattern for many women's working lives will consist of episodes of work interspersed with career breaks. If you are considering such a break and plan to return to work at some stage, you can activate strategies for ensuring your long-term employability. Consider the following.

Before leaving work

- *Do you want to return?* Think about the job and company you are in and whether or not you wish to return to either.

- *What are the policies?* Check with the person that looks after human resources in your organisation whether there are any policies on career breaks. If there are none, you may have to convince your employer to allow you to return to the organisation. Argue the benefits – for instance, it costs far more to recruit and train a replacement than to allow an experienced professional to take a managed career break. Nationwide Building Society, for example, estimated that a 30 per cent increase in their rate of return from maternity leave saved them over £3 million. Additionally, people on career breaks are a source of qualified staff that can provide relief cover.
- *Consider your benefits.* If you are planning to return to the organisation ensure you arrange any benefits, such as pensions, to be put on hold until you return. If you don't plan to return, get advice on maintaining your pension while away from work.
- *Social security.* Identify any social security or related benefits you may be entitled to during your career break.
- *Will you ever need a reference?* Check if it's okay to quote your employer as a reference in the future.
- *Maternity leave.* If leaving to have a child, ensure you are up to date with maternity leave entitlements and policies for extending your leave.

During your break

If you don't want to return to the same job or company then take time to evaluate your future options. Make an appointment to see a careers consultant – many good recruitment firms offer this service. Also consider the following:

- *New skills.* If you are changing career you may need to acquire new skills. If so, you might consider participating in learning activities during your break. Even if you are returning to your old job, you may need refresher courses if your break has been a lengthy one.
- *Keep networking.* Arrange to meet your colleagues regularly. If you can't get out so easily to meet them, phone them or invite them round to your place at the weekend. It will make it easier when you do go back to work. Make a point of reading any relevant professional journals. Keep up membership of any professional networks you participate in.

- *Keep learning.* Check out any local learning opportunities in your area. Often, these are free to unemployed adults at local colleges of further education or training providers. Many colleges run specific courses for women returners.
- *Keep your hand in.* If time and inclination allow, keep your skills in practice by engaging in voluntary work or similar activities. However unrelated to your career, this will still allow you to maintain your key employability skills.
- *Evaluate the benefits of non-work activities.* Managing a family, for instance, can be a particularly useful means of developing expertise in multi-tasking. See Chapter 4 for ideas on what looking after a family brings to the workplace. Also, liaising with benefits agencies, schools, parents groups, etc. can enhance interpersonal skills.
- *Enjoy your time away from work.* It will help you appreciate the value of your life and the work you do, helping you return to work refreshed and eager, qualities every employer wants.

Before you return to work

- *Have a plan*! Returning to work after a lengthy break may prove difficult on both a practical and a psychological level. On the one hand, your skills may be out of date and you may have lost touch with the labour market. On the other hand, you may have lost some confidence in your own abilities and may need to build this up gradually. Check Chapter 4 on women returning to work for more advice.

The Employers' Perspective – Outplacement Consultancy

Today, outplacement consultancy to help keep a career on track is more often being offered as part of the severance package. Outplacement has progressed considerably in recent years and is being offered to many more people, not just senior executives. With a buoyant job market and fierce competition among companies for high-calibre employees, the emphasis has shifted from helping candidates get a job to helping them manage their careers. New technology is affecting the way that outplacement is delivered; much more is available online than ever before. Access to company information, links to recruitment sites, online e-learning materials and access to consultants are among the growing initiatives available for people going through career transitions. Displaced employees can have access to a helpline and can contact consultants for additional support by e-mail and telephone. Audio and video materials, designed to help people assess and develop behavioural skills, also form part of the package, together with face-to-face counselling and group workshops. The approach is not so much helping employees to get another job, it is about helping people cope with change, to manage their own careers and take responsibility for their own development.

Employers' Guide to Exit Interviews

Many organisations consider using exit interviews to help them find out why staff are leaving of their own accord, quite apart from managing the redundancy process. They may help in highlighting problem areas within the organisation and in identifying any characteristics that may be common to early leavers. As well as recording classification details about leavers, they should be asked why they are leaving and what they think is good and bad about the firm. For example:

- The job itself
- Supervision and management
- Training and career prospects with the organisation
- Working conditions and amenities
- Equal opportunities
- Pay and other terms and conditions of work.

However, it should be kept in mind that workers may not always disclose the real reasons for leaving or their true views about the organisation. To minimise 'distortion', it can help to:

- Have the interviews carried out by a person other than the immediate line manager
- Conduct them away from the normal place of work
- Explain fully the reason for the interview
- Explain that the interview is confidential
- Explain that the reasons for leaving will not affect any future references or offers to work again for the organisation.

Best practice in managing the process might include the following 10 tips:

- *Make employees aware.* Publicising that the firm is going to conduct exit interviews is a positive move, as it shows that it is a listening organisation.
- *Make it all inclusive.* While one might be happy to see some leave, it is unwise to ignore these people. There should be no such thing as 'wanted' attrition; either the employer has recruited the wrong person or done something to limit their performance. Leavers should be offered a questionnaire and the interview can be combined with personnel tasks such as handing out the P45 and recovering the laptop, etc.
- *If you want to keep them.* Act quickly. By their final week, it will be too late to change their mind, so conduct an early meeting to see if they can be encouraged to stay. If not, keep the exit interview separate.
- *Choose a neutral.* Not the line manager, they may have been the problem! In order to talk openly, the employee must feel that they have the confidence of the interviewer.
- *Agree some rules.* Make it clear that the interview is confidential and what will happen to feedback given.
- *Apply a structure.* Ensure that you are able to learn about your recruitment process, career development, performance measurement and succession planning approaches in the exit interview. This information can be used to improve your processes and the perceptions people have of the organisation.
- *Why are they leaving?* Are they going to a competitor or client? Is it for more money or – as one engineering firm found – is it because they do not have the right tools to do a professional job?
- *Listen, don't react.* While it may be tempting to get into a slanging match with the exit interview being used as a way for the leaver to vent their spleen, it is best to stay calm and objective.
- *Act on the information.* Analyse the data from exit interviews to look for trends, but act immediately if a specific issue is raised.
- *Be positive.* Rather than think of it as an opportunity to give the individual a good talking to, value the feedback on their time with the firm and their reasons for leaving.

More ideas and suggestions can be found on the government's appointed agency, ACAS, site (www.acas.org.uk).

Summary

In this chapter you have:

- Considered the removal of people from your organisation from a number of perspectives, both as an employee and as a manager of people
- Covered a guide on how to leave an organisation on a high
- Explored the role that outplacement consultancies can offer
- Reviewed a series of ideas on how to manage exit interviews.

Questions

1. Consider the practices of your organisation, or one with which you are familiar, and consider whether they meet best practice in the removal of people. What recommendations can you make for improvement?
2. Do you have a succession plan for your position in your organisation? What are the main features to consider?
3. With an ever-increasing number of people reaching retirement – and the government increasing statutory pension age – what are the options for older workers? Critique your organisation on its policies for assisting in the removal such people.
4. What would be the key questions to cover in an exit interview? Prepare an exit interview plan for someone who has been with the firm for several years and is moving to a new, non-competitive sector.

Further Reading

Back, S. (ed.) (2005) *Managing Human Resources: Personnel Management in Transition*, Blackwell Publishing.

Fowler, A. (1999) *Managing Redundancy*, Chartered Institute of Personnel and Development.

Jay, L. (1999) *Retirement Redundancy Removal*, Croner's Guide to Managing Redundancy, Croner.

12

The Future of Work

Reviewing a book about the future is as dangerous as writing one, since neither the assertions nor the criticisms of them can be proved.

Hermann Hauser, *Management Today*, December 2003, p. 30

Learning Outcomes

Let's talk about the future – as that is where I plan to spend the rest of my life! This chapter has been written with tomorrow in mind to cover particular elements of the National Occupational Standards for Management and Leadership: *Providing Direction*; most sections of *Facilitating Change*; and many sections of *Working with People*. It also provides a resource to many of the requirements of the Chartered Management Institute's Diploma in Management and the CIPD Professional Development Scheme in as far as 'managing in the future' is the basis for all professional management qualifications.

By the end of this chapter you will:

- Have had a short review of the past as a prediction for the future
- Know something about information technology and its influence in the workplace activity, particularly e-collaborating
- Recognise that e-learning is making inroads and also consider how to help it find its place
- Discover the importance of flexible working
- Know some of the pitfalls of working from home and how to manage a virtual team
- Review interim working and discover its attractions for many people

- Have considered future trends in work and children, pensions, incapacity benefit and older workers
- Have looked further at women in work in the future
- Understand the importance of a work/life balance and approaches to achieving it
- Know what is meant by work with meaning.

Tracking Future Trends

Any view of the future will be someone's personal selection of often contradictory predictions made by distinguished people in different fields. From such ramblings will emerge a picture that will be as much influenced by the writer's ability to comprehend complex technological issues as by emphasis on one scenario over another.

As author, I have tried to be as objective as possible in selecting ideas for this final selection for the text, recognising that the predictions might not be right, or if they are, will anyone take any heed of the warnings or opportunities identified? History suggests not.

Given that many of the current changes in the business environment were predicted well in advance, how can we excuse the fact that we are continually caught out by changes in the world around us? There have been any number of 'surprises' that have wrong-footed some of Britain's major industries. These include:

- Legislation on business largely compromises business rather than *enables* business
- The growth in information technology does not mean we have more leisure time
- A diet consisting mainly of fat, sugar and salt is bad for children
- Bank customers prefer to talk to human beings face to face in a branch
- Financial services people working on commission have not generally had the customer's best interests at heart when selling products that mature in 25 years' time
- Low-cost airlines have altered holiday and leisure behaviour
- The population of Europe has been ageing demographically.

Since all of these issues have been precisely pointed out by trend analysts (see Hayward, 2004), why have they all been cited as reasons for commercial underperformance and consumer dissatisfaction?

Here are some further 'surprises' yet to hit the headlines:

- Governments cannot continue to spend more than they earn each year – neither can consumers.
- With waste sites filling and resources becoming scarcer, unnecessary packaging will have to be reduced.
- Within a generation, the concept of finishing 'work' and spending 20 or more years in full retirement will be unheard of.
- Ever-increasing rates of staff turnover at all levels in organisations and continued outsourcing of services abroad will severely diminish customer satisfaction.
- The current welfare state in the UK is unsustainable as the increasing numbers of people in retirement or on other benefits, aligned with the growing numbers of civil servants employed to administer it, outstrips the number of people in work to pay for it.
- The continued pressure to reduce costs will lead to a reduction in the quality of food and goods.
- Some lesser educated indigenous people of Western Europe will not do some fundamental work that Eastern European, Asian or Chinese will be only too happy to do (or the services that can will be outsourced overseas) to the detriment of Western society – someone working in a call-centre in Lahore does not pay UK income tax and national insurance.

So, why don't businesses heed the warnings? As suggested later this chapter, there is a lot going on in the business environment but not much action. There are three reasons for this.

Firstly, *inflexibility* – many companies are inflexible and unable to respond appropriately or quickly to changes, assuming they notice them in the first place. Companies need communication channels to permit messages about changes to affect their tactical and strategic responses to the influences. There are some other problems the author has witnessed in organisations of late:

- The data about the need for changes so often does not rise above administrative levels.
- Data is collected and filtered so that it only reinforces decisions already made in a self-congratulatory way, rather than challenge the status quo.

- Even if the information reaches decision-makers, they often don't know what to do with it, as their organisation structure is not able to respond to change in the most effective way.
- 'Another reorganisation' is often a lame attempt at progress.
- Customer feedback (complaints or praise) and staff opinions are rarely systematically tracked; if they are, the results are frequently only given lip service.

Second, there is a worrying *lack of competence* – despite considerable salaries and people's best intentions, many organisations and senior people in them are unable to comprehend the information they are given. While there is a glut of data available to executives, the 'wheat and chaff' are not separated, analysis-paralysis is rife, little data is digested, less is understood and very little acted upon. The more a person sees, the less they understand. Moreover, the feeling is that if someone understands, they haven't grasped the whole picture; the sheer size of the task means that it is harder and harder to assess what is really important.

In an age where the corporate philosophy is to 'get closer to the customer' (see page 3 of your company's annual report), it appears that as organisations get bigger, they get more bureaucratic and more anonymous, yet still they continue to grow.

Third and most worrying is *short-term self-interest* – too many senior people in organisations ignore obvious signals of the future because of their cynical self-interest. Who cares about the long term when the average marketing director is in place for only 18 months and the average employee in the UK has been in eight different jobs by the age of 32? Added to this, it seems that the current business culture rewards failure (Equitable Life directors or Roger Holmes and others at Marks & Spencer), so who cares about the long term? Even if someone noticed the future trends, they probably don't plan to be around to deal with the consequences.

Why are organisations surprised when consumer trust and respect for the financial services industry, the oil industry, the food industry, the media, transport infrastructure, the government and its politicians are so fragile when they all have so obviously not responded to the signals consumers have been giving them about their products, services and their behaviour?

The consumer response has been to lower their loyalty; the next generation of consumers (your employees) is being brought up to switch brands and suppliers at the drop of a hat, to be as short-term and expedient as the companies they deal with – and this is being seen in the workplace too. This is altering the dynamics of commerce, taking away the inertia of core business that allowed trends to be ignored yet companies to still prosper.

For long-term corporate health, a longer-term perspective in thinking and acting is fundamental. The data is available; action is required to sustain us into a more secure future – beyond the next 18 months, that is! The more senior a person is in an organisation, the more he or she should be focusing on the future. It is crucial that relevant knowledge management is in place to track what is changing and what is not (and what ought to change), and that this is effectively exploited. The effectiveness of senior managements' strategies will depend on their ability to ask the right questions and how they have been listening to, and acting on, the answers.

So how do you protect yourself in an ever-changing world (and help your staff cope too)? Box 12.1 suggests some future changes.

The first step will be to stop relying entirely on the judgements of other people and start being a trend-spotter yourself. Keeping one's eyes and ears open (to view one's own situation as an outsider might) will be crucial, finding a few moments every now and then to look beyond the daily challenges to get a sense of what is going on beyond the horizon. Perhaps this means finding dedicated time and space to see the broader perspective. Look behind

---

Box 12.1: Foresight's view of the next 50 years

A government think-tank, Foresight, published its 50-year predictions in January 2006. With four scenarios outlined, the world of work will become very different than it is today. So, will we be going to an office building at all, and if we do, will it be by horse following a global energy crisis? Will the transport infrastructure change as much as suggested to cope with congestion and climate change? Will there be sophisticated urban colonies where most people will live with more local food supplied by the rural hinterland? It is suggested that 'pay as you go' road pricing will be countrywide by 2015 – it was being trialled in 2006 in central London. Some of the report's critics said that much of the report was just 'pie-in-the-sky' imagination and unlikely to be realised – just as 'flying' personal cars predicted 50 years ago are not a feature of today's society.

---

the work that you are doing and challenge the assumptions that underpin what you do. Look for what others might not have seen, a better way to achieve the objectives, perhaps redefine the objectives. Build a network to keep abreast of what others in your profession are doing and thinking.

However, it is not enough to see the future – you need to be prepared to be part of it. While it is easy to be comfortable in a given role or function, suppose someone else decides to shift your comfort zone? Two fundamental approaches will increase your ability to cope:

- *Self-belief.* Trust yourself and have the confidence that you can make the right choices in the long term, even against short-term setbacks.
- *Justify your employability.* You have to make sure that you reinvest in your learning. If an organisation is not willing to make sufficient investment, as the saying goes: *if it is going to be – it is down to thee!*

The Growth of Legislation

In the last section we identified future trends that had been largely overlooked by businesses. As Patience Wheatcroft, Business and City Editor of *The Times* observed in *Management Today*, in November 2005, Lord Turner of Ecchinswell produced a report on the state of the UK pension system, yet some 18 months later, when this text was being written, what has been done to implement his proposals?

While some pension issues may be too far ahead for most politicians now in power to address, with some companies collapsing and members of their pension schemes losing their pension entitlement, the UK government launched the Pension Protection Fund. Companies are likely to have to pay £1 billion into the fund in the first year and the bill will keep rising.

But the new regulation on pensions is but the tip of a massive iceberg of legislation in the past few years; we have a whole gamut of new regulations that companies must pay for (see Box 12.2).

Manchester Business School estimated that the cost of new regulations introduced since 1988 is over £20 billion (*Management Today*, 2003), with a further £10 billion for the minimum wage and £4 billion for the increases in employers' National Insurance contributions. New parental employment rights alone could add a further £300 million a year.

Box 12.2: A selection of the new legislation affecting British business since 1988

- 48-hour working week
- A reduction in the qualifying period for unfair dismissal
- A new public interest disclosure act
- A higher cap on unfair dismissal payouts
- The introduction of European-style working councils
- New range of restrictions on the dismissal of striking staff
- Restrictions on repeated fixed-term working contracts
- A working family tax credit – paid through company payrolls
- The minimum wage
- A new right to take time off to study
- Changes to student loan regulations
- Enhanced trade union recognition
- The right to accompaniment to company hearings
- The creation of complex stakeholder pensions.

There are further measures likely to be welcomed by families – from increases in statutory maternity leave, maternity pay, unpaid maternity leave to the introduction of paternity leave, possibly transference of unused maternity leave, up to 13 weeks unpaid paternity leave, and a new right to adoption leave – all paid for in some way by employers. But what of those employees who don't have children – they have to fit the bill (via taxation and lost income from stretched employers) and provide cover while colleagues are away.

The cumulative effect of these legislative changes for business, especially small businesses, could be devastating. There is more in the pipeline from Brussels with new rules on worker consultation (yet to be fully clarified), rules on employing temporary agency staff, new discrimination legislation and much more.

All of this is on top of a rising tax burden (windfall taxes, £5 billion pension levy, extra oil taxes, National Insurance, carbon emissions, etc.), coupled with an ageing population moving out of full-time employment and an increase in state employment with proportionally less people working in the private sector.

As reported in *The Independent* (25 January 2006), the Institute of Fiscal Studies concluded that, despite recent increases in taxation (mainly on companies), the Chancellor (Gordon Brown) will have to raise taxes still further to fund his long-term spending commitments.

Ruth Lea, director of the Centre for Policy Studies, observed that there has been a range of complicated regulations from the EU on anti-discrimination measures, working time, working conditions, and information and consultation procedures (*The Daily Telegraph*, 2006). She went on to say that 'the EU, intent on creating a socialist workers' paradise, continues to harass the UK about its opt-out from the compulsory maximum 48-hour week and is undoubtedly going ahead with implementing the employee-friendly Charter of Fundamental Rights'.

It is not any easier for the individual 'man in the street'. In the lead editorial of the same newspaper, it suggested that there has been a 'surreptitious' creation of a DNA database, an 'explosion' of anti-terrorist legislation, increases in the 'discredited' methods of stop and search by British police, and the proposal for a 'compulsory' national ID scheme. The editorial suggested that we might have to justify our existence to the state, rather than the other way round, the country becoming less free, but less safe as well. Something has got to give!

Information Technology and Working Practices

Mobile technology is already revolutionising working life – and whatever one writes about it is out of date as soon as it is published. But imagine the scenario: you are sitting in a virtual office with a virtual representation of yourself and your colleagues around you. Someone in another office across the world has hard copy of a document that they want you to comment on so they insert it into a slot and, instantly, the same image is there for you and everyone else to view.

Not so amazing; you probably have had a fax machine sitting quietly in the corner of your office and virtual images are part of gaming technology already. But with computing capabilities doubling every 18 months or less, we will see 'digital dust' monitoring your stress levels and rescheduling your work for you, chairs with electronic monitoring of your posture to spot when you need a check-up, and a digital 'helper' to automatically update you on the actions that it has taken on your behalf.

'In the future we will see intelligent agents acting as personal assistants, sifting and dealing with information, while digital dust will mean that even the tiniest thing can be connected,' according to John Ames, managing consultant to BTexact Technologies, the R&D arm of BT (*Professional Manager*, 2003). It is likely that the manager of the future will be someone who has a personal area network wherever they are, always connected to the Internet.

Over 50 per cent of managers in larger businesses are estimated to be using Personal Digital Assistants (PDAs) – hand-held mobile devices that can access the Internet and act as a basic personal organiser by setting up diary appointments. Most modest mobile phones have an appointment/calendar function with an alarm. While the limit is the size of the screen, voice entry is just around the corner. See a glossary of some terms in Box 12.3.

Box 12.3: A selection of technology for mobile communications (find more information through your favourite search engine)

- *ADSL/WiFi/3G/GSM/GPRS/xDSL*. Different forms of broadband connectivity, each for different environments and applications.
- *Convergence*. A group of technologies to integrate voice and data services, permitting easy access to e-mail and redirecting voice mail to PDAs.
- *Dial-up*. A slow method for connecting to the office that requires the opening of a telephone line between the two sites. Insecure, it is only for back-up.
- *Encryption*. Essential security technology that scrambles data over wireless networks; the greater the encryption, the slower the transmission.
- *IM*. Instant messaging permits something you type into a PC to be instantly seen on another.
- *PDA*. Personal Digital Assistant or hand-held computer; ranges from a BlackBerry to a Palm Pilot.
- *SMS*. Short Message Service used for text from e-mail to mobile phones and back. Used by traders wanting prices, procurement managers closing deals and service organisations keeping clients informed.
- *Voiceover IP (VoIP)*. Voice and data transmission travelling over telephone wires, but the information is in packets – like the Internet. Benefits include cost reductions ('always on', like the Web), mobile connectivity (logging on is simply 'plug-and-play') and better call quality (termed hi-fi telephony).

Comment has already been made in Chapter 8 about 'blogging' and 'podcasts' from employees as a cause of grievance and discipline. While the ability to access e-mail during downtime spent travelling or waiting for meetings can bring vast time savings and speeds of response to busy managers, there is a worrying trend. HP called it 'infomania' – an obsessive desire to receive and respond to e-mail communications however trivial: laptops on the beach, PDAs at breakfast while on weekend retreats. Moreover, there is a risk of alienation of many people working remotely too much – both from the employee feeling isolated not having the direct human contact and the manager fearing they are losing control of their staff. Personal contact is vital and managers must make time to get together and speak to people – have that coffee in contact with other people, not just in the company of your e-mails.

Telephones

Looking recently for a new mobile phone for my wife, I was surprised to find that the 'feature-driven' displays showed devices that had built-in cameras and a torch, ready to download videos and music, play games, and watch news and sports clips – the clam-shell designs would have come in handy at the winter festive season: they are strong enough to crack walnuts. The shop assistant missed the irony when I asked if these devices could be used to make and receive telephone calls!

Every 3G device contains an application unmatched by any other consumer electronics gadget – you can make telephone calls with it. Wireless telephony brings in annual global revenues exceeding £1000 billion – perhaps that is the 'killer application'. Indeed, there are good reasons why 3G capacity could be used more to provide cheap calls – even substituting for calls over fixed-line connections that we are seeing BT offer already – than any other small-screen entertainment services on which many operators are focused. Not only could this bring in more revenue, it could help operators defend against emerging competition from Internet technologies such as Wi-Fi and WiMax, a long-range broadband technology.

Back in 2004, Vodafone launched 3G in the UK with subscription packages that included both entertainment and cheaper calls. Who can blame them; they spent £13 billion on acquiring 3G licences earlier in the new millennium. However, as long as voice tariffs remain high, operators face a long-term threat from wireless calls being routed over the Internet via Wi-Fi or WiMax, not over their networks. Indeed, BT Group incorporated Wi-Fi technology into mobile phones, allowing Voiceover Internet Protocols to be made from 25 000 Wi-Fi hotspots.

So, what of this for the business manager? Recognising that e-mail or text dialogue is not as powerful as voice communications, encourages text messaging only for finite one-way messages where a response by text is not required but a call. It is those people who can undertake a conversation with confidence and clarity that people will want to do business with. Recommend the use of text sparingly – we risk having a generation of today's teenagers entering the workplace in a decade or so who not only have poor written communication skills, but are also lacking in the ability to express themselves in conversation.

MP3 theft

Apple's iPod and MP3 players are increasingly popular as mobile entertainment and storage devices – indeed, many mobile telephones have an MP3 facility to download music and film. The original 150 000-word text for this book and its companion web pages travelled with me on trains and planes while it was being developed – all saved on a 256 MB memory stick no bigger than a disposable gas cigarette lighter.

Gloriously fast and easy to use, they can be plugged into a PC and used to copy data, often bypassing firewalls or password protection. Therefore, they pose significant potential risks for companies. Disaffected employees could use such MP3s to download numerous files of their employer's confidential information and intellectual property with the intention of selling it to a competitor, moving to that competitor, or starting up their own business.

So, what can employers do to protect themselves from such abuse and what does the law offer as protection? Start with clear confidentiality, anti-competition and IT policies that are reflected in the text of staff contracts. The use of electronic storage devices and other media, including CDs, pen drives and hard drives, needs to be properly controlled, possibly prohibited in sensitive areas, with clear and strictly enforced guidelines on employees taking information away to work in home PCs. Get good legal advice to precisely draft restrictive contractual clauses that can be enforced in the courts to clamp down on misuse of sensitive data and damaging competitive activity by current or former employees, or contractors and consultants.

Mobile communications

Mobile working has been around for a long time – wireless-capable laptops and smart phones are easy and relatively cheap to acquire. However, the everyday nature of access to e-mail, diary functions and the ability to book a holiday on the move hides the fact that the truly mobile business needs more than the latest flashy gizmo for key people. There are two routes to becoming 'mobile'.

There is *ad hoc*. Here someone gets a new device or management gets a brainwave and purchases some new kit, but shrinks away from the cost and complexity of the support systems and training necessary to make it work effectively. Faced with a fear of not seeing junior staff at their desks in the morning and losing control, managers get cold feet and try to grab back the reins.

The 'official' route involves a more thorough approach: management makes a value judgement; laptops, mobile phones and PDAs are acquired along with the essential in-house organisational and security systems; the people to be mobilised are trained and equipped to work out of the office. Concomitant with this tangible activity is the hope for increased corporate productivity rising alongside employee freedom, with individual effectiveness growing alongside a better work/life balance. There is also the potential to save money and streamline processes by improving the surrounding management systems.

Of major concern is that the former *ad hoc* approach is more common. While there are theoretical benefits of allowing people to work remotely, nearly one-third of mobile workers report losing money through missing messages and more than half have missed a meeting (*Management Today*, 2005). In order to become fully mobile, organisations need everything from secure, always available IT connectivity to the transformation of the work culture and management processes. Experience suggests that the former cannot be relied on or the latter achieved. Four case studies to illustrate how firms are grappling with the problems are given below:

- Siemens Communications equipped 110 000 people in the UK civil service with an IP profile – a mobile computer identity that travels with them around the organisation. This means that whether they are working from home, in a different office or move to another department, the individual can immediately log on without having to gain special access or be allocated a new ID by the IT department.

- Continental Airlines has mobilised cabin crews and pilots with wireless PDAs to help them share flight information more effectively. Naturally, the major concern is security following the atrocities of 9/11, particularly as all employees have access to operational data, passenger and flight plans. So, replacing their four icons on their desktops for differing remote access, Fiberlink provided a secure, easy-to-manage, one-click remote access solution.

- With more than 600 field-service technicians making over 2500 service visits a day throughout the UK, the imaging and copier technology distributor Ikon was looking for a mobile solution. An application from Dexterra allows data on products, customers and problems to follow the mobile people making their service calls. Moreover, the new system means that the average parts order takes seconds rather than five minutes, saving 15 700 person-minutes each day and more than £40 000 per year in telephone costs.

- While these types of mobile communication are relatively straightforward, the bank Kleinwort Benson's Channel Island division required something different. They have many high-net-worth clients that value 'personal home visits' from fiduciary managers, investment staff and client advisors. Although they need a central system that is flexible, it must also be global and secure. Their solution was to opt for a system from OpenHand that was more secure than BlackBerry PDAs; these carry risks from theft and data hacking, while OpenHand keeps information centrally and more secure, plus the e-mail function can operate with different network standards, so maintaining service standards globally.

So, many companies are going mobile to achieve differing ends, and it seems that mobile technology (devices, connectivity and manageability) is developing rapidly yet has already outstripped organisational ability, or willingness, to use it. Security is paramount, which leads to a question of management. This is a major consideration, since mobility changes the nature of organisations. Businesses should implement an effective wireless asset management (WAM) strategy and treat wireless assets like any other. However, management is also about people – managers and employees.

Mobility shows up bad management – the productive knowledge workers who thrive on mobile working practices will inevitably gravitate towards better managed, better mobilised companies. Dickensian management will be exposed and results-orientated management will be rewarded.

Pros and cons of e-collaborating

IBM and the Economist Intelligence Unit interviewed over 350 remote workers across Europe, and discovered that nearly half feel they lack access to what might be called corporate social capital – chatting over lunch and informal office networks. (When the author's firm were called in to do a staff audit of a business with high staff turnover, they discovered that the loss of a staff canteen in their smart new office building contributed to a feeling of isolation from the 'grapevine', yet all staff still populated one building, albeit distributed by department on selected floors of a massive eight-floor complex.)

People need informal collaboration to get ahead and to form relationships with colleagues. Workers can feel alienated and under-appreciated when working away from the office because of a lack of appropriate management support, technologies, skills and performance measurements necessary to work effectively and productively.

Mobile technology can assist with some of the problems of remote workers. Hi-fi telephony – which uses broadband technology to facilitate phone conversations in pin-sharp CD-quality stereo – helps people connect more effectively, communicating emotionally and factually. At another level, some companies use instant messaging and video-conferencing to have virtual coffee breaks – regular times when mobile workers can meet online to exchange ideas and chat informally.

Box 12.4: Sources for collaboration browsing – find more information through your favourite search engine

Office suites
Lotus – www.lotus.com
Microsoft – www.microsoft.com
WordPerfect – www.corel.com

Net meetings
Microsoft – www.microsoft.com
Netscape – www.netscape.com

Collaboration companies
eRoom – www.eroom.com
ICL – www.icl.com
Lotus – www.lotus.com

However, deeper cultural problems remain for managers. If employees think that what counts is 'presenteeism' – simply being seen to be at work – then they will grow more anxious about more remote working practices such that the improved work/life balance and improved productivity might not be realised. Conversely, if managers can learn to trust and empower employees to be more self-directing, relinquishing micro-management control over them – and be seen to do so – mobility can begin to reap rewards.

The technology for e-collaborating is the easy part – you probably have an office suite of software that allows one document to be amended by a group of people, storing a version that tracks each person's changes in a different colour (see Box 12.4). Bulletin boards have been around for a while: a series of e-mails, some with documents attached, are presented in a conversational structure where onlookers can add their own dialogue. They have their limits as they are not in real time (although useful across time zones) and they are passive, requiring an individual to seek out the board or they might miss something. At the other extreme is the Net meeting, where people are connected in real time; the dialogue can be text (confusingly called 'chat'), spoken voice or video link. Some Net meeting software offers shared white boards appearing on each collaborator's screen, and they can host other software. The ultimate is bespoke collaboration software, working in tandem with office suites to provide collaborative support in a unified environment.

For the future, a clear trend is an increasing ability to make electronic collaboration more like the real thing. This might involve, for example, small pictures of each group member when they are logged on (perhaps live video images), which can be clicked on to initiate a quick chat or dragged together to form informal meetings. A further enhancement is to make it easier to collaborate with the right people. Software could monitor your type of work to build a profile of the topics dealt with; then, when you need to collaborate with a specific resource, the system puts you in touch with the right person – and you control the profile that you want the system to track or advertise a specialism without identifying yourself to the person asking for help.

Whatever the technology, it is developing the right 'culture' that must take the top spot for managers to get right.

Electronic communities need to be voluntary rather than imposed. At ICL, the Fujitsu-owned British company, they major on their support for collaboration, with over 350 electronic communities within the organisation – groups using a dedicated part of the company's intranet, bulletin boards, shared documents and Net meeting groups. They provide a new community with the tools to add discussion forums, Net meetings and shared documents, and to manage intranet content; all this is pushed out to the communities themselves so that they take ownership. With the massive amount of information flowing, it would be a nightmare to manage centrally, so people have to be encouraged to willingly share knowledge.

In such environments, chatting needs to be encouraged; managers need to remove the initial suspicion, educating the organisation into realising that the exchange of information is an essential activity for a modern business.

When setting out to improve e-collaboration, take each stage in turn:

- Explore the capabilities of your office suite of software first.
- Then, without investing more, look to see what can be achieved from your intranet, from Web discussion forums and from Net meetings.
- Once you have explored the pros and cons of your situation – as each business differs – approach collaboration vendors to get them to show you how and if they can add value for each level of extra expenditure (see Box 12.4 for some ideas).

E-learning

On the back of increased efficiency and lower cost per learner, corporations are pursuing the installation of e-learning systems. Given that e-learning is a technology-driven solution, it is all too easy to assume that the solution lies in the technology. However, all too often when learning systems have been installed they have had a negligible response. Imagine the classroom analogy – a major event is organised with a popular keynote speaker, all the visual aids and a fine lunch prepared, but no one turns up as you did no marketing. The high visibility of failure of instructor-led training (ILT) pushes marketing of the event to the fore; with technology-based training (TBT) it is often overlooked but perhaps needs to be more important.

The literature shows some successes – but these are for self-selecting, highly-motivated people who are generally technologically aware. With a mixed-ability organisation in the real world, the introduction of e-learning will involve not only telling people that it is there, but also how and why to use it. Successful e-learning systems involve organisations that invest heavily in the culture shift in perception, they take time and they involve people at all levels from the outset. It requires the top people getting face to face with people to let them know how important the change of approach is and what the individual and collective benefits are – and that message needs to be sustained. Managers need to 'talk the talk' *and* 'walk the walk'.

While classroom-based training is the traditional approach, bringing people together in an appropriate environment and allowing people to focus on their own learning, it is limited by time and travelling in congested cities. E-learning, delivered to the desktop, has its attractions. Online tutoring and peer-group interaction, via e-mail and chat rooms or video-conferencing, may be the way forward but there are costs: online networks, courseware, and the cost of monitoring and evaluation. Some firms are literally taking to the road and delivering their training through e-learning from mobile vehicles that can add the people element that aims to achieve the all-important winning of hearts and minds of the learner. Tesco has used mobile training vehicles from PC Coaching to entice customers into seeing what e-commerce can do for them, aiming to increase the number of online shoppers. But it is not just the UK that is developing e-learning.

Norway has invested in a programme to improve the IT skills of 4 million people. Established by the 'The Competence Network of Norwegian Business and Industry', the installation of the Saba e-learning infrastructure is the first time that a country has modelled the practices of successful global corporations to provide greater training and skills aimed at improving customer, partner, employee and supplier productivity. The system links employees throughout the country, providing flexibility, speed of delivery of training solutions and the ability to integrate multidiscipline learning applications – all on a platform that is accessible to all who desire, or require, training. More than 40 content providers have come together on the platform to offer training and re-education skills that will not only reduce the time-to-competency of Norway's workers, but also, it is hoped, reduce the amount that companies, governments and schools spend on training.

While the global corporate and government spend on learning is estimated to be more than $300 billion, it is growing – with more and more on e-learning. However, as most readers probably admit, when they have a problem with something they don't understand, they would still prefer to turn to a friendly face to help them out.

Flexible Working

Ten years ago it was predicted that by today the plc was going to be history, replaced by global chains of IT-enabled, flexible workers. If the 'firm' was the organising economic unit of the 20th century, the 'network' was to provide the economic architecture of the 21st. Yet it seems that in most areas of economic life we remain non-networked – glued to old-style organisations, big brands and standard jobs. While there have been major shake-ups in some capitalist dynamics, not least in finance itself, there have been none in ordinary economic processes and social systems. The 'network economy' is a term that has been used to describe a range of separate issues such as 'globalisation', the impact of IT, corporate organisation and labour market change.

So why have traditional companies not lost out to networked economies? There are two reasons:

- Employees like to belong and feel part of a community. An organisation provides the solidarity that most people welcome – Maslow's sense of belonging. While they may not be as sexy, they are more secure.
- A company offers brand value that even a network of highly-talented individuals cannot. No one ever got fired for buying IBM or hiring McKinsey. The brand from an established organisation provides security for cautious purchasers.

From an economic standpoint this leads to gross inefficiencies – consider advertising agencies. Big firms need big brands so they invest in grand offices, generous hospitality, sponsorship and so forth – all of which needs to be paid for by the big-brand client in higher fees, yet no one will get fired for engaging a big agency. However, most creative people in advertising agencies don't like the large agency mentality so they go solo, but without the big agency name behind them they can struggle.

While IT has revolutionised capital markets, its potential to reconfigure the world of work remains almost entirely unrealised. We have not been turned into networked knowledge workers; many of the jobs created as a result of computer technology are less knowledge-based than pre-industrial farming – particularly in contemporary service jobs.

Empirically, the network economy is as much a mirage as the new economy. Networking offers us so much that the opportunity should not be ignored, but the difference between networking and not working is one vowel.

There are some high-profile organisations that have embraced networking with open arms. BT has 63 000 people in some form of flexible working and over 12 000 employees working from home. Legislation and concerns about logistics seem to worry managers – they see flexible working as just another problem rather than an option that can be a motivational, performance-enhancing and overhead cost-saving opportunity.

Of course, it would help if transport, industry, environment and educational officials worked together to create a framework that is good for the economy, good for the environment and reflects an increasingly integrated lifestyle – rather than penalise people for commuting at peak times, which deals with the symptom of congestion and not the cause. Workers are moving around too much because organisations enforce work patterns where everyone has to be there at the same time to get work done. Why struggle to get into work to e-mail the person next door or phone and leave a message to someone stuck in traffic?

In a recent report from the CBI, nearly one-half of organisations said that transport problems were having a detrimental impact on profitability, 40 per cent reported that their business growth was held back and 33 per cent said that transport problems were having a notable effect on investment in their business (*Professional Manager*, 2006). The survey reported that many organisations have tried to address the problems – 57 per cent have introduced more flexible working and nearly a half has altered delivery schedules or logistics. However, 93 per cent of employers and 86 per cent of staff believe that these measures alone cannot overcome the problems and extra transport infrastructure investment is necessary.

If everyone that went into an office to sit at a workstation and use their phone, e-mail and a PC worked remotely just one day a week it would reduce their commuting by 20 per cent at a stroke. While this approach would not work for manufacturing, plumbers or retailers, it would work for knowledge workers.

The benefits of flexible working include:

- Employee attraction and retention
- Employee motivation and loyalty
- Increased productivity
- Increased heath benefits with reduced stress and a better work/life balance

- Reduction in cost and time commuting
- Reduced absenteeism
- Less office costs.

The business issues that need to be considered before adopting flexible working include:

- Impact on teamworking
- Communication issues
- Coordination of resources
- Employee disenfranchisement and loss of identity
- Fewer informal communications
- Resentment from employees not flexi-working
- Performance management.

On the issue of motivation, a recent report from the Chartered Management Institute suggests that there is a link between adopting modern work patterns, business performance and motivating employees (see www.managers.org.uk). The study found that one-half of organisations that were growing and dynamic offered facilities for regular flexible working, while only 36 per cent of the declining organisations offer it. The study also found that options for flexible working were one of the top 10 factors that influenced managers to join their current employer. Respondents indicated that they could cope with the long working hours culture if they had some flexibility about when and where they put in the hours. See Box 12.5 for ideas for introducing flexible working.

Managers need to ensure that staff have the appropriate information to do their job, as many flexible workers cite isolation and lagging behind others as the biggest drawbacks to doing their job properly. Managers need good communication, trust and sound objective setting as the key skills to manage flexible workers; they also need greater than usual skills in motivating, ability development and confidence building, along with good planning and team-building skills. Managers therefore need to manage much more by outputs and results, rather than by inputs and the time people put in. Organisations need to look to the training and coaching given to managers to build their skills in these areas for flexible working to reap its potential benefits.

Box 12.5: Key thoughts when introducing flexible working

- *Look for mutual gain.* There could be gains for the organisation in terms of opportunity to broaden customer access to the service by longer opening, cover over lunchtimes, even easier access to the staff car park, better morale and better recruitment and retention; there are many benefits for staff, including a better life/work balance, easier commuting and a greater sense of ownership of their job.
- *Keep flexible.* Every organisation and all staff are different, so start by finding out what staff want and how the organisation might meet those needs – parents might want time off in holidays, single people may prefer later hours or a sabbatical for travelling.
- *Set clear guidelines.* Avoid resistance through line managers being unclear about what is possible. Consider flexitime, annualised hours, a compressed working week, job-sharing options or term-time working, and ensure managers apply the options objectively and consistently.
- *Plan flexibility.* In customer-facing jobs shifts must be covered, but in an office environment, managers need to plan ahead and ask for staff to play their part in the deal by being responsible in keeping to agreed arrangements.
- *Think outside of the box.* Use flexible working as an opportunity to review current working practices. While this can uncover jobs that suit flexible working, if their job does not easily lend itself to flexible working consider moving someone (rather than sidelining them).
- *Take legal advice.* There is a raft of legislation, including the Employment Act, that you need to make sure you comply with; sound legal advice is good security against problems.
- *Walk before running.* Start with small groups as a 'test' rather than convert the whole organisation; use them as role models and iron out any glitches. Make sure that there are no 'favourites' and keep people informed about trials.
- *Measure the outputs.* Monitor key areas such as absenteeism, morale, staff turnover and key performance indicators to establish a case for flexible working, looking for a sound cost/benefit case.

Working from Home

There are already 8 million people working from home and a further 2 million working from home at least one day a week (report by Standard Life, 2006). It is expected that this figure will rise to 12 million by 2020 with 'demuting' as a significant trend. However, not all organisations have adopted the practice, with one-third of employers reported as not making any provision for home working (Workplace Survey, 2003 – see www.managers.org.uk).

Twenty years ago we expected so much: but the reality of the paperless office recedes every day, little manufacturing is done in outer space, teleworking from tele-villages has been slow to materialise, and anyone that experienced both boarding and day pupils at school would not be surprised. Home working is not all it might be.

While one can work very well at home without interruptions, less gossip, and no time-consuming and energy-draining commute, the human instinct is to form teams and stick with like-minded others. We did it at school; we do it as adults at work; 'day-bugs' were frowned upon as an inferior species by boarders – even if we consistently won the inter-house competition. Working from home means that people miss out on the all-important informal information networks.

Moreover, many homes have children or animals, sometimes both, and they don't mix well with the committed home worker. Finding a truly comfortable space separate from your daily life can be a big problem – sat in the third bedroom on your own all day is maybe not quite what you had in mind! If it is not soundproofed, it means it's the garden shed for you. Don't be too dismayed, you'll be in the good company of George Bernard Shaw, Roald Dahl and Daphne du Maurier – they all worked in a shed. And don't answer the front door. This is not so much a security issue but it is so easy to get distracted by double-glazing salespeople, political and market research canvassers, delivery drivers wanting you to take something because your neighbours are 'at work', charity collectors, relatives and friends 'just passing', and meter readers. Then there is the temptation to sort the garden/garage/house before settling down to a coffee and biscuits – then there is the kitchen to clear, put on some washing, feed the cat – and now it is time to collect the children.

From a management perspective, there are two crucial issues:

- Measurement – are they actually working?
- The usefulness of technology – who is it best suited for?

When it comes to home workers, not all jobs are the same. At the fundamental level are 'white-collar', process-driven activities like call-centre operatives. Here it is about software-driven processes undertaken over the Internet. Wherever your people are (Aberdeen or Andover, London or Lahore), these people do easily managed activities; the technology to quantify what they do is straightforward.

At the other end of the spectrum you have highly motivated knowledge workers who adapt well to the technology and prefer to be measured by results (outputs) rather than do work that can be realistically measured on a daily basis. Measurement of daily activity is a moot point – when did you last look over the shoulder of a talented web designer or copywriter?

For the middle group, it is more difficult. Unusually, they need more supervision as their work is neither routine nor project based and their problems will probably be more complex to manage. Add to this that everyone is their own systems administrator – they have to save and back up their own work, be their own security, and deal with many everyday system problems; someone cannot come running along the corridor to sort a defunct mouse!

However, the technology is getting better. At the author's consultancy we have virtual IT support from someone that can navigate the LAN, sort technical problems and 'see' what the people are doing to sort technical problems. We have software to manage collaborative projects with associates and can engage talented people wherever they are to provide creative and competitive solutions to client problems.

There are a few things worth reminding prospective or current home workers. They need to call up a greater degree of self-management and discipline than comparable people in the workplace. They have to compartmentalise their working time and place to keep the two separate. Many home workers actually put in more hours than their workplace colleagues – upsetting their work/life balance when they took flexible home working to help deal with an imbalance. When a home worker spends 10 hours a day in the company of their PC and e-mails, in time they may not have the rich fund of stories with which to entertain friends.

For the employer, most want creative, problem-solving team players; while solitary confinement may boost the balance sheet, it is probably not the best answer. Moreover, many firms have dress-down workdays; few people have the acting skills to remain professional when dressed in a kimono!

Top 10 tips for home working can be found in Box 12.6.

Box 12.6: Top 10 tips when working from home

- *Get the right tools.* This means computing with broadband, printing and facsimile – and a telephone line separate from the domestic line.
- *Get the right space.* Separate home and work as much as possible physically and set times for work and play.
- *Keep in touch.* Make sure that the office knows that you are there; also, keep in touch with chat and gossip as much as possible; informal networks are crucial.
- *Develop a routine.* Develop a structure for the day and make sure your partner and/or family respect the fact that you are working and don't take advantage of you being around.
- *Identify black holes.* Analyse your time and work out where you waste time, then eliminate that black time from your day.
- *Get others to buy in.* Make sure friends and family know that you being at home does not mean that you are available for a chat or chores.
- *Beware the guilt trips.* While you can take advantage of some flexibility, don't beat yourself up over taking time off provided you are achieving the outputs you need to achieve.
- *Develop allegiances.* Seek out others who are also home workers to learn from them and gain a sense of identity; they are a valuable source of moral support and problem solving.
- *Don't let it fester.* If you feel that there is a problem with head office, get on to it immediately – clarify it and stop the problem escalating. Perhaps organise a face-to-face meeting if you don't have access to video-conferencing tools.
- *Spread the word.* Become an advocate of home working both within your organisation and outside; the more people do it, the more you will become the 'norm'.

Managing virtual teams

How do managers build and maintain virtual teams of people that they don't see every day and how does this differ from face-to-face working?

Of course, managing 'virtual' people is nothing new. Any national sales manager will have had experience of managing groups of people necessarily spread across the country, whether the people themselves worked at a remote site – like a network of restaurants – or a team of people making sales calls in a geographical region. Managing overseas operations is similar, save for differing distances, possibly time zones and frequently languages. However, today, as we have seen, there are many more people working from home, often on their own, with no particular need to go out and make personal calls on customers or suppliers or travel into a place of work where they regularly meet others. It is managing these people that will be our focus.

As with any communication, the media and the message are the crucial dimensions to explore. Those that have been effective face to face cannot assume that they will be effective in a virtual environment. It is essential that the leader establishes and maintains 'influence' in the group, yet must remember that 'power-playing' will have little or no value in virtual teams – it may be severely damaging.

Three 'rules' for managing virtual teams can be found in Box 12.7.

Media

Managers' first need to understand the media employed to communicate with their people and recognise patterns of usage. Some media allow communications in 'real time' – that is, 'live' (such as the telephone) – allowing a richness of content. Others such as e-mail and an intranet have a time

---

Box 12.7: Three 'rules' for managing virtual teams

1. Make sure that you invest time into 'building' the team through online socialising – there is a human behind the message.
2. Online leadership requires a careful consideration of the media and the message – aim to be more of a coach rather than dominate all the time.
3. Your leadership authority will be different online – work to establish trust and mutual respect for all.

delay – as does an SMS communication to a mobile device (phones, etc.). A manager needs to decide which is best for a given purpose given the time zone and any organisational boundaries.

When people have time to consider their response without the immediacy of 'live' communications, there is opportunity to develop clarity and richness in the message. This will be particularly useful in managing cross-cultural groups, where team members are using a common language that may not be their 'mother tongue'. Conversely, those methods that require immediate 'real-time' interactions do speed up dialogue and can shift delays. Remember, using a conference call or a video-conference, with software that can facilitate immediate data transfer, can achieve rapid consensus on critical decisions.

One of the obvious differences in virtual working that computer-based media facilitates is that the team member can literally disengage from the technology without the leader or the other team members knowing immediately.

Message

With the nuances of the media, leaders need to consider their messages carefully, so that a mutual trust is developed between the parties. To this end, managers need to try to capture, in virtual working, the 'social' nature of the organisation. This does not mean sending jokes around or inviting people to play virtual games. Managers need to find ways to stimulate relationships online and develop mutual understanding.

Virtual working has the advantage of being largely free of race, age and gender disadvantages. Thus, the leader – whether imposed or elected – needs to minimise explicit directive behaviours, since any hierarchies can fade online. Looking at the three Development Models in the MAC Factors (Motivation in Chapter 9, Ability in Chapter 14 and Confidence in Chapter 19 of Mackay, 2007), one can see that with a virtual team, a manager needs to have a lower task control orientation in any of the three key factors. A leader will find more success in a democratic approach of shared control and consensual decision-taking, particularly in the early stages of a new virtual project group.

The leader's role in this situation is more subtle; the 'conversation' (either in real time or delayed) is more subtle, focused on the business processes and allowing 'buy-in' to ideas to achieve a solution rather than direction on what to do. Hence, the effective virtual leader adopts the role and style of a coach – in this way helping the group establish clear procedures and goals, modelling desired behaviours and actions, and asking appropriate questions – just as we saw in the 'Level 3' styles of each of the three Development Models.

Disengagement

As the virtual environment gives the leader little early warning of people withdrawing temporarily or completely from the group, it requires clearer and more structured processes with clear roles and a careful consideration of the communication technologies and patterns of use than with face-to-face environments. Also, managers need to consider how to maintain business processes, decision-taking and the progress towards objectives if the technology should fail.

As with a face-to-face group, a clear set of objectives needs to be agreed by each individual; a clear set of working protocols, and clear individual tasks and responsibilities, will all assist the virtual team. However, in some more complex virtual working environments, to reach a clear summary the leader may need to interlace the communication threads and develop a consensus, ensuring that any patterns, interpretations and conflicts are resolved to ensure agreement. While interpreting an individual's contributions may not seem to be a new task, dealing with online 'silence' must be dealt with, requiring subtlety and emotional intelligence.

When there is mild conflict in face-to-face situations, appropriate humour and irony may help to resolve the problem – these may lead to quite the opposite in a virtual environment; deepening misunderstanding and resentment may develop, leading to more disengagement. Thus, decisions are likely to be delayed, buy-in may not be unanimous, and frustration can prompt ill-considered reaction from leaders and team members. The manager needs more patience; critical paths need to reflect the nuances and decision-making may need to wait until a face-to-face opportunity.

Good news is acceptable online, bad news is not – especially when delivered to a mobile phone – which is not secure anyway!

Working Part-time

So, someone in your department asks you if they can go part-time. How should you respond? Clearly, if you ignore the request, you'll be inviting trouble. The individual may leave – if that is what you wanted, all to the good? Maybe not! After all, before they leave they are a major source of discontent and that dissatisfaction can spread. If they do leave you'll have to accept that their knowledge and know-how leaves along with their contacts, plus you will have the cost and effort of hiring a replacement – and the stress on those (probably mostly you) that 'cover' key tasks until a replacement is found.

One of the first steps will be to gently enquire why they are aiming to go part-time. Child and parent care are two obvious examples, but think about those who are aiming for extended study periods. While child/parent care may be lower on your list of good reasons to accept a case for part-time working, a high proportion of those who study an MBA leave their companies within 18 months of completing a qualification.

While you may be able to sympathise with a person's need for a better work/life balance, you probably have your needs too. Naturally, one might view with suspicion those that want to start their own business to supplement their income or those that just want more time for themselves – their loyalty might be in question.

Ask them what is in it for the organisation? Your primary concerns will be logistical: how does the person aim to achieve in four days or fewer what they did in five? If they will not be able to do it all, who can? You might have to consider if there are others with spare capacity who can handle additional tasks and responsibilities. Get them involved in thinking through the departmental impact and make a robust case before deciding – they might come up with some surprises to assist your decision; if they can't, it softens your refusal.

Naturally, many roles do not lend themselves to part-time working, particularly daily customer-facing functions – that is, unless there is someone to provide competent support or a job-share scheme.

There are some head-of-department roles that can be successfully handled in fewer than five days a week. Mia Kennedy, the strategic planning director of AMV BBDO, the UK's largest advertising agency, was able to move to a three-day week after the birth of her first child. It required a highly organised approach and a really efficient PA, ensuring that she was involved in the important things where she could add most value, but delegating other areas where her direct involvement was not vital. It required good 'lieutenants' who needed support in developing their management skills. Obviously, she needed to be very diligent and make the most of the time she was in the office, and used travel time for business reading to keep up to date and a PDA BlackBerry to manage her electronic communications.

When it comes to your staff, as with any negotiation, work out what they want and what they are willing to trade with their employer. What concessions are they willing to concede and what value are they to the organisation. For example, are they willing to take a salary *pro-rata* as the savings may be helpful? Would they be willing to trial it for, say, three months, with an objective review? Do be careful not to use the ultimate sanction and 'let them go', as they might have a case for unfair dismissal (see Chapter 8).

Interim Working

For many looking for long-term security, flexible working and a choice of assignments, they turn their backs on a permanent job and become an interim manager. Here, the person gets involved in specific projects on behalf of a client organisation with defined parameters and deliverables. Some assignments still entail long hours and often nights away from home, but the option of taking time out between clients more than compensates for any negatives.

The author, having been made redundant three times in six years in the 1980s/1990s, confirmed that companies often do not take a caring, paternalistic attitude – one just accepts the financial reality of the global marketplace, where companies have to flex to meet rising or falling demand. With thousands of final pension salary schemes being shut down, more and more employees realise that they have to put 'number one' first. Moreover, the transition into interim work is easier for managers in the mid-2000s because they are already working in bite-sized chunks on a project basis, often with different teams of colleagues.

As one interim manager commented (*Professional Manager*, 2004):

I am not tempted by the money; it is wonderful being free to express my views to clients without fear – as an outsider I have no axe to grind, there is relatively little stress, no psychological contract, you have objectivity and no baggage.

Research by human resources consulting firm Chiumento (*Professional Manager*, 2004) among interim managers found that 17 per cent chose that route seeking a better work/life balance (see later in this chapter).

The current trend is for client firms not to consider individuals under 35 years old, as they tend to be viewed by some as interim people and not interim managers. The Institute of Interim Managers (IIM; see www.ioim.org.uk and www.interimmanagement.uk.com) has seen an increase in younger members in their mid-thirties and forties in recent years – that category making up nearly one-quarter of their membership. It needs to be recognised that there will be periods of feast and famine; one cannot expect assignments to appear when wanted and, like buses, several may come along at once. This can put pressure on the financial front and the uncertainty can put a strain on personal relationships at home. However, there has been an increase in younger women entering the interim market and they can be particularly good at it – they tend to be more focused than men on the challenge of the role itself, rather than the status of a title or climbing the corporate ladder.

People embarking on interim management need to recognise that it requires considerable self-discipline to put in the marketing effort during 'rest' periods. The interim manager needs to keep in touch with their clients, set themselves targets and take the time to invest in themselves.

Family Fortunes

In a study sponsored by nine investment banks, Shell and the Metropolitan Police (*The Daily Telegraph*, 2005), it was found that most female bosses (about 70 per cent) think that women's need to balance work and family is a barrier to career progression, while most male managers (more than half) disagree. This suggests that female managers are more downbeat than their male colleagues about the obstacles to equality that exist at work.

Women managers are more critical of the behaviour of senior leaders in relation to equality and are less convinced of their commitment to the ethos. Other studies have shown that many managers consider maternity leave to be a 'serious risk' for their business – particularly small to medium-sized enterprises. Given the UK government's Parental Rights Bill extends maternity rights from six to nine and ultimately 12 months leave, the concerns of business managers deepen. Moreover, the then Trade Secretary unveiled plans to allow mothers to transfer 'spare' maternity rights to the child's father if she chose to return to work within the year (Work and Families

Bill, 19 October 2005). Clearly, with many parents working for different organisations, dividing the allowance between them would be complex and potentially unenforceable. While such measures are welcome as they raise the profile of 'family-friendly' approaches to management in organisations, there are costs both to organisations and taxation – and there are concerns in other quarters too.

Employers need to make sure that they not only cover staff on maternity or paternity leave, but also that they are aware of and respect employees' legal rights. In Britain in 2003, some £4.3 million in damages was awarded by employment tribunals, which grew to £6.2 million in 2004.

Children

While the combination of tax breaks, tax credits, higher child benefit and free pre-school education, expanded maternity, paternity and parental leave is good for parents, is it best for children? Some 'tough' questions raised by Richard Reeves (2005), writing in *Management Today*, included:

- How do we really want children to be raised – by their parents or by professional and semi-professional childcare workers?
- Why should parents – especially affluent ones – receive tax handouts partially paid for by the childless?
- What are the real costs to business and national competitiveness of high levels of support by parents?
- Are we all prepared to pay for it?

He went on to argue that children's needs are best served by parents as a first resort, yet official attitudes seem to favour dawn-to-dusk childcare based around schools. Rather than restructure working lives or the labour market to meet the needs of children, he feels that children's pattern of life is altered. While expected to adapt to the needs of the market economy when still in short trousers, far from adopting a family-friendly economy it seems we are adapting economy-friendly families. Surely the gains of a stable, loving start for our children is worth the costs – even, dare one suggest, a degree of personal sacrifice – otherwise, we will have lost the right to consider ourselves a civilised society.

Pensions

Perhaps children of today need to be brought into 'economic line' as early as possible, since it is suggested that a child born today is likely to live to 100 and will need to be 'in work' for more than 40 or so years to support such longevity – and staying in one organisation will be almost unheard of. In the past, retirement funds were expected to provide for individuals a few years into retirement. The contributions from the unfortunates that died a couple of years after retiring provided for the others that survived. Equally, it is predicted over the next decade that there will be 0.8 million less 16- to 34-year-olds in work making National Insurance contributions.

Some interesting, and worrying, statistics emerged from the Prudential:

- A quarter of people between 55 and 64 feel they cannot retire at 60 (women) or 65 (men) because they do not have a big enough pension or sufficient savings.
- A third of women think they will have to work beyond the state pension age.
- More than a million people are currently working beyond the state pension age.
- By 2015, 2.5 million people are predicted to be working beyond the state retirement age.

With Britain's pension industry's £130 billion shortfall, it can only be filled by increasing the retirement age and giving better tax breaks to people who save for private schemes (*Evening Standard*, 2005). Most firms believe that it will take more than a decade to repair the damage to pension funds caused by the abolition of tax breaks and poor stock market performance.

Older workers

A labour market report published by the Department of Work and Pensions and the Office for National Statistics (see www.statistics. gov.uk/focuson/olderpeople, accessed March 2006) revealed that one in five 'older workers' over 50 is self-employed, compared to only 14 per cent of people aged 25–49. The report showed that the employment rates of men and women aged between 50 and state pension age in Great Britain were 72 and 68 per cent respectively in Spring 2004, compared with 64 and 60 per cent in 1994.

With an ageing workforce, there needs to be a culture shift in how managers and employees view 'older people' generally – particularly in as far as it affects the organisation and the contribution these people make to the workplace. Naturally, many will be looking for part-time work and they may be more flexible than employees with young children.

For all employees throughout their working lives – and the older person today – retraining will be mandatory to maintain employability; tomorrow's worker may have more than one 'career' and will work for many more organisations. Career breaks to raise children will be less 'damaging' as new careers in middle age with mature students in further education become more commonplace. Older workers will have much to give, whether in commerce, industry, social services or charities.

Self-*motivation*, lifelong learning enhancing *ability* and developing the *confidence* to face the challenges of new technology and changing working practices will be necessary to provide financial security, maintain intellectual capacity and physical well-being into the latter parts of a century lifespan.

Incapacity benefit

One problem that has to be addressed is that far too many families – 2.7 million British claimants – have become dependent on incapacity benefits. A green paper (January 2006) disclosed that the sick and disabled could be paid about £20 a week less than at present unless they took advantage of a £360 million package of help, advice and rehabilitation.

But why have so many people fallen into a poverty trap? Why do they prefer a mix of benefit and black economy to the little-respected dignity or low-paid straight (i.e. taxable) work? It has been suggested that, much of the time, people stay on benefits even though they have sporadic work because they need security as well as money (Orr, 2006), not just because staying on or around the poverty line is predictable.

Unfortunately, many of the services available are not as attractive as they might be for getting people back to work.

- Job Centres, for example, tend to get the least attractive jobs as they have a reputation for attracting the least dynamic jobseekers.
- An out-of-work person inspired by a 'small business advisor' will have to provide financial resources for the assistance before claiming reimbursement from the state against receipts.
- Do banks lend generously to the long-term unemployed?

Sadly, one-third of new claimants on incapacity benefits claim depression; recovering depressives cannot be pushed too hard, too fast. Life can be very hard for many people, they become wounded and damaged, and need understanding from compassionate managers. Box 12.8 summarises the real benefits of being in work but remember: there are good jobs and bad ones. Badly paid, antisocial, low-status, menial labour is unlikely to provide many benefits – it may be that many people on incapacity benefit today were in this type of employment.

Box 12.8: The real benefits of being in work

1. *Structure and purpose.* Our education system develops a sense of a 'nine-to-five, five days a week' working culture. Work continues to provide a shape to the day, the week and the month, while being out of work leaves the person with poor time management and extended, restless sleep patterns.
2. *Man is a complex, social animal.* Work provides an expanded friendship network, colleagues providing a source of support and interest, conversation and shared feelings. Home workers miss it, the unemployed can't find it – they are left feeling isolated, forgotten and friendless.
3. *Social identity.* For men especially, you are what you do, which explains all the fuss over job titles. Many people define themselves in terms of the exact job they do and who they work for – being on benefit may have lost its stigma but it implies another loss.
4. *Sense of achievement.* Work often channels our skills and talents; the most satisfied at work are artists, potters and gardeners, because so much of them is in their work.
5. *Physical and mental agility.* Research shows that maintaining both wards off disease, both physical and mental; being on benefit is not stimulating.

(After Adrian Furnham, Professor of Psychology at University College London)

The Future for Women in Work

While Chapter 4, on women returning to work, looked at organisations making provision for today's returners, what of tomorrow? There are a number of issues affecting the future of women in work.

Many of the jobs that women do now, in shops and offices for example, will either not be there or will have changed out of all recognition in the coming years. Just look at the current increased popularity of shopping online, the growth of technology in the workplace and the outsourcing of key skills overseas. Organisations need to address how best to anticipate and prepare for this situation. Moreover, there are clear indications that there are fewer jobs in women's traditional work areas such as clerical/secretarial work and sales assistants, yet an increase in managerial and professional levels. Women need to become aware of where new opportunities lie, so that they can build on their existing skills during any break in employment to give them the best chance of making a valuable contribution to the workplace on their return.

We have seen statistics showing that women are having their children at a later age, so it follows that they will be returning to work older – yet with more years of earlier experience. Organisations need to harness this experience and counter issues of women returning and ageism.

While this chapter has reviewed the changing and increasing variety of work arrangements, particularly in the 'knowledge' and service sectors, how do businesses and women's organisations ensure that women do not have a disproportionate share of the less well paid and less secure part of a two-tier workforce?

There is a need to build 'return to work' strategies and advice into future educational programmes for mature women students – and to make them available to all women, irrespective of ethnicity, before a course starts so that they have the best informed choice before enrolment.

The pattern for the majority of people over their longer working lives will become more fragmented – episodes of work interspersed with breaks for caring responsibilities, education and so on are forecast to become the norm. In these circumstances, it will be even more difficult for employers to justify the disparity in pay between the genders. At the same time, a competency approach is moving towards pay and rewards for achievement in place of time served; this means that all organisations' pay strategies really must reflect fair pay for work done.

With such widespread changes in working practices, being a 'returner' will become less exceptional; this means that organisations need to consider how 'exit', 'keeping in touch', 'training and modernisation of skills', as well as 're-entry' processes are made widely available to all returners, irrespective of gender.

Since women are well placed to benefit from the structural changes taking place in the world of work, have particular lifestyle needs, are more comfortable with variety and are generally less committed to positions of 'status' at work, organisations must be ready to make changes to their employment policies and practices to capitalise on the benefits that women offer.

Work/Life Balance

In March 2000, the Prime Minister launched the government's Work/Life Balance campaign. Its purpose was to 'help parents balance their work and family responsibilities' and its solutions included 'the reform of the ways in which the tax and benefit system supports families with children and those on a low income'. It was therefore a 'work/*family* life' balance campaign. Much of this chapter has addressed some of the issues that enable the policy to work and considered some of the concerns – but what of those working people who don't have children or whose children have 'flown the nest'? Should not organisations consider them? Are they not also allowed a work/*personal* life balance or don't they want one?

The newspapers and management journals are full of stories about working hours getting longer, difficulties in commuting adding to the hours, job security being non-existent, targets getting tougher, we are all teetering on that work/life balance, just managing to save ourselves from plunging into divorce, alcoholism, impotence and financial ruin if we don't 'keep our noses to the corporate grindstone'.

Sadly, it is not quite as it seems and we need to 'wake up and smell the coffee' on this one. A 2004 Web@work survey revealed that over 50 per cent of US workers spend between one and five hours online each day for personal reasons. In one month in 2002, 7.9 million workplace Internet users viewed online dating sites. Also in the USA, 35.2 per cent of the workforce received more than five personal e-mails a day and 10.3 per cent received over 20.

In the UK, some employees' Internet use is limited by their ability to get into work: two-thirds of UK young professionals admitted in one survey that they had called in sick due to hangovers at least once in the preceding month. In another study, it was discovered that 9 million 'questionable' or 'suspicious' requests for sick notes are made each year to UK doctors – 9 million represents one-third of the UK workforce! When it comes to a 'sickie', Monday and Friday are the most popular (23 and 25 per cent respectively), while Wednesdays only account for 8 per cent – it must be severe toxicity from being at home. There are many thousands of chat rooms, web logs and sites on the Internet set up specifically for the millions of people who spend hours not working at work (Bolchover, 2005).

So why don't people admit their poor 'work/life balance' is largely of their own making? Most employees are in mass denial:

- We have bored junior staff pretending to all around them that they are occupied and motivated for fear of losing their jobs.
- Middle managers are too busy forming political alliances with those in power above them to worry too much about their underlings.
- Senior managers are blissfully unaware of the grassroots disquiet, surrounded by yes-men (but fewer yes-women), their heads swelled by the advances of ambitious middle managers and filled with the latest management text drivel about how easy it is to get to the top (not this one I hope!).

As Sir Winston Churchill observed: 'Men occasionally stumble over the truth, but most of them pick themselves up and hurry off as if nothing has happened.'

Perhaps we should seek the truth and look at it a while! One truth is that there are many sad cases of 'presenteeism' in the workplace, but with Blackberry and Palmtops on the beach we now also have 'virtual presenteeism'.

The sad fact is that, despite the suggestion that people are at work far too long – and perhaps the fact that British workers spend more time at work than any other European counterpart yet their productivity is not the highest suggests that they may have a point – people do 'work' long hours. At least, they are 'at work' for a long time. In the same study mentioned earlier in the chapter, it was found that one in five managers were working for more than 60 hours a week. The report recommended that companies 'identify role models for work/life balance'. In particular, firms should consider a 'mentor-buddying scheme' for those wanting to change their working patterns to 'guide them through making a business case and negotiating with their manager, and providing them with work advice about how to make a new work schedule work for them and their team'.

Achieving the balance

It may be that you are quite happy working 15 hours a day, five or six days a week. But remember all those clichés – very few people on their deathbed wished they had spent more time in the office. If you really feel that no other aspect of your life is suffering because of your work, you have probably got your work/life balance right.

But if, like most of us, you sometimes feel torn between finding time for your business and the other things – and people – that are important to you, then your work/life balance is something you need to work on. This is particularly true if you feel that some areas of your life are actually suffering because of your working hours.

Ask yourself the following questions. Do you:

- Feel stressed most of the time?
- Find it difficult to delegate work tasks to others?
- Feel guilty about not being able to 'do it all' – even when you know your expectations of yourself are unreasonable?
- Find it difficult to 'switch off' from work?
- Feel that your relationships with your family/friends are suffering because of the time you spend working?
- Find it difficult or impossible to fit leisure activities into your schedule?

If you have answered 'yes' to any of these, you need to start thinking about improving your work/life balance. Perhaps use your diary and record those other non-work activities that you have undertaken; then, after a month, review your activity and work out what proportion of time you have had for the other things in life – like family, friends, exercise, hobbies, yourself. Then you will be better able to decide what areas you need to change.

241

If you own your own business, the idea of completely changing the way you work can seem impossible. Instead, to improve your work/life balance, try focusing on specific areas and improving them, one at a time. Aim towards:

- Recognising your own limitations. You have to understand that you can't do everything perfectly and that the in-tray will never be completely empty – adjust your expectations accordingly.
- Doing that which makes most money first, then meet your legal obligations – question the need to do the rest.
- Separating work and home – for example, not taking your work home with you, leaving work by a certain time, not working weekends.
- Scheduling and taking holidays.
- Taking commitments to family and friends seriously.
- Delegating work – hiring the right people, developing them and managing them appropriately.
- Learning time and stress management techniques.
- Setting aside 'me' time – this is time for you and you alone.

Box 12.9 has some further suggestions on how to gain a better work/life balance but still manage your career upwards.

Box 12.9: Top 10 tips for managing a career and getting a work/life balance

- *Blur the boundaries.* Make work part of your life rather than a separate entity.
- *Manage expectations.* If you are going to be working late, be honest and let people know in advance, then aim for payback.
- *Keep a clear head.* Make a 'to-achieve' list before you leave work and leave it there. Then think ahead towards your destination.
- *Show your humanity.* Show other people in each part of your life that you have another side; 'take five' and share your day and experiences, then move on – you don't want to be a bore.
- *Set challenging goals.* You have these at work, so why not set a personal challenge that motivates you? Learn to play the piano or run a marathon – and get in to it.

- *Talent transfer.* Use your skills in one area of work to enrich another. Good at organising – organise your son's rugby tour. You can write reports – do one for your residents' association.
- *Get focused.* Charming people have time for others; copy them and get the same reputation. At work, focus on your staff, not the weekend dinner party; at home, focus on your partner, not the sales meeting.
- *Set a reasonable pace.* Busy times need your full effort for best effect, but schedule time to recharge the batteries; aim to smooth the flow.
- *Call time-out.* A change is as good as a rest, so schedule something out of work and rethink what and who is really important to you.
- *Share goals.* Look at what you want to achieve and how well you are doing; use the guide in the chapters on self-esteem and achievement.

Work/life balance and your staff

Staff that do not take their leave can also be vulnerable to burnout, and lack of holiday can cause low morale and resentment. Therefore, it makes sense to encourage staff to use their holiday entitlement as well as take any other statutory leave they may have. Only allow weekend working for special circumstances when there are particularly important projects in progress or you are in seasonally busy periods, and always make sure 'time off in lieu' is taken. Provided you have an efficient system of planning for leave, this should not cause your business any major problems.

Good practice will include:

- Reminding staff to take their leave. Do not let it stack up at the end of the year and discourage people from carrying over leave from one year into the next unless they have planned something special, like extended travel, honeymoon, study leave, etc.
- Keeping a holiday diary for staff to enter their leave dates in so that everyone can see when people are away.
- Encouraging staff to book their leave as far in advance as possible.
- If your company is very small, don't allow more than one person to be away at once.

Work with Meaning

In a recent survey by Roffey Park (*Management Today*, 2004), it was found that 70 per cent of managers are looking for more meaning in their working lives. The history of mankind has always been about the search of some answer to the meaning to life – *The Hitchhiker's Guide to the Galaxy* enthusiasts know the answer is 42 – but today we are looking for 'meaning' in the workplace. The Roffey Park annual 'Management Agenda' survey has been running since 1996, but recent results show that there has been a trend of growing disillusionment at work and a desire to be doing something more meaningful.

While over two-thirds are looking for more meaning, a startling 42 per cent of respondents said that they would be looking to change jobs in the following 12 months. Eighty per cent said that it was personally important to them that their companies are environmentally and socially responsible, yet more than half (52 per cent) are sceptical about their company's value statements. Not surprisingly, 39 per cent say that they experience tension between the 'spiritual' aspect of their values and their daily work.

So, what does it mean – 'meaning' in work? Different people have different definitions: for some it is about personal values and ideals, for others it is spiritual beliefs or personal fulfilment.

When MI5 advertised for new recruits in 2004 – on a starting salary of just £20 000 – thousands of higher paid people applied. Perhaps they wanted to do something for the UK rather than just work for a fat pay-cheque. The Joseph Rowntree Foundation research backs this up; they described 'Generation X' as depressed. Other research identified 'TIREDs' – Thirty-something, Independent, Radical, Educated Dropouts – people with good prospects leaving their high-flying jobs to do something more meaningful with their lives. Meanwhile, Voluntary Service Overseas (VSO) regularly targets its recruitment programmes at Britain's managers – fertile ground for new helpers.

So, what prompted the introspection and feelings that a good job with prospects and a stable salary couldn't satisfy our deeper needs? Is it that we spend so much of our waking time involved with getting to and from as well as at work? Roffey Park research showed that 83 per cent of managers work longer than their contracted hours, leaving less time for other pursuits that might offer a sense of meaning, whether that is more time with home and family, doing volunteer work, travelling or learning a new skill.

A 45-year-old today is around one-half of their way through their working life – why spend the second half doing something meaningless? Given the time and duration of work, it is hardly surprising that 'work' is so central to our lives. It provides a sense of community and identity; we expect to make friends and meet partners there. Yet previous generations worked long hours, often in monotonous jobs in unpleasant conditions, and fully expected a shorter retirement. So, are we better off and just don't see it or are we more demanding?

Frank Furedi, Professor of Psychology at Kent University and author of *Therapy Culture*, concluded that higher expectations are crucial – we expect work to be more than just work. People have always tried to find meaning in work, which is understandable, but work cannot always meet all our needs. The media provides a steady diet of people actively changing their lives, whether that is building properties aboard, travelling round the world on a motorcycle, switching jobs (even wives!) or downshifting.

Couple that rising expectation of life's meaning, the time commitment people give to their work, with the sad fact that companies are generally not treating their people that much better and we have a nation of cynical 'Dilberts' counting the hours until they can go home.

There are a number of employer practices that can exacerbate a sense of meaningless in work:

- Demanding longer hours
- Increased demands leading to stress
- Lack of appreciation for individual effort
- Relentless focus on shareholders
- Managers that do not do what they say they will (walk the talk)
- A lack of adherence to stated organisational values – such as corporate social responsibility
- Mismanagement of change.

Such practices lead to employee cynicism, particularly following the Enron and WorldCom scandals and evidence of widespread fat-cattery. The Roffey Park research found that nearly one-half of managers say these events have made them more cynical, while one-quarter have lost trust in corporate leaders.

There is a strong business case for helping staff find meaning in their work. Companies can benefit by:

- Change of management being more successful
- Retaining staff better
- Having greater staff engagement
- Improved employee performance
- More productive workforce
- Greater creativity
- More commitment.

So, what are the activities that companies can do to engender a sense of meaning? These include:

- A strong customer focus – as opposed to shareholders
- A clear role for individuals
- Flexible working practices
- Recognition by managers of work well done
- Giving employees room to develop and grow in the company
- Paying more than lip service to company values.

Companies that manage change effectively and have 'clarity of purpose' provide employees with a greater sense of meaning. Companies where employees feel a sense of belonging can also have a positive effect – although having Yahoo! tattooed on yourself as some proud US employees of that Internet portal have done is probably a step too far.

A few UK companies have tried to help staff find meaning through encouraging them to take sabbaticals or spend office time on charitable causes. Unilever and Deutsche Bank are two that have staff involved with 'Arts and Kids', a new venture to enable staff to work with children and the arts.

Blaming companies that do not do such things sidesteps the personal responsibility people need to take for their own destiny. People are generally pretty grown up; they do not have such a patriarchal relationship with their employers. While companies can do nice things to make their people valued, that does not make their work and lives meaningful. Many people are unhappy as they feel trapped in the wrong job and get stressed as they cannot see an exit route – many cannot even see when their next holiday will be. As we saw in the section on confidence building, self-esteem and achievement, people need to make a coherent plan and set about doing it – once they start, say, exercising more, they begin to feel a change to spur them on further.

Clearly individual needs and circumstances affect what can be planned. While people cannot change their lives completely overnight, there may be small gains that one can achieve – even if it is cutting down on 'down time' wasted at work and getting out to explore other interests. While employers should do what they can, it is up to each individual to make their own decisions about life and work out what is best for them. Those that are not happy are doing something that is not right for them.

So, find your own *motivation*, develop your *ability* to do it, and have the *confidence* to see it through and build your own future – and, if you are a manager, help your people do it too.

Good luck!

Summary

In this chapter you have:

- Explored some factors that will have an impact on organisations in the future
- Reviewed information technology and its influence in the workplace activity, particularly e-collaborating
- Seen that e-learning is making inroads and have considered how to help it find its place
- Reviewed the importance of flexible working and recognised some of the pitfalls of working from home and how to manage a virtual team
- Reviewed interim working and discovered its attractions for many people
- Considered future trends in work regarding children, pensions, incapacity benefit and older workers
- Looked further at women in work in the future
- Seen the importance of a work/life balance and approaches to achieving it
- Reviewed the term 'work with meaning'.

Questions

1. Consider events over the last five years that have affected your organisation, or one with which you are familiar. How many were 'predictable' and how well did your chosen organisation deal with them? Then, what do you feel is likely to be the range of 'issues' that need to be managed over the next five years?
2. Imagine that you or one of your colleagues wishes to work more flexible hours. Make a written case to management for that change.
3. Imagine that you or one of your colleagues wishes to work more remotely/from home more often. Make a written case to management for that change.
4. Consider how you might help your people discover more meaning to the work that your organisation is engaged in. What would you do to help them feel more committed?

References

Bolchover, D. (2005) *The Daily Telegraph*, 29 September, p. B7.

The Daily Telegraph (2005) 5 October, p. 10.

The Daily Telegraph (2006) 23 January, p. B2.

Evening Standard (2005) 6 October 2005, p. 25.

Hayward, M. (2004) *Management Today*, September, p. 69.

Mackay, A. R. (2007) *Motivation, Ability and Confidence Building in People*, Butterworth-Heinemann.

Management Today (2003) June, p. 33.

Management Today (2004) May, p. 46.

Management Today (2005) July, p. 70.

Orr, D. (2006) *The Independent*, 25 January, p. 27.

Professional Manager (2003) March, p. 20.

Professional Manager (2004) Chiumento report 'Coming of Age', September, p. 29.

Professional Manager (2006), January, p. 23.

Reeves, R. (2005) *Management Today*, April, p. 29.

Further Reading

Covey, S. (1999) *Seven Habits of Highly Effective People*, Simon & Schuster.

Drucker, P. (2001) *Management Challenges for the 21st Century*, Harper Business.

Duarte, D. L. and Snyder, T. (2001) *Mastering Virtual Teams: Strategies, Tools and Techniques That Succeed*, Jossey-Bass Wiley.

Fisher, K. and Fisher, M. (2000) *The Distance Manager: A Hands-on Guide to Managing Off-site Employees and Virtual Teams*, McGraw-Hill Education.

Houston, D. (ed.) (2005) *Work–Life Balance in the 21st Century*, Palgrave Macmillan.

Mackay, A. R. (2007) *Motivation, Ability and Confidence Building in People,* Butterworth-Heinemann.

Index